CHERISH THE SEA

Cherish the Sea

A HISTORY OF SAIL

BY JEAN DE LA VARENDE

TRANSLATED FROM THE FRENCH BY MERVYN SAVILL

with technical sketches by the author

NEW YORK
THE VIKING PRESS
1956

La Navigation Sentimentale
Copyright 1952 by Ernest Flammarion
Cherish the Sea
Copyright © in all countries of the
International Copyright Union
PUBLISHED BY THE VIKING PRESS IN FEBRUARY, 1956

Printed in Great Britain
Library of Congress catalog card number : 55-9786

TO

MY GREAT-UNCLES
Marshal de Tourville
Bailli de Laval-Montmorency
Bailli de Cintray
Commander le Roy
Commander de Bonneville-Chamblac
Commander de Mallard

MY GRANDFATHERS
Chevalier Fleuriot de Langle
Rear-Admiral Fleuriot de Langle

MY UNCLES
Vice-Admiral Fleuriot de Langle
Captain Fleuriot de Langle
Lieutenant Fleuriot de Langle
Captain de la Monneraye

MY GREAT FRIEND
Vice-Admiral Galibert

MY FATHER
Lieutenant Mallard de la Varende

MY NEPHEW
Sub-Lieutenant Fleuriot de Langle

I dedicate these musings
born of their actions
L.V.

CONTENTS

CONTENTS

LIST OF PLATES

ILLUSTRATIONS IN THE TEXT

CHERISH THE SEA

CHAPTER I
The Art of Sail

THE child at the water's edge reveals the primitive in us; the child and water are dangerously allied. He immediately wants to possess the element. The bits of wood, rubbish and leaves he flings in the stream become his ships. He boards them in his imagination as, bright-eyed, he follows them, in their flight. There you have the source of all voyages, and floundering is merely the first act of nautical adventure.

Soon the child will go further and will realise his confused but imperious dream. He will navigate. He will succeed with no

1. The Infancy of Sail

matter what, audaciously making use of the most unlikely objects. I myself, who admittedly came of a long line of sailors, launched old barrels and wash-tubs on the muddy waves. I crouched at the bottom of them feeling very sick, advancing in giddy circles, at the same time triumphant because I was afloat and making progress. The joy of sailing comes before that of swimming. Many sailors cannot swim. Sailing is quite another matter. You see a child fling himself into the water supported by water-wings which give a complete guarantee that he will not

3

sink: he does not experience the same pleasure as in his tub—in that tub from which he dominates the waves (1).

Our imagination is aroused by those first men at the water's edge, those violent and terrible children, in the moist shade of forbidding jungles, irresistibly attracted by that second heaven, the pond or the river. It reflected their prognathous faces and their eyes were fixed on the motionless or flowing expanse of water. For many centuries they were only lake or river dwellers, for whom the sea was a desert while the lake formed a comfortable haven. The cave was too far from the springs and difficult to defend, whereas the lake dwelling to some extent enjoyed flowing water and once his bridge was raised man could sleep in peace. Our moated castles are a distant reminder of this lacustrian security.

The river also gave these pedestrians another pleasure—that of easy migration: the mobile lake dwelling, the river caravan.

They had looked with jealous eyes at the swans as they glided gently on the water; admired the squirrels on their strip of bark, like those small grey ones, which embarked in their thousands, mentioned by Regnard in his journey to Lapland. The man who dared imitate them by entrusting himself to some weighty sapling blown down by the storm must have felt very proud of himself! So much so that in the ancient mythologies this audacity was always attributed to a god: the Phoenician Sankionaton wrote two thousand years before the Christian era: 'Great storms broke on the forest of Tyre, several trees struck by lightning caught fire and the flames devoured the wood. In his terror, Osöus took one of these tree trunks, tore off the branches and, clinging to it, was the first to venture on the waves.' It had been done; the rest was merely a question of craftsmanship.

So man collected branches and made fascines and entrusted himself to their emergent masses. He could sit on the treacherous surface and by enlarging this mysterious apparatus could instal his belongings and his family and travel down the river. For the first time he could move without *personal movement*, without fatigue and out of reach of the dangers on land. On both banks the ounces, leopards and wolves watched with hungry disappointment as the king of the animals passed by.

*   *   *

4

By using his tub, the child was already an instinctive follower
of Archimedes. Ideas of this nature are now taken for granted,
but they did not exist in antiquity. Primitive man attributed to
plant life a sort of miraculous property which would not allow it
to sink. The idea of buoyancy took a long time to establish.
When the first iron ships were built, most simple people, women,
children, peasants, even certain sailors, considered the undertaking to be insane. When I was a child this prejudice was still
current. I was once given a toy boat made of iron, painted red,
with a metal deck made to look like wood. All the servants
came out rather superciliously to witness the shipwreck. How
terribly disturbed these simple souls were when the cutter did
not sink below the water line and floated triumphantly!

But what vegetable matter was to be used, for primitive man
did not consider cutting down trees an easy task? In fact, it was
the faggot which, on fresh water, first became the most popular
float: the bundle of reeds which the river and the lake banks so
kindly offered for the picking. Our ancestors hoisted themselves
on these bundles of reeds or rushes, which were more in the
nature of a buoy than a ship or a vessel; but they were quickly
contrived and did not require too much effort.

However, with the raft of reeds, shaped like a crescent to enable it to float, we see appear the prototype of the barque. And
this will be found among all peoples, at different epochs in
time, but at contemporary stages of civilisation, whether in
Chaldaea, in Egypt, in Colombia, in Australia or in the Polar
seas. In Colombia this still holds good today and you straddle a
log, propelling it forward with your legs, just as you find on the
bas-reliefs of Nineveh a skiff almost identical with that used by
the fowlers in the marshes. The Chinese pirates also use this
method for crossing rivers and carrying out surprise attacks.

The lozenge form of the fascine was obtained by two end
bindings which joined the framework together. The curvature
was soon found to be necessary since the extremities of the craft
had to be out of the water. In practice, the reeds available were
smooth, empty canes; hence it became indispensable that the
extremities of these tubes should be above the surface so as not
to ship water and make the whole craft too heavy. They were
well plugged with some plastic material but nothing could
resist the infiltration of the water for very long— we know that

B

even rubber will not remain watertight for four days if subjected to any pressure. This is why, by the very nature of the
stalks, this form of vertical crescent developed so swiftly everywhere—a form which experience would prove to be so marvel-
lously suited to the movements of the waves, to facilitate progress and seaworthiness, that it remained that of the 'trimmest'
craft, such as the Indian and Norwegian canoes and the
barque of Amon. At the very first attempt the best design was
discovered.

We must note that the curve came naturally from the hand
of the shipwright. When one of our shepherds makes a reed boat
for a child in the meadows, it will be an exact replica of the
Egyptian barques, even to the position of the whippings fore and
aft. A little cow dung smeared on it makes the green sides
watertight and the vessel sails away. . . . The boats of Lake
Chad are still made like this and they too evoke the Pharaonic
line.

*   *   *

Slowly, very slowly, man made his way down to the sea on
these floats. Paddling cautiously, he always beached his craft at
the mouth of the estuary and from there, standing on some rock
or sandbank, he watched the terrible monster with the countless arms—that sea with bestial and hungry waves which snap-
ped and rocked his small pathetic skiff. The whole immensity of
the world and its restlessness appalled him as he faced these
growling expanses, whose horizon must hide some chasm into
which the waters gushed, whose din filled his ears. The roundness of the globe, above which objects suddenly appeared,
seemed to him like an engulfment. For certain savage races, the
sea was an immense cooking pot surrounded by cataracts, and
the whole art of coasting, which they practised with a circum-
spection that can be imagined, consisted in hugging the shore
far from the rim of this fabulous cauldron.

At the mouth of the river, the pleasure trip was over and they
had to return up-stream. Over the rapids the boatman used his
pole; in slow-flowing waters the paddle, which replaced the
webbed foot of the duck or the hand of the man astride his
floating log.

6

But this nautical caution could not last very long and primitive man, to brave the waters, created the raft, a vessel large enough to protect him from the waves and more durable than his bundle of reeds. Homer reveals the technique when he describes the construction of the raft of Ulysses, who was already a skilful navigator.

* * *

The King of Ithaca chose twenty trees with great discernment. He selected poplars and pines. Certain woods are buoyant while others sink. Oak is one of the latter, its density being 1·17 times that of water, whereas for conifers this factor decreases from 0·55 to 0·45 (for spruce) and for the poplar does not exceed 0·36. Ulysses used the olive tree, which was to be found in great abundance, only to haft his adze—the essential tool of the naval carpenter, an axe whose blade is set at right angles to the handle. The Egyptians of the first dynasties already used it.

Twenty trees. Ulysses intended to build an impressive and solid raft for he planed his logs until they were perfectly smooth so that there would be none of that play between them which was an ever-increasing problem of assembly. He joined them not only by rope wooldings but also with dowel pins, piercing the holes with an auger. Homer must have got his information from sailors, for the raft was reputed to be thirty feet by nine—the exact proportions today of rapid sailing craft—and it was pointed at both ends. Better still, to resist the waves, on the first bed of beams which formed the hull and gave it buoyancy, the master-builder placed athwartships a few bridging-joists, on which he nailed planks, thus forming a deck sheltered from the sea. He surrounded this deck by a wall to strengthen and defend it. Finally, in the centre, he placed a curious apparatus that may have been a kind of dropkeel, with a movable paddle which could be plunged into the water according to the strength of the wind. And he established a mast, a sail and a steering oar.

This would indicate the use of the wind, an early discovery; but one can divine something even more significant. Did Ulysses, with his raft, create the first real deck and give it watertightness? Did he use the air as a float? Did he employ a

7

volume of free or enclosed air, to which the water had no access? That, perhaps, was his immense discovery.

*   *   *

The hollowed-out tree trunk was heralded by the Assyrian use of certain reeds large enough, when cut in two and coupled, to serve for the transport of a man, each end being sealed with clay. The *monoxylon*, the boat in a single piece, is incredibly ancient. It achieved the watertightness that would remain for a long time the major anxiety of the sailing novice—there is no vessel which does not ship water—and the tree trunk, the dug-out, gave some hope that the bottom would remain dry. The rudimentary system still employed by the Polynesian natives is ingenious enough to warrant description. Fire accomplished the hardest part of the work. Burning coals were placed all along the piece of wood which had to be hollowed out and, taking care to protect the two side walls with a strong coat of damp clay, two men fanned the embers lengthwise. This human bellows produced the effect of a pipe, the flame lengthened, grew to a point and charred the wood. The clay wall was made lower as the inside grew more hollow. Each evening they scraped out the burnt wood, which crumbled quite easily. Fashioning

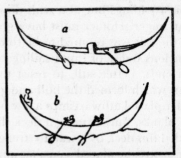

2. Primitive Barques
(*a*) Ur of the Chaldees ; (*b*) Aggeby

the pointed ends was a more delicate operation, and these were hollowed out with the aid of a red-hot stone.

But however skilful and practised these builders, and however much they scraped, they could only produce a very heavy craft because they were afraid of damaging the wall. Moreover, the dugout was always narrow and could carry little weight. It was the reed and the goatskin more than wood which led to progress in ship-building.

The goatskin (19a) was used for short and easy crossings because of the delicate buoyancy of these inflated skins, which must have delighted men. The best skins remained watertight for only a short time. However, the Assyrians used them by placing them underneath their rafts (16) so as to raise them on the water and to make them bear a bigger load. The really light, safe barque emerged from the outer covering of the reed. It was achieved by reducing the timbers to a minimum and covering them with skins, smearing them with a waterproof coating to prevent any leakage or at least to prevent the water entering more quickly than it could be baled out. This was the birth of the modern ship. Now it was merely a question of building it of stronger and less fragile materials. Man progressed from the hollow skiff to the ship, from the vessel to the man-of-war.

The most curious thing about this development is that every country followed the same sequence in construction. We reproduce here two drawings illustrating this. One was taken from the Aggeby stone (2b) in Sweden and the other is of a silver model barque found at Ur (2a) in Mesopotamia. The design

3. The Barque of Rê

from the Bronze Age is closely related to that of the Euphrates (2a), both of them having a special form of crescent, and the votive barque from Egypt (3) seems to have come from the same shipyard as the vessels sculptured on the rock in Bohuslän (2b).

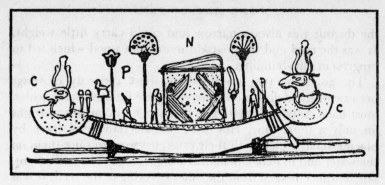

4. The Ark of Amon

CHAPTER II

Egypt

EGYPT, that narrow nation which was once so great, which has lingered nostalgically in the memory of man as an ideal of unattainable perfection; Egypt, which, by her art, her science and her culture, had such an enormous influence on the minds of antiquity, was also the chosen fatherland of the ship. It was the country of the river and the barge.

We must have recourse to figures in order to realise how rare dry land was. Admittedly Egypt extended over a thousand miles in length, but it was merely a narrow corridor between the two walls formed by the Arabian and Libyan mountain ranges, with the Nile like a moving stairway, and it did not exceed four leagues in breadth. From the beginning of July to the end of November, no more shores, no more pavements— nothing but a vast lake. The towns, villages and hamlets became islands joined by causeways or fordable crossings. This inundation, which took place at the driest and most torrid season of the year, in a country whose rainfall in a century did not reach that of France in one year, reduced the nation to an archipelago.

When in December the fecund waters retired, leaving behind them that famous black slime which in April and June would give two successive harvests, Egypt became a twin quayside of three hundred leagues stretching from north to south. Traffic

10

was composed entirely of boats. Only China had a similar need for ships and barges.

The kingdom of Pharaoh for many centuries knew no other vehicle except the boat. Occasionally the sledge was used (5) for hauling the huge stones of the buildings to their sites. As for the wheel, it was only introduced into Egypt at the time of the Hittite invasions.

*　　*　　*

This essentially aquatic tradition has been an incidental cause of civilisation. The Egyptian city first arose among the nomad peoples. The houses must have been placed on hillocks out of reach of the floods. They were fortified for self-defence and there the caste system, that incomparable civiliser, took root. More than this, Egypt, entirely dependent for its existence on an incomprehensible phenomenon reputed to be miraculous—in those days they were ignorant of the immense

5. Hearse-sledge

equatorial rains which fed the flood—assumed before the mystery a kind of humility of a religious character, although this is not quite what I wish to suggest. Exercising its power on Pharaoh and *fellahin* alike, this submission to unknown forces, this renunciation of pride in being a human, inclined the race to the most delicate sensitivity, preserving it in that semi-infancy without which man—we have grown aware of this too late and perhaps as a result the world will crumble—becomes the most evil of the beasts and bears within himself the seeds of his own destruction. Had humanity been subjected to the influence of Egypt more than to Chaldaean or Phoenician leadership, the world would perhaps have known neither this bitterness, this frenzy, nor these hideous dreams. Egyptian culture preserved the golden mean between the fever of Europe and Hindu torpor. Greek civilisation itself had at its peak but feeble influence on the Mediterranean masses. Its action only affected a very small *élite*. Moreover, Attica was spoiled by a sterile taste for words and the taint of artifice. For the masses, the Greek visage bore no resemblance to the great, almost divine features of Plato, but on the contrary lengthened into the cunning profile of Ulysses. . . . The character of the masses and the humble in origin was formed by the Phoenicians, those lecherous, greedy and choleric adventurers. No one can say how far the contagion spread in detail: the dozen, that strange figure to which we remain irresistibly attached in spite of the decimal system, is the unit of Phoenician reckoning.

Christ broke away from the Chaldaeans by spending his childhood in Egypt. They were Egyptian themes that He developed and opposed to Chaldaeo-Phoenician violence . . . from Egypt which recognised a Trinity; which had, as we have the Virgin, a goddess of Indulgence whose tiny hand leant gently on the scale of virtue when the soul was being judged before Osiris and weighed for its merits and its crimes. . . . What nation has ever put into the mouth of its dead such justifications as these: 'I have never killed. . . . I have never diverted a canal. . . . I have never stolen milk from a child. . . . I HAVE NEVER MADE ANYONE WEEP!'

*   *   *

Egyptian mythology took possession of the vessel; Phaëton's chariot, which the Greeks portrayed harnessed to white stallions rippling with light and champing through incandescent heavens, would have been incomprehensible here because they had no knowledge of the carriage. It was replaced by the barque of Rê (3), the solar demon of midday, while Horus was the incarnation of the morning and Osiris the deity of the dusk. The people of Egypt represented the rise of their master and the orbit of his flaming journey in the form of a crescent-shaped boat. A huge, bright disc gleamed in the centre of the barque (3). Everything took on a nautical appearance; their tabernacles were boats such as the Jewish Ark of the Covenant may have resembled before the *diaspora*, before the need to house the tables of the law reduced it to a jewelled coffer. In the temple at Luxor they worshipped the Ark of Amon (4): a complete hull placed on the altar at the far end of the enormous edifice. After crossing the portico and entering the Hall of the Apparition, the central part of the gigantic hypostyle basilica with capitals seventy feet in girth, one finally arrived at the Hall of Mysteries where, on the silver floor, the priest could salute the Great God. It was a true barque, gilded, but even more carefully caulked and perhaps slightly more elongated; its overhang stressed in the ancient fashion; at the bow and the poop a ram's head adorned with the divine tiara and bearing round its neck flat, circular necklaces of gold (4c), typically Egyptian and used by no other race for embellishment, enlarged like fans and perhaps intended to cool by their contact. Small figures can be seen in it; royal servants to chase away the flies with peacock feathers; a lotus has been fixed to the end of a lance; and in the bows, this time, out of humility, represented in miniature without the complete *pschent*, without insignia, Pharaoh adoring his father (4p).

The *naos* (n), the roof of this barque, was in the shape of an Egyptian ogee, which had developed from the early use of reeds—reeds which were bent backwards and took on this characteristic curvature. Inside, once the panels fanned by the wings of Isis and Nephthys were opened, the god appeared, a jointed statue of gold which sometimes deigned to pronounce oracles or to wave its hands. The whole effect of the colossal temple, diminution of light and altitude, the incredible differences of volume, were only contrived to facilitate the sacred deceit by means of shadow and a sudden surge of awe. The high priests knew, but they judged it unwise to tempt the god and expose him to profane minds. They did well. How often in my life would I have liked some old *curé*, aided by some holy ruse, to make me believe in all the miracles!

In any case, Egypt was the only country in the world to conceive her Creator in the form of a mariner and sailors must respect her for this. On his feast day, the god steered the vessel. His barque was solemnly carried down to the water and he made contact once more with the life-giving river.

* * *

The Egyptian boat has always retained the primitive form mentioned by Herodotus: the bundle of reeds covered with leather or papyrus. We see the boats evolve slowly but surely, sometimes even reverting to ancient types. When the joined stalks were replaced by planking, the primitive form was not destroyed. It was an eminently nautical form, whatever may be said. The shipwrights were so respectful that they even remained faithful to the ancient appearance when there was no longer any justification for it. A clear proof of this is the persistent decoration of the boats as far as the spot where in olden days the whippings kept the craft together fore and aft. Imitation ropes often continued to appear.

Still retaining the feeling of primitive construction, the typical ornaments at the extremities bore the trace of ancient requirements. As a general rule, stem and stern were not in one piece with the main structure except in very small boats. They stuck out of the brushwood, one might say. One can easily realise that in the age of reed bundles the insertion of these solid, compact parts must have been necessary, for example, for mooring, when coming aboard, or to prevent a direct collision which might have wrecked the delicate sheathing of the vessel. What we see in the Egyptian Golden Age as a perpendicular bronze spur could formerly only have been a stout carved plank, well secured to the hull.

For thousands of years one merely finds the same form being exploited: a half-moon or a half-ellipse. Flat bottoms have been mentioned, but I do not believe in them. Although a few models in low-caste tombs have displayed flattened keels, it was merely because the bottoms were cut off with the object of making them stand upright. Our shop models today still suffer the same degrading mutilation, whereas the lover of ships respects above all this part of the hull which in the expressive language of seamen is known as 'the vitals'. On the marvellous models in the tombs of the kings one finds only tapered keels: the flat bottom does not exist. It would in fact have weakened the construction by breaking the line; it would have impeded the natural movement and disturbed the overall elasticity. It would not have been understood in Egypt, where river navigation was not subject to tides. In Holland and China, where the coasters beach twice a day, one realises that the shipwrights found it necessary to build an underwater platform on which the ship could rest and balance. The Red Sea has little tide and even today one meets with an infinitesimal number of ships with flat floor timbers. On the contrary, the keels of *sambuks* and *baggalas* exaggerate their tapering.

I must mention that the curve of the Egyptian vessel is irregular. The ship has a higher angle forward and takes the shape of a boomerang. As in China, the midship frame, the widest part of the vessel, is therefore nearer the stern on the pattern of the waterfowl. Again in common with the Chinese, the Egyptian sailing ship could hardly advance except with the wind aft. Thus, under the pressure of the breeze, the bow dips. This lengthens the waterline and without plunging in the wave, without impediment, the vessel preserves a happy balance, speeds over the water and is easy to steer. In any case, one invariably returns to those forms which have so long been decried. Modern yachts, too, are in the form of *gendarmes'* hats. The Egyptian shape, admittedly ritual in a country that observed rites in everything, was also extremely practical.

*   *   *

The demands of navigation and its increasing skill led to a rapid increase in tonnage. The largest ships of the Middle Kingdom do not seem to have exceeded 120 feet, the length of the European galley, but this increase entailed a speedy transition from paddle to oar.

The Egyptians must have invented the oar at a very early date. Its adoption has been fixed in the sixth dynasty, 2500 B.C. This was inevitable as soon as the ship grew taller and the rowers were removed from the surface of the water. It was an important discovery: it was a step towards modern navigation. The paddle demands more effort for less return; it brings the whole body into play and lacks the leverage of an oar. In fact, the paddle is irreplaceable in rivers with rapids dotted with rocks, between which the boat has to slip. Then the action which propels and steers the craft must be performed close to the hull and cannot be at some distance from it. Furthermore, the stroke of the paddle is much more lively and more intelligent than that of an oar, which always remains a trifle mechanical. The paddle burrows, raises and twists, rather like a hand. But none of this was necessary on the Father of all Rivers and the oar lent power-ful and majestic wings to the sinews which cleft the waters.

These wings were to remain the basic 'engine' of the ship for four thousand years. It was only in the seventeenth century of our era that the artists in sail dared to give them up and rely for the future entirely on the wind: an admirable but costly audacity which was paid for very dearly. How many ships ran aground for lack of oars at the moment of a difficult manoeuvre? How many delays from ships being forced to wait in a sheltered roadstead for the arrival of a favourable wind instead of going out to find it. It was only the skill of the northern sailor which enabled him to do without oars, whereas the 'Moko', the Mediterranean sailor never entirely abandoned them.

* * *

The Egyptian sailors rowed, as ours do, with their backs to the bows. Along the whole length of the ship they made a sombre, gleaming frieze of polished mahogany, relieved only by their small clouts of white cotton. We do not know their rhythm. Probably they did not exceed 26 strokes to the minute at full speed, nor impel their vessels forward at more than 5 knots. The Egyptian ship, however, remained essentially a craft with oars. It always remained pliable and without rounded sides.

As for sail, which we are told was the offspring of the Thinite

6. Hunting in the Marsh

period, I dare not protest too much, as I am unwilling to com-pare my slight work with that of the true scholars, but I will accept this date only as a general point of departure. The sail and the vessel were obviously evolved simultaneously. That admirable engine the wind was there for the asking. Even a child who lives far removed from the shores, the rivers and from ships, as soon as he floats a walnut shell on the water, blows on it, or graces it with a flower petal if he is a poet or a leaf if he is prosaic, so that the wind may bear it away. The wind was a natural agent. Across any open expanse it revealed its strength and showed its impulsive nature. The beasts used it, the squirrel used it and the tree also took account of it. One merely has to look at the propellers on a sycamore seed. The water is intimately bound up with the wind. The breeze hurls the autumn leaves into it, then collects them in a huge sheet which it blows away like a wildly distended spanker. The most primitive sailors put to sea with a sail and a following wind, marvelling at the unaccustomed calm.

In the case of the canoe, one finds little change from the original fascine type. Its handiness as well as its lightness probably kept it in use for a long time. Certain hunting or fishing boats, individual vessels, even Pharaoh's barque, seem to have been these craft which lay low in the water and which could be tucked beneath the arm (6). The most important types, carrying several passengers, vary only in their decoration, the emblems sported fore and aft, and the arrangement of the stem and stern posts supporting them: more or less bent back, splayed or vertical. The most humble boats seem to have been decorated with these motifs, which varied with their uses and which were often most graceful. Lotuses appear to have been reserved for funeral barges; the hearse-sloop was amply decorated with them: they were the symbols of purity and peace. One fact is certain: these insignia were detachable. On many vessels the

7. Poop Variations

empty notch, the mortice in which they were fixed, can be seen. Modern modellers are wrong always to reproduce them in relief: most of them were rounded and were real works of

17

art. One could make a charming collection of the insignia of all the votive barques; for the barque of Amon (4) the wilting lotus, the crown of Lower Egypt aft and the tiara of Luxor on the bow; the goat's head, the antelope, the big lotus bud that has just blossomed and the head of a sparrow-hawk with two plumes (7).

Perhaps too, in the Great Epoch, these subjects were weighty and of metal, used as counterweight, like the *iron* of the Venetian gondolas in olden days. They were delicate barques, calling for great care to attain their best performance. In a certain picture from the eighteenth dynasty representing a whole squadron with sails furled, the ten ships, with the exception of one, have abandoned the enormous curved lotuses on the stern and the mortices are empty, while in another drawing of ships under sail they can be seen in position in all their splendour. Did they wish, by adding this weight, to diminish the hogging of the vessel driven before the wind? The drawing is so accurate that by comparing this picture with the others, one can see very clearly the difference in the waterlines. Free of its spur, and no longer subjected to the breeze, the vessel which has retained its stern iron has raised its nose.

*   *   *

The river must have teemed with boats great and small, medium-sized barges and ferries—Maspéro has discovered only one bridge in Egypt—passenger boats, local omnibuses, special craft and pleasure boats, the only method of transporting the nobility; cargo hulls descending or making their way up river with various commodities; market boats, entertainment boats. . . . One could see veritable convoys of ships: a funeral procession used five for the officiants and an unspecified number for the friends. Religion sped up and down the river. . . . There were packets for pilgrims crossing between Memphis and Thebes, or visiting the great sanctuary of Abydos. Processions, companies and 'societies' went by water; a priest blessed the crocodiles while the archers shot a goose or a fisherman harpooned a pike. The whole of Egypt splashed about in the Nile God, under the gaze of the Sun God, with cries, prayers and songs. The river must be envisaged as one of our main roads,

considerably enlarged, which would have to serve the entire
nation. Egypt had about the same population as Belgium and
everyone repaired to the river. They all foregathered there. One

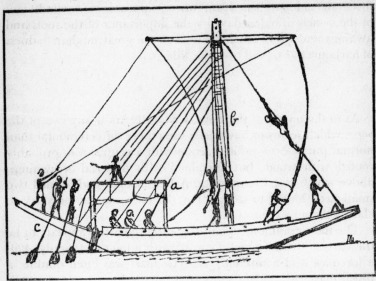

8. Fifth Dynasty

caught a glimpse beneath the mosquito net of the thick lips of
some great lord in the shelter of the *naos*; the fat paunches of the
scribes and peering through the canvas roof (8*a*) the pointed
nose of a young girl or the huge slanting eyes of a courtesan. . . .
The only concession to comfort was protection from the sun;

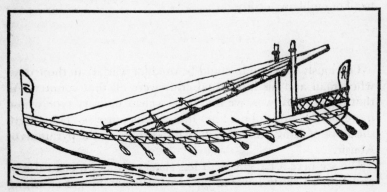

9. Fifth Dynasty

19

even the cattle on the barques were in the shade. The thorough-breds on the barges had their covered boxes.

Today, the watery expanses are deserted. You occasionally meet an indolent *dahabiyeh*, whose appearance reminds you of the vessels of olden days by the importance of the roofs and awnings and the pointed bows; but the great modern sadness of harbours has spread over the Nile. . . .

*　　　*　　　*

As to the names of the ships, we hardly know any except the *baris*, which seems to have been used more for ceremonial than normal purposes: a noble barque with a central *naos* probably roofed with wood, but curtained with material or awnings, above which rose the masting. A tent at each end formed two small deck houses or poops. For the rest, one can only try to classify them by their sails.

The most common type in the early dynasties appears to be the barge. The mast well forward with a long rectangular sail, a foremast and a mizzen. . . . The mast was often double: a biped-mast (8*b*) partly supported on the forepart of the roof. It was composed of two spars joining at the masthead, forming a very acute angle, with cross-bars which may have served for ratlines. Such was the barque of the fifth dynasty, 3500 B.C. (8) which seems already to be singularly complete: a common, all-service boat, with few decorations, no poop or bow emblems, snub-nosed and, as one might say of a vessel devoid of figure-head or emblem, 'utility'.

*　　　*　　　*

Obviously such a ship could be used for warfare in those days when man and his individual craft were all that counted. At that period, however, we find a very clear military type whose more slender and robust lines indicate its purpose. These were the ships of King Sahu-Rê, drawn in profile on the pyramids of Abusir.

We see here a barque with less sheer, without a central roof and with an easily lowered biped-mast which hinges on strong stanchions and comes to rest aft on a crutch. In all Egyptian

ships the mast could be lowered, but in the warships the operation must have been made particularly easy, while in cargo
vessels one simply finds it lashed to a large stanchion rising
from the deck. The mast is a hindrance in getting to windward
under oars—particularly a biped-mast; they fought with decks
cleared like the French galleys. It might be that this apparatus
was more perfect in a warship because it was customary to
return to depot as soon as the ship made port. Had the mast
remained aloft gigantic sheds would have been needed. In the
case of merchant ships, the deck house often prevented this
operation.

Sahu-Rê's ship (9) has only two posts, fore and aft, unadorned
except for the ritual eye of Osiris, and this confirms my instinct
that these decorations, with the progress of navigation, must
have served a utilitarian purpose, at least in the big ships.

Another detail concerning the warship. All the military
oarsmen seem to have rowed standing up, whereas for merchant
and pleasure ships we normally find them seated. This is
logical: more strength, more impetus and no hindering thwarts.

* * *

In the eighteenth dynasty, a thousand years later, was born,
fully armed, the most beautiful type of Egyptian ship, that of

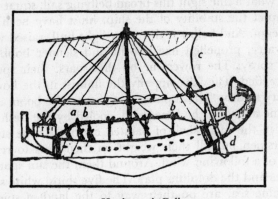

10. Hatshepsut's Galley

Queen Hatshepsut (10), which was reproduced on the cliffs of
the Valley of the Kings, at Thebes, on the walls of her tomb.

The Queen must have been a great sea-amazon. The ship portrayed by the artists, who were as painstaking as they were skilful, will remain for all time as a magnificent nautical achievement. There is little change, but the vessel has been brought to perfection. It is more sensitive, more keen. It tends towards an instrument of total warfare. It must have been far swifter than those of King Sahu- Rê. Its slim hull needs a far smaller press of sail to throw up a fine wake. Every effort has been made to achieve efficiency.

It seems better balanced and more sensitive to the waves. It is sharper, its bows are razor-edged and must have made a ram capable of grievously wounding the enemy when the beautiful, elongated vessel was borne forward by the strength of its rowers, pulling for all their worth with the aid of its sail—a sail tightly lashed to the curved yards. On the stern can be seen the hieratic lotus, so secure that were the hand of a giant to seize it, the whole ship could be lifted up. Clear, unencumbered, muscular lines; watertight joints: the ships of Hatshepsut are thoroughbreds.

The rigging was composed of a sail with both yard and boom, rectangular and curved like a shield (10c): this is rather rare and is a feature of ocean-going vessels. The rock carving represents it rigged fore and aft but we know that this is merely the clumsy Egyptian style of drawing everything in profile. One can imagine what a fine sight this broad bellying sail, squat enough not to upset the stability of the ship, must have been with a wind abeam. And below it this ultra-light hull, raised well out of the water, propelled like a swift and slender bobbin in a whirl of spray. The rowers lie on their oars: their speed has been exceeded. They accompany the flautist in the bows with their lusty shanty. The topmen cling on to the boom and the lifts, borne away on the blue flood, cooled by the fresh breeze sporting in the huge shell of painted cotton. At the stern the two steersmen put all their weight on their oars to resist the caprices of a following wind. Around them the sun sparkles on the waves and the dolphins play. The five ships, white spots on a dark blue sea, are on their way to the land of spices and incense....

Ultra-light we said: yes and more so than any other craft; frail yet sturdily built, braced to dispense with a heavy keel or

coarse timber-work. In Egypt, for the first time, and the last
time to my knowledge, appeared a superb piece of audacity:
external reinforcement by the hogging truss. The two extremities of the ship are joined by a very powerful hawser, one of
those master ropes from Byblos or Sidon, designed to ensure the
stability of the craft; to maintain on a taut rope the curve of the
beautiful arc. And more than this: to achieve sensitivity at any
given moment, it will be seen that a lever remains permanently
among the strands on the principle of the batten used to set a saw.
A few turns suffice to flex that slender and resonant hull which the
heel of a rower could make vibrate like a lute string (10*b*, *b*).

This is not literary hyperbole. I have made a model of one of
these beautiful ships, with a joy akin to that felt by the sailors
who originally sailed in them. It was under three feet long and
did not weigh more than a pound. When its batten had tight-
ened the hair cable, a flick would make the shell of polished
wood tremble. In this way I was able to study the shape of

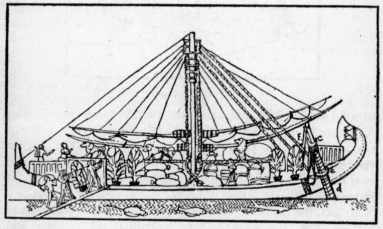

11. A Cargo of Incense Shrubs

Egyptian ships. I saw that the waist could be used for a light
cargo because it was placed very low. I also found out that the
lifts which led to the lower yard to keep a true balance could be
secured with two complete turns and a half-hitch. Thus they
took on the exact aspect they had on the sculpture and allowed
a rapid change or topping up. I realised how well this delicate

23

ship must behave on the water, with its huge steering oars to ensure a straight course.

* * *

The solid steering oars (10*d*) were a novelty. In the smaller boats, an oar was fixed to the quarter and served to direct the movement. But there was nothing of the scull about it. The fixture did not allow the figure-of-eight movement of the scull— its 'screw'. Previously, on the barges (8*c*), one saw the multiple oars plied with all the weight of the body, which replaced to a certain extent the nimbleness of the paddle. Later, we meet a port and starboard fixture of two oars, attached at a single point

12. Twentieth Dynasty

to solid posts, which still permitted the twist of a man's body. And here at last was the rudder, firmly fixed to resist a heavy sea but confined to the rotation of a 'cheek'. It is the modern rudder. One no longer rows with it, one steers. The craft will now respond to the least touch on the water which streams past its smooth hull.

In fact, the heart of this rudder (11*d*), its central post, rests at first on a fork (11*c*), where it turns, is bound loosely to a spar and finally—a novelty—moves through a ring fixture (11*e*) which keeps it absolutely straight. The shore, the 'helm' of our ships (11*f*), descends at right angles to the deck, forming a very acute angle with the post. The steersman grips it with both hands and turns the ship by the simultaneous action of two rudders.

This time there is no decoration; lightness above all. But on other vessels, the upper part of the rudder reveals the most

24

charming fantasies. Usually these are variations on a woman's head, as if she alone were needed to steer: heads of queens even wearing the *pschent* and the false royal beard in its holder; the great wig or a little fleece, curled and smooth, which reminds one of the young Numidia at the age of sixteen; streamers, too, which were the first poop flags.

* * *

I could not resist reproducing the stone carving which portrays the cargo of one of these lovely ships (11); it is a complete Egyptian conversation piece. Divine Hatshepsut has demanded perfumes. Her subjects, highly excited, have left for the south; they have taken in a full load, an overload. Panniers and sacks are piled up on deck, ivory; everywhere incense shrubs packed up to protect them from the burning sun. The ship is so overloaded that the line of its cross beams is hidden below the water: the line of the beams (10 *s, s*)—placed athwartships—to support the deck. And a charming touch, some fine baboons have adopted the ship with its crew: baboons are particularly fierce, but now they seem to be at home balancing on the famous cable, on this ingenious invention which they apparently consider was built entirely for their pleasure. A little further off, the sailors are taking a giraffe aboard.

Rameses III provides us with a special document on the warship in the composition representing his victory over the 'Peoples of the Sea'. The beautiful warlike yacht has grown less attractive in two hundred years. The rowers are sheltered behind a high *pavesade* (12 *p, p*) which protects and hides them. On the upperworks can be seen two houses (12 *d, d*), real 'castles', the forerunners of those which will appear later in the Middle Ages. The mast still carries a lenticular sail, which seems to have become entirely a war sail; but here, too, is a novelty—one of the first crow's nests, in the shape of a lotus, rather like the half-top of the galleys, a practical device for a lookout man or a soldier. Finally, the ritual form seems to have been transformed and the stem post has been replaced by a leopard's head, (12*c*). This type begins to evoke the Mediterranean fleet which very soon decided upon the spur for ramming purposes. The vessel carries a single yard in the Greek manner.

The construction of the Egyptian barque remains an irritating little problem: it has aroused much interest. However, we possess pictorial and descriptive documents and the text of Herodotus which says: 'Their transport vessels were built with thornwood [or acacia] which weeps tears of resin. They take

13. Building a Barque, Twentieth Dynasty

planks [pieces no doubt] of two cubits which they place one on top of each other like bricks. They bind them with long, stout ropes; on the prepared surface they place beams, making them fast inboard with ropes from Byblos' (13).

But 'bricks' is the revealing word. The Egyptians possessed only mediocre materials for their medium-sized cargo boats, since good planks were a rarity, so they clamped these half-fashioned pieces together in corbelling, one on top of the other like bricks in vaulting (13a). They then had merely to round off the protruding angles, following the line of the small ship. This is precisely what we can see the men doing with their axes. All builders of models have used this technique. Model ships are built today for American children on exactly the same principle. The Egyptian adze is an admirable tool which I have used successfully (13b).

To reinforce the whole structure, the Egyptians introduced what landsmen translators have called the joists and what sailors call the beams. The side planking is secured to these beams by lashings, as we shall find on so many other primitive ships, Scandinavian, Hindu or Malay. By cutting away the inboard ends the shipwright creates a nut (13c), a cleat, which is then drilled to take the woolding. Finally, the Egyptians, who were experts in natrons and pitch, carefully caulked the entire hull. The result was a vessel created from the resources of the country, a 'maid-of-all-work' as they say in the ports.

On the other hand, it is certain that for the warships, where nothing was stinted, for the delicate instruments we have seen, the finest woods were brought from Syria just as in the old French navy all the masts of the government ships were made with wood from Riga; just as today the luxury canoe is made of mahogany.

This explanation would seem to tally completely with the drawing I have reproduced and accounts to a certain extent for this planking which for once, in its shoddiness, does not typify the Egyptian precision.

*   *   *

Admirable ships these Egyptians, graceful and refined, invariably decorated with taste and invention; but, fundamentally, river ships. The sacred Nile so influenced the whole Egyptian marine that, in spirit, they never really left its banks. The proud Pharaohs had no interest in cargo vessels. They entrusted all their imports to the Phoenicians, or at least a very great part of them. The people of Sidon, among others, were their official couriers. The port of Suez and the two others they had built on the harsh coast, attempting to join them to the Nile by canals which were always silted up, contained more foreign ships than native craft. The Egyptians, aristocrats to their finger tips, despised the rumbustious men who took pleasure in the sordid occupation of commerce. Their ships sported with the sea and did not till it. They preferred to pile up perfumes on their decks rather than commercial travellers' carpet bags, to redden them with blood and not with cochineal. But what happened? The Semites took the place they disdained and transmitted their ideas by selling their rubbish. The modern world, instead of imitating the negation and grandeur of Egypt, has fallen for the Chaldaean huckster, his baseness and buffoonery, his nervous unreliability, mockery and cynicism, his commercial drive and baker's dozen.

14. Assyria

CHAPTER III

Chaldaeo-Phoenicia

CHALDAEANS and Phoenicians are sufficiently alike for them to be considered of the same origin, or they inter-married so extensively that they became of the same blood. Whether they are called Chaldaeans, Assyrians or Phoenicians, they had the same black metallic locks, the same thick skins, the same sloe-like eyes. They all had hooked noses, a rancid olive tint and thick, sensual lips. They all dressed the same, in a jumble of wool, pompoms and fringes like Henry II dining-room curtains. When they went further afield the Phoenicians wore complicated, greasy greatcoats. They had the same character: a never-satisfied pride combined with a secret anxiety which nothing could allay. This made them quick to kneel before their gods and cringe before the customs officers. They invariably felt that they were on remand. Their mythology was abominable, for they insisted that they were pursued by demons and threatened by a Gehenna whose cruelty increased with each generation. No race has ever been less contemplative, and thus no race has ever been less civilised. They rushed about as though their woollen clothes and baggy trousers were on fire. Eager to grab something in their doomed hands, they flung themselves on their neighbours, on women and on gold.

Historians try to explain the Chaldaeo-Assyrians by their climate. Admittedly theirs was not an ideal country; situated between a fiery desert to the west and south and icy mountains to the east and north, they were frozen on one side and roasted on the other. The country was irrigated by powerful, muddy rivers, as furious and dirty as the inhabitants. They were plagued by vast marshes, and their costume may have been designed to protect them from the mosquitoes.

The first to emerge from secular shadow were the people of Chaldaea, from the country of the plain, because, as usual, it was easier to live there; but they expanded rapidly, in ruthless

15. Assyrian *Gufa*

conquest. Contrary to the usual procedure, we see an estuary people from the Delta conquering the interior. They soon became very powerful politically and commercially. In fact they were admirably placed at the junction between the eastern world and the Mediterranean basin.

Their entire marine started in Chaldaea. They, too, began with fascines but they were lucky in having a kind of exceptionally large mangrove. The Tigris and the Euphrates, before joining as they do today, felt their way through a marshy swamp full of reed thickets: dense undergrowth which allowed oppressed peoples to take refuge in them and to live as outlaws. In these hideouts, they could make a twin skiff from a split stem. They also profited from local adhesive and watertight products. One has only to think today of the famous Mosul oilfields. They had plenty of resins and pitch.

The 'round ship' soon appeared, built on a wicker frame. In drawings 14 and 15 we see the change over to the pitch or

29

leather-covered pannier. Furthermore we possess an astonishingly accurate document, particularly if we compare it with the pictures of almost circular barques to be found on the palace of Nimrod. This was the explanation given by Herodotus. It shows what great value we must put on the Father of History when he speaks of craftsmanship: 'The boats which serve for the journey to Babylon are round and made of skins. They are built in that

16. Cargo Raft on Skins

part of Armenia north of Assyria with willows, from which the keels and ribs are made, and lined with skins. The skins themselves are given the shape of ships' sides.' (This can clearly be seen in my drawing: on the original, the stitching and the cross threads are visible.) 'The ship is rounded like a shield with neither bow nor stern. The bottom is filled with straw. . . . When the merchants arrive at Babylon they sell their cargo, with the hulk and the straw. Then they load their skins on asses and return to Armenia' (15).

With this people, we can tranquilly study the floating skin. The goat skin, blown up like a balloon, was in common usage. We see that these people took to the water on their strange craft (19a) at the slightest opportunity. They were almost amphibious. Perhaps a part of their liking for wool came from this inclination to paddle, since damp wool does not chill like cotton. They were absolutely at home on their skins. We even find a good man, wearing a tiara, fishing with a line, astride his four-footed bladder, which seems itself to be swimming. A strange feature of these craft is their balance. One would think they carried ballast.

But the skin was used on a grand scale and we can see it in the sketch of the cargo raft (16). One should note the mattress, supported by a second set of ropes, to preserve the skins from collision or damage (16*m*).

In these countries there was not the same lack of big timber as in Egypt. They received floating trunks from the Armenian

17. Assyrian Trader

and Syrian mountains. The solid hull was easily built with long planks. This rapidly became common commercial practice and is perhaps the reason for the paucity of documents we possess. They are confined to a few reliefs on the palaces of Kings Sargon, Nimrod and Sennacherib. The Assyrians appear to have invented nothing new and there is nothing particularly national about their marine.

The historians distinguish between two types: the so-called commercial (17) and the military (18), because the latter has a spur. However, the commercial vessel also carries a *pavesade* of shields (17 *p, p*). It is not certain that the spur was a weapon of war. These documents are in any case of only comparative antiquity and date from a few centuries B.C. Ramming is out of the question unless there is great perfection in the craft's construction. It is possible that this spur may be a ritual design, like the Egyptian crescent, evoking their god Oannes. All the Mediterranean types of the Iron Age were designed in this manner. Could this not be the representation of a fish?

I have tried to reproduce one of these ships under way. The apparent novelty of two rows of oars may be due to the displacement of the rowers. The double deck is clearly Hellenic. I have lowered the trellis above the rowers; this must have been a protection and at the same time have provided ventilation. I must bear this slight responsibility; not that I am afraid to back my opinion, but because one must respect the original.

We have little more information about the Phoenicians. We know that they were closely linked with the Chaldaeans and Assyrians. For the most part it was the Phoenicians who built their fleets. It was an easy journey. The Euphrates was not more than 120 miles from the coast and we know that in addition to being great sailors they were excellent caravan leaders, capable of bringing the cargo to their ports. They quickly descended upon Babylon, which was to become a universal symbol of wealth and vice. They were influenced by the Chaldaeans, who consulted the stars so that the Phoenicians could exploit them. The Chaldaeans counted the stars so that they could calculate their hoards better and they may possibly have invented alphabetic writing in order to draw up their bills of exchange.

The Phoenicians were only colonials on Syrian soil. They are not considered sufficiently from this aspect. All they wanted was the strip of land necessary for their port installations and for the manufactures they exploited. They acted as the British did in China with Hong Kong and Shanghai, and behind them lay the Chaldaean might to supply them with orders. Their national feelings were very weak and each of their towns was a separate entity. Carthage, their pride, very quickly seceded from Syria. Merchants and pirates, they built their gulls' nests on the edge of the cliff without a care for the fields that lay behind.

They, too, were no innovators. They never invented—they watched and served others. They copied the Egyptian marine and enlarged it. The Phoenicians possessed everything necessary for success. We still speak of the cedars of Lebanon when we think of them and this points an irrefutable truth. They had wood just as England had coal and, in the universal and ridiculous battle for supremacy, geography is always the grandmother of history.

These shipwrights could surround their vessels with single planking. Sennacherib entrusted his equipment to them. Solomon himself founded—or perhaps improved, for it is one of the oldest ports in the world—the harbour of Ezion-geber, situated at the far end of Lake Sinai, from where the fleets left for Ophir to bring back gold, precious stones and rare woods for the mighty Emperor of Israel. The voyage lasted a year .

We can safely say that the organisation of the journey was left to the Phoenicians, apparently the only mariners in the ancient world who were used to ocean navigation: they built their famous Tharsis fleet which made a voyage lasting three years. It is difficult to accept the modern location of these still hypothetical places, Tharsis and Ophir. It is believed that Tharsis was Spain with its silver and mercury mines; but the journey would have taken only two months. The old legends tell us much more, and even suggest that the Phoenicians knew the route to an unknown continent from which they obtained

18. Assyrian Galley, 700 B.C.

their riches. Diodorus Siculus mentions Ethiopian voyages towards the southern ocean and Seneca himself, in his famous passage: *Venient annis saecula feris quibus oceanis* . . . , heralds the new world. Modern geography locates Ophir in Arabia, but this position does not at all explain 'the great voyage', and the maritime importance attributed to it by sailors. Far more likely it was the country of Goa, Ceylon or Bengal where Ophir, son of Jactan, had established a trading centre; the fabulous riches of India and its remoteness conform very much better to the legend.

In the Bible, Tharsis is the Western Ocean and Ophir the Southern.

*   *   *

In any case, the Phoenicians were quite capable of fostering every maritime legend. Not content with exploiting the sea to a greater extent than any other people of their period, they knew how to preserve the secret of their goals and their routes. The ancient world could only be surprised by their cargoes without knowing where they came from. They remained an unknown race—not even a race, for they never possessed any spirit of cohesion. The ten towns they inhabited on the Syrian coast with barely a few leagues of land around them, soon felt completely independent. Carthage, as soon as she rose to greatness despised them. The Phoenicians constituted a secret society more than a nation. The invention of freemasonry, still so fashionable in the ships of the nineteenth century, has been attributed to them. They created widely spread reserves as the Knights Templar—who also, perhaps, exploited America—were to to do later, following their example.

One discovers Phoenician traces everywhere, as far as India, and the sons of Melkhart have left their mark on Europe. No present-day port in the Mediterranean escaped their attention. They passed the Strait of Gabes, sailed northwards and entered the Channel; they penetrated far into the Baltic. The similarity between the *drakkar* and the Mediterranean ship proves that their hulls moored in these countries where they came in search of succin, the yellow amber so beloved by antiquity. They must have wintered there and left their shipwrights behind.

In the south—at a later date it is true—under Necho, they circumnavigated Africa. Leaving the Red Sea, they knew that they had rounded Africa when the sun rose obstinately to starboard. They took three years for the trip.

When the Flemings colonised the Azores they found on the point of the westernmost island a gigantic horseman carved in the rock, stretching his arm westwards to point the way. The horse was the Punic emblem which, according to Herodotus, adorned the bows and, so that no one might remain ignorant of this, the stonemason had engraved on the armed man's chest a huge letter: 'K', signifying Karthago.

*   *   *

We have very few details of the vessels which carried the Phoenicians beyond the known limits of the world. One has to interpret those which everyone knows: the rickety ships in the Louvre, taken from the bas-reliefs of Sargon's Palace, which show us a vessel taking in a cargo of cedar trunks in the port of Tyre. Obviously we must make allowance for the sculptor who got his information only by hearsay and by description. We find what we can logically expect of the Phoenicians, who created nothing and copied everything, who were exploiters and pirates, a basically Egyptian form. The emblematic side is modified with the horse's head *which is never met with on the Nile,* but the principle of the vessel with stem and stern posts is maintained (19).

The documents obviously exaggerate the height of these fore and aft posts. Their proportions should be restored to conform to their necessary aims, both ritual and practical: for mooring or strengthening. We might perhaps grant the Phoenicians, as a distinctive mark, taller and eminently practical perpendicular posts, such as the 'Peoples of the Sea' carried when Rameses III defied them in a pitched battle in the twentieth dynasty and which the Assyrians seem to have preserved.

Furthermore, one of the bas-reliefs shows a main top such as we saw in Egyptian ships of the same period.

In addition, we possess Egyptian documents of the thirteenth dynasty (1900 B.C.) figuring Phoenician vessels which are portrayed with Egypt's usual accuracy, skill and sense of colour. We find an enlargement of the Nile boats, a notable increase in tonnage. It is no longer a nacelle but a cargo ship (19). The delicate almond has become a coconut. The heavy planking of the hull curves round a thickened bottom. The sheer of the Egyptian ships has been noticeably flattened. We are looking at solid travelling chests. Their rigging is what we considered to have been reserved to the Egyptian ocean-going ship: the rectangular sail, well spread by two yards. The stem and stern posts are quite vertical and broad enough for the pilot to climb on top of them (19*h*), and to remain aloft to take soundings of

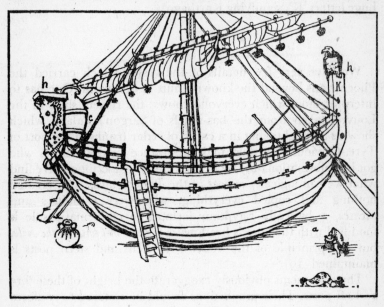

19. Phoenician Vessel, 800 B.C.

the channel with his eye or with a pole. Near the stem seems to be the ritual place for the amphora (19*c*). For the first time we meet with gangways (19*d*) made of timber.

There is no doubt as to the nationality of the sailors: on board are bales of rich materials which will buy the skipper his clearance papers and permission to sell his wares even on the quayside to the merchants who are haggling about his prices.

These Phoenicians knew how to keep their secrets even as regards their hulls. They came and went on the high seas, half traders, half pirates.

Tin traffickers and purveyors of human flesh, they supplied slaves to all the palaces and harems and they often had to hide from the police. They inspired admiration for their nautical skill and disgust for their commercialism and cruelty. It is

36

an historical fact that they sacrificed hosts of children; Flau-
bert, alas, did not invent their Baal of red hot bronze who consumed their first-born by reducing them to ashes.

Perhaps they were haunted or soured, perhaps they shoul-
dered an incubus of inextinguishable bitterness? Homeric and
Platonic tradition maintains that they were the sole survivors
of Atlantis. There is no longer any doubt of the existence in
olden days of a very large island extending from the Azores
to the vicinity of little Brittany. Soundings at 1,500 fathoms
have brought up tachylite lavas which could not have vitrified
in this way, without crystallisation, except in the open air.
Were the Phoenicians survivors of the appalling cataclysm?
Did they beach at the end of their journey on the Syrian coast
where, as indifferent sailors, they merely wanted to establish
temporary quarters? It was they who christened Gades, who
called the Straits the Gadiric Gates in memory of Gadirus, the
brother of Atlas and ruler of Atlantis. Was their alliance with
the Asiatics to prove disastrous? They would assume some
grandeur were one to see them as eternal exiles of a lost Fatherland in an endless search for their national soil which had been
swallowed up, for some kind of promised land.

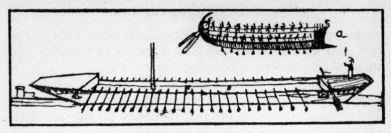

20. Raft and Primitive Bireme

CHAPTER IV

Greece

THE Athenians, according to sublime Plato, were of the same origin as the inhabitants of Saïs: the Pelasgi were also Atlanteans. Are we to see in this one of the elements which contributed to the superior civilisation of Attica? With a more lively and nimble intellect, we find in them something of that grandeur which stamps Egypt with a sacred seal. On the other hand, they were colonised, or partially so, by the Phoenicians; Cadmus came to Boeotia and, although I know that the Boeotians aroused the sarcasm of the mocking Athenian, this encroaching occupation, so near Attica, could not have continued without having some influence. It is perhaps to be found in a taste for gossip, a love of change and in ingratitude.

This, too, doubtless developed in the Hellenes a naval sense which, with the intelligence that sparkled in this creative and poetic folk, allowed them to win maritime successes comparable with those of the famous Hatshepsut, and even to surpass them in the warship. The Mediterranean has never produced anything superior in efficiency and hardiness to the famous Greek trireme of the time of Themistocles, in fact, as a work of art.

Furthermore, the Greek, even if he used the sea with the science of the Phoenician, knew how to enjoy it. The description of his pleasure has enabled us in turn to appreciate and love it better by recapturing his songs and discovering his images. The Phoenician was the pimp of the sea, the Greeks were its lovers. We are still thrilled today by the Greek naval epithalamia and still submit to the charm of Hellenic imagery. Its symbolism, far from dulling its poetry, on the contrary enhances it.

38

They pondered long upon the sea and the gods they made of its changing moods incarnate their memories and feelings. From the summit of promontories and the inlets of the Attic shore with its gleaming temples, they knew how to appreciate the blue and violet, restless expanse, glittering with golden crests; they delighted in the sea, furling and unfurling its foamy, echoing waves, reft the wonders from it, divided its beauties the better to savour them, and the profusion of their oceanic gods reflected the diversity of their joys.

These gods are at the same time very old and very young, thus symbolising the eternity of the waves and their perpetual youth; gods and goddesses sport in the foam, born of the limitless force and matchless gentleness of the great element. Poseidon, whose attributes were the Punic horse and the Greek dolphin, was highly respectable but possessed a dauntless vigour which could cleave mountains. He shared with Proteus and Glaucus the epithet θαλάσσης γέρων, 'the old man of the sea', although like them he possessed the most youthful ardour when raising storms or begetting monsters. Proteus watched the flocks of the sea and when he paid a visit to the shores, his seals—the Mediterranean at that time abounded with them—lined up in serried ranks to defend him. Like the waves, he could take on all disguises: phosphorescent, serpentiform and even winged like the spray. Glaucus reigned over the deep. His unfathomable gaze followed you from the bottom of green abysses, terrible yet reassuring.

But the Greeks reserved their greatest fervour for the daughters of old Nereus, the Nereides, who at first, in the time of Homer, numbered thirty-four; then forty-five according to Apollodorus; while Hesiod raised the number to fifty, as though there could never be enough to express the varied whims and charms of the waves. First Amphitrite, who softly girdled the earth with her warm arms; Thetis, whose silver heels pranced on the shore with the rising tide, and Kumo who danced on the crests of the swell; Actaea, who flayed the rocks; Protho, who impelled the ships with a hand full of pearls, and smiled in their wake; and then, pale Speio, no less moving, who penetrated deep into the grottos, whose eyes were the colour of beryls or sun-stones and whose transparent flesh shone like mother-of-pearl. . . . Brilliant imagery which the Greeks caught up from the waves in their swift course and transformed into ageless poetry.

They immediately applied their sensibility and skill to the construction of their craft and they seem to have surpassed all others in the success of their light ships, so pliant and strangely modern. Of course, fortunately for our love of tradition, generalisation and transformation, they include clumsy, rounded, primitive forms (21) in which can be felt the Assyrian

21. Early Greek Galley

influence and the shortcomings of osier with leather or pitch. But this was purely transitory; one is bewildered by the elegance—one might almost say the *morbidezza*—of their Iron Age ships. They created these subtle craft at a period when other nations were building clumsy, bloated vessels, and their warship, πλοῖον μακρόν, responded to these syllables which echo and glide like a shuttle weaving a passage through the waves.

Tradition maintains that the Greeks made a great advance in the art of the raft. They are supposed to have perfected this rudimentary instrument: from it perhaps emerged those slender spurred ships which we are so amazed to find on their clay amphorae. For the idea of the raft, buoyant because of the difference in density between its timber and the water, they substituted a craft which kept afloat through the air imprisoned inside it. We have already seen that Ulysses' raft was almost watertight; when he fashioned those trees so carefully, a little resin or moss would have sufficed to prevent the water from passing between them so that the planking of the deck would have formed a real hull. The authors of antiquity seemed to think that the Greek ships of the Trojan period were built with flat bottoms (20) tapered fore and aft. They even give the proportions and the designs. Their beam was a seventh of their length, which remains a good dimension for ships in general. They were propelled by fifty rowers; they called this vessel, rather pompously, 'the long imperishable ship' because numerous watertight compartments divided, protected and strengthened it. Since each small compartment was kept well sealed, damage could be plugged or repaired without any dire conse-

22. Egyptian Influence

quences. The vessel therefore remained manoeuvrable and light, easy to haul ashore, as was the general custom in antiquity. We find mention of this in Homer.

So I accept this quinquereme. I accept it even more readily since it can explain and give credence to the famous Greek beak which has been so strangely decried and declared to be impossible. When we examine the Trojan quinquereme, we see how easy it is to transform it into a vessel with a prolongation forward; how its silhouette can determine that of others without great change (20a): the boats portrayed on the vases from ancient Dipylon, in the Louvre and at Athens. To deny the value of these documents, which are so numerous, is to deny the evidence.

I accept also, as a special type, a plausible version painted by a fashionable artist on a vase, for I find in it details still reminiscent of the vessels from the south. Of this nature is the small boat with its *naos* and its Nilotic crescent-shape (22) and that other on a Carian vase which, reduced to nautical requirements, could give us a true Assyrian craft like those we have already met (21). Furthermore, we must note a very pronounced tendency to the cataphract galley and the galley with a *catastroma*, i.e. decked, with a gallery above the rowers, sheltering them and allowing the hoplites to fight overhead

41

with an unencumbered combat ground. The small figures on
this vase are performing evolutions which today look merely
comical, but which were exceedingly bloody (23). It was at the
Ionian port of Thasos that decks were used for the first time in
the Mediterranean. They seem, however, to have been abandoned in the transition period and to have been reserved for
costly and delicate warships. We find them only in the trireme,
probably at the moment when progress in naval shipbuilding
allowed them to be built without risk.

On the Minoan seals we see once more a type of ship which
corresponds strangely with the vessels defeated by Rameses III
when he gave battle to the 'People of the Seas'. It is possible
that our dear Greeks were taught a dreadful lesson.

*   *   *

Doubtless it was one of these solid and handy ships which
served Jason's thrice famous expedition in quest of the wealth
of Colchis: a medium craft, seaworthy and light, able to sail
anywhere, with fifty men aboard but, as the epic tells, harnessed to the oars in pairs. Thus, counting 3 feet in spacing,
12 benches and 12 feet fore and aft, a ship of 60 feet—but
manned by immortals! A crew for once which had not been
harvested in the cafés or the harbour dives: all demi-gods,
heroes and princes. . . . Hercules, whose feats of strength cannot
be disdained at the tiller; Orpheus, whose lyre distracted the
men on watch and calmed the waves; Peleus, the future father
of Achilles; Telamon, the father of Ajax, and the two dazzling
Dioscuri, the twin sons of Zeus and Leda. . . .

And they made their way towards that legendary wealth in a
pine ship—the red pine which flourished in Greece. A single
one was sufficient for Argus, who fitted out the *Argo* in the
port of Pelusium: for the bows, Athene herself had provided an
oak. The mast, taken from a sacred tree which used to pronounce oracles, continued to prognosticate and everyone lent an
ear to it, even Orpheus.

When I wanted to build my model of the *Argo*, I tried to
procure Greek wood—a wood which had grown on that incomparable soil and which preserved, if not the power of
augury, the scent and a little of its soul. So I wrote to the friend

of a friend, to M. Topazi who, in response to my request, went in person with his daughter to Mount Pelion. 'Alas,' he wrote, 'wooded Pelion possesses only a copse of pines, a very small copse which today is sacrosanct. I could not even approach it.' I was not able to procure a branch big enough to make a yard arm. But later I was given a sprig of myrtle and from it I made Peleus' lance, which Achilles was to inherit. My *Argo* is merely of limewood from the Pays d'Ouche.

As regards the streamlined form of the ship, we cannot ignore the influence of mimicry, an imitation of the dolphin which is so common in the Mediterranean where it plays on the waves as squirrels play among the waves of the forests. The nose, the

23. Early Greece

prominent lower lip, the kind of trumpet we find in the dolphin, would give a satisfactory explanation for the beak of the ship (23). We must not forget that here a sense of cult as well as reverent imitation might intervene. These creatures were considered to possess the attributes of divinity and, in view of their agility and their speed, the Greeks might very easily have copied their form to endow their ships with their qualities.

Does not this little academic drawing show the striking resemblance (23*a*)? Does not this enlarged eye on the bows of the galley, at the same time ritual and reminiscent of the eye of Osiris on Egyptian barges, add to the face of the dolphin the ironic and cunning gleam of its glance? It has always been a tradition, even in modern ships, to copy the lines of fishes. Le

Roy, the old shipwright from Brest, replied to my grandfather who congratulated him on the performance of one of his thoroughbreds, 'I based my design on a mackerel; only the tail and head are missing.' The Greeks retained the head.

Aboard the ships, the hoplites, in close-fitting helmets and narrow greaves, displayed magnificent and highly artistic shields with warrior, hunting or marine motifs: the crab, the agile bonito, the furious charging bull and the surly boar.

In any case, from the sixth century onwards, the galley without *catastroma*, without a double deck, was established and

24. Greek Galley, 500 B.C.

standardised in its frail perfection. We find the purest models on the great Exekias *dinos* in the Louvre, around whose rim rival vessels revolve at full speed: two dolphins with forty fins, who seem to leave their orbit under the centrifugal force with which the painter's art has endowed their hull (24). The type has been rationalised and lightened again, remaining aesthetic but becoming solid, well-ribbed and eager. The ships were launched at extreme speed and one feels that this speed must swiftly have reached its maximum.

One would think of the racing yacht, of regattas, if the great number of rowers did not exclude the idea: such expense would never be wasted on any but a military or a commercial goal. The general shape is lengthened, as though by its speed, and its length necessitates flattening. Here we obviously have a vessel more than 60 feet long. The *aphlaston* rises high in the stern in the form of a fish's tail but is lightened and reduced, as can be seen in my sketch (24a). The bows have a superstructure

44

ASSYRIAN NAVAL EXPEDITION
Bas-relief of King Sargon II at Khorsabad. *Louvre*

PLATE I

PLATE II

CREW OF

Bas-relief from

TIAN SHIP

gdom. *Louvre*

Photo Archives photographiques

(a)

GREEK SAILING SHIPS

From a Greek vase. *Louvre*

Photo Giraudon

(b)

ROWERS IN A TRIREME

Bas-relief from the Acropolis. *Louvre*

PLATE III

which may have been useful in battle but whose purpose seems to be more nautical than warlike: to prevent the galley from wallowing in the waves and to provide a bulwark with the idea of ploughing through them. Also to protect the crew from the spray. The beak is in the shape of a pike's jowl. The sail is the same as to be found in Egyptian ships, but the boom is missing.

It is a boat race, whereas the famous Nicosthenes cup (25) portrays a sailing regatta. This time the rowers have been put ashore. The skiffs are manned only by a helmsman and a topman. Some of the ships have only a coxswain. These are the

25. Athenian Galley, 400 B.C.

fine documentations we possess on the intermediate Greek ship. With the revival of interest in nautical matters (which takes place every 60 years) the cup of Nicosthenes has become famous. It has been constantly reproduced, whereas many years ago I was one of those few privileged people to know and admire it. Thanks to its precision, we can flout the official restorers, many of whom denied the possibility of a beak on primitive Greek ships. I was helped by family influence. One of my relations, a pupil of the famous Admiral Paris, with the humanistic interest of his age, profited by a spell ashore in Athens to study the marine of antiquity. My father, himself a sailor and always eager to learn, brought back from his travels in Greece rough but terribly painstaking sketches. My grandfather, the Admiral, who certainly never read Didymus, constantly spoke of Attic ships with boars' heads. In fact, the vessels of Nicosthenes (26 and 27) sported a wolf's head; but my grandfather was no

26. Boar's Head on the Prow

huntsman. On the banks of the Eurotas he even killed a very young donkey which he had taken for a giant hare among the

27. 500 B.C.

oleanders. This experience allowed him to see Greece in its proper proportions and to convince himself that the admiration of the world had really been exaggerated.

It was by starting with the cup of Nicosthenes that I was able to build my best Greek model, and that I became inspired by this construction. Note the elegant and practical angle of the boar's head with its ears and collarette of bristles sutured to the ship's lines (26), its snout prolonged, circled and ringed in different colours, ending in a metal plate. It is a trifle lowered to burrow in the adversary's hull without becoming entangled in the collision. It is already in a position to administer the blow in the fashion of the spokes of a bicycle wheel. Notice too, right aft, the *aphlaston*, a very strange oval form (25a) which I have never seen elsewhere: an ellipse which finishes in a swan's neck. When I built it on my model I thought that it should be hollow and serve as a counterweight. With lead ballast it could counteract a certain over-loading and re-establish the requirements of navigation. It is obvious that this charming craft, 75 to 90 feet long, must have been as sensitive as a leaf. A trifle could modify her waterline and in consequence her steering. Every canoeist knows that one can steer merely by changing one's position and I am convinced that we have here the model of a racing yacht which took part in those Roman *naumachiae* described by Virgil.

In the stern again, the gangway (25e) is clearly to be seen, that gangway which so many old and even modern designers, as well as certain model builders, have taken for a poop rail and incorporated with the main upperworks as a fixture of the galley. It was placed in the extreme stern of the ship and could on occasion have served as a counterweight. It always remained in this position, however, because the crew went aboard from the stern. I found the gangway in position on a splendid Greek vase, a fourteenth century *crater* portraying the death of the giant Tatos; the ship is beached on the fatal shore and the youth is lying on the deck (28). The ladder leads to a poop, the epitome of the slender delicacy of Greek design and the end process of that hereditary skill which each generation perfected. Faced with this refinement, one is amazed to find certain reproductions or reconstructions where, carried away as we have been by strength during the past few years, the feminine Greek

galley has been transformed into a barbarous instrument made
of the very toughest timber when in reality it was constructed
rather of three-ply than of planks. The wind could have lifted
my model! I shall always remember the disapproval expressed
by the genial Maurice Larrouy at my house when he saw the
sinewy delicacy of my ship and its beak. He did not understand

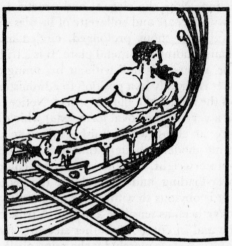

28. Couch on the Poop, 400 B.C.

the slenderness of the antique ship and this beak grieved him.
'The beak is impossible', he assured me sententiously, 'in view
of frequent beaching.' And I, who had just copied my Tatos
poop, made no reply, secretly enjoying my little private knowledge. They always beached stern first (28).

This is the moment when the Greek ship appeared in its
flower, in this period before it became fussy and over-decorated.
For this *featherweight*, it is possible that construction took place,
without frames or ribs, on a mould which was removed once the
planks were in position and grooved and tongued, held together
only by the spring of their compressed fibres: typically Attic
approach to ship-building, intelligent, and daring.

Aft, these stalks and curved pistils added to the slenderness
of her lines. It is probable that these points, these unbound
blades, recalled the ancient reed construction. They could also
be retained as defences for the stern as it lay, vulnerable, on the

shore, or again, they could be used to secure the fishing lines towed in the water as one finds in certain modern ships of the West Indies. On feast days they could be decorated with flowers or some form of bunting or flags (30*d*). A *crater* from London shows us an ornamental carpet (29*a*). The little model is of an ordinary ship, neither skiff nor yawl; a solid little craft with

29. Small Galley, 500 B.C.

modest curves at the stern. It might have been on these pistils that Jason displayed his trophy, and that the Argonauts, rowing with their faces to stern, saw the waves, 'tossing the flashes of the Golden Fleece'.

*　　　*　　　*

And now I must mention the famous triremes (30, 32), which brought immortal glory to Themistocles on the wine-dark waters of Salamis. Unfortunately, these ships have been the cause of great scientific argument. They have incited one against the other in a mordant wrangle which still continues among all specialists of the marine of antiquity: were they

triremes with several tiers of oars? 'True ships,' say the anti-
quarians. 'Impossible ships,' reply the naval experts. It is a
most curious joust between men of letters and men with nautical
experience. What ingenuity has been used to torture the words
and the weight of syntax; what subtlety displayed in an attempt
to reconcile the contradictions!

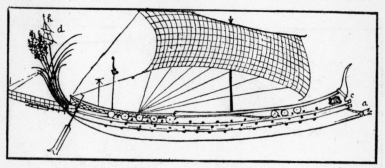

30. Trireme from Delos, 88 B.C.

It has sometimes been a tiresome struggle due to the vanity
displayed on both sides, to the insufficiency of knowledge and
the self-sufficiency of the combatants. Can the translators be
sure of their dictionary when it is a question of expressions and
words of a technical nature? Are sailors entitled to oppose their
actual knowledge to the customs of antiquity? The sea is always
the same, of course, but can this be said for the men who tame
it? A loaded launch would find difficulty in cleaving a passage
with oars in a choppy sea, but the sailors who manned the skiff
of antiquity might be infinitely better trained than the modern
crews and naturally and by heredity more able since the oar
was their natural means of propulsion. What naval officer, unless he had seen the present-day exploits of the Eskimos in their
kayaks, which they use like amphibians, would believe the tales
brought back by the travellers?

How can one deny so many testimonies? Towards the twentieth Olympiad (700 B.C.) Amenocles of Corinth is reputed to
have built the first trireme, the first ship with three banks of
oars. Lucian and Arrian speak of outsize upper oars in ships of
which Xenophon mentions the successive *palamentes,* the
tiers. We find names given to the different tiers of rowers: the

thranites on the top; the *zygites* in the centre; the *thalamites* below, and this last term does not derive from the word θαλάσσα for the sea but from θάλαμος, meaning a bed chamber. Virgil and Thucydides assure us that the first triremes had three rows of oars, with a single man to each oar. The Syracusans, according to Diodorus Siculus, went beyond this at the time of the Punic wars, and managed to build quinqueremes, with five banks of oars. Pausanias certifies that the famous ship of Delos was equipped with no fewer than nine tiers of rowers from bottom to top. Finally, Athenaeus analyses a famous ship belonging to Hiero and, although it is possible he may have exaggerated, it is equally impossible that he could have invented it. It is enlightening as regards the importance of the Greek ship and as regards Greek facilities in the order of nautical construction.

For this famous prototype, the wood used would have been enough for *sixty galleys*. They had recourse to the forests of Etna: incidentally, the men of the Mediterranean had little respect for trees and managed to strip their mountains bare and we cannot picture the antique world from the deserted aspect these land-scapes have today.

The ship was built very strangely, in two parts: the hull and the upperworks. Hiero wanted to immerse the hull first and since his engineers differed in opinion about how to launch such a mass, Archimedes was entrusted with the operation. He solved it without touching the structure (another proof of its size). Instead of bringing it down to the water, he brought the water up to it by means of the famous internal screw pumps which have borne his name ever since. This reminds us how a detail which has not been invented can make the rest credible! To secure the planking, copper rivets with blunt heads, weighing 10 lbs., were used. On the deck, mosaics portrayed scenes from the Iliad and a temple to Venus had been erected there. We have not been given its length and perhaps this is another proof of veracity. Admiral Serres considers that it might have reached 270 feet and that such a ship would displace at least 6,000 tons since it made the crossing from Africa with a 3,000-ton load. Now Athenaeus speaks of *20 tiers* of oars.

* * *

Sailors, with Jal, the father of nautical archaeology, in the van, reply: 'Athenaeus made a mistake or he was deceiving us. Such a construction could never be seaworthy.' Without taking into account the difficulty of getting so many people to row in unison, it would be impossible to house so many oarsmen permanently. 'The men of letters are wrong', maintains Jal. 'They are always making mistakes.'

But what about the plastic sources? Well, one of the most vigorous arguments of the opposition is that we do not possess a single picture of a vessel larger than a trireme. Sculptors and

31. Salamis

painters, they say, have shown themselves to be less fantastic than writers and have not tried to portray what did not exist. The argument bears weight. It is, however, strongly diminished by the fact that there exist a mass of perfectly clear documents on the trireme and that these ships, also, have been denied. I shall not mention the famous bas-relief of the Acropolis which, after careful examination, a frigate captain, M. Carlini, has restored to a simple galley. There are incontestable Greek and Roman pictures and, for the moment, dealing with the trireme alone, we have a certain modern experience: the trireme which Napoleon III, who was very interested in antiquity, ordered from Dupuy de Lôme and which sailed up the Seine in 1851. It had an unqualified success in calm water, even if this did not apply entirely in the roadstead of Cherbourg. But were they really sure of the qualities of the crew that manned it? Can we compare rowers trained in a few months with those oarsmen of antiquity who possessed the concentrated experience of twenty generations?

The fact that this trireme, which in a coarse and ugly manner reproduced fairly accurately the shape of the Roman vessels, made headway and could be steered, should have been sufficient. Do we know, for example, whether with a big sea running they did not put out of action a certain section or several sections of the oars to avoid disorder and jostling? We must not forget that the galleys, which were perfected by the seventeenth century, never went out except in fine weather. They went into dock at the beginning of October. This does not seem much,

32. Greek Galley
Reconstruction by Admiral Serres

but in practice it is very significant. It meant confining the use of the multiple oar to a calm sea. The short sail of the triremes may have been their only means of propulsion in the event of a gale at sea, to enable them to reach less disturbed water where the rowers could resume their efforts.

Admiral Serres, for his part, managed to build a Greek model which passes as plausible. The *thalamite* stands at the bottom of the galley (32). Near his wall and above him, two men are seated on steps, the *zygite* and the *thranite*. This is the model used in the Larousse dictionary, whose attention to naval detail is particularly worthy of respect.

The general shape is quite credible. It is not lacking in subtlety but remains, in comparison with Greek grace, fantasy and art, what Empire style is to the antique—poor and withered. I have given a sketch of this to show the essential elements. We can see the *catastroma* (32a, a), the military deck which protects the soldiers and aids in combat; the probable wales; a stern with a very lanky *aphlaston* (32b) which would

E   53

have disgusted the Greeks; a squat *stolos* to carry a really impertinent jib set on a bowsprit. With his sails, Admiral Serres has shown at least as great imagination as the literary men have been reproached for; such rigging is pure and simple invention. A sailor, of course, could not make it ridiculous, but it is no longer archaeology. The Admiral has rigged his trireme as a Dutch shipwright would have rigged a galliot.

*   *   *

Jal reaches a solution with two different decks: the lower one carried the *thalamites*, bent and doubled up, the second the *zygites*, on low benches, with the *thranites* on other benches,

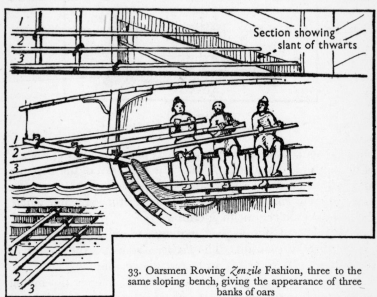

33. Oarsmen Rowing *Zenzile* Fashion, three to the same sloping bench, giving the appearance of three banks of oars

slightly higher and staggered. The explanation given by Serres seems the most acceptable, but the best solution is undoubtedly the one found by Commander Carlini in 1934, which had already been hinted at by Paccini in 1844 and well illustrated by the drawings of Morel Fatio, one of the head librarians at the Musée de la Marine.

This is taken from *zenzile* rowing which I shall deal with later in my chapter on modern galleys. Let me mention here that by placing the rowers' benches obliquely, the rowing vessels of the fifteenth century allowed an oar each to be entrusted to three oarsmen on the same thwart. It is a difficult thing to explain, but a mere glimpse at the drawing will make it comprehensible: here you have a trireme and what a simple one (33)!

What gives weight to this solution comes from a very close observation—it is astonishing it was seen so late—of one of our best-known works of art, one of the most revered and the most obvious, which has been staring us in the face since 1879: the base on which stands the sublime Winged Victory of Samothrace. This figure quivers in an incomparable *élan*, the incarnation of triumphant flight, and yet everyone knew that it stood on the prow of a galley. American scholars brought out their glasses, but Commander Carlini studied it as a naval engineer who possessed a great knowledge of antique drawings. Today we can see how little it needed, by starting from existing data and by making use of contemporary medallions, to restore to the pedestal the appearance of a galley of the period. We can see that the Greek galley was very similar to that of the sixteenth century, using an outrigger on its flanks to support the oars, a salient, a kind of longitudinal fin, the *parodos*.

Now this *parodos* on the Victory bears two rows of oar ports, separated vertically by only five to six inches. We must conclude that the vertical staggering of the rowers themselves must have been of the same order inboard. Thus, by returning to Paccini's solution and also by raising the seats, by staggering them laterally as well as vertically, one sees that banks of oars could be superimposed in a very restricted vertical space: eight tiers to reach a height of $4\frac{1}{2}$ feet, for example.

The disposition is easy. Commander Carlini has solved the famous architectural problem: there only remains the problem of the handling of tiered oars: this is made easier by their compression.

To Commander Carlini we owe, furthermore, other discoveries of great value: rubbings of the *graffiti* from Delos discovered in sumptuous interiors which at some time had been invaded by sailors. For these images, engraved with a knife or a stiletto point, were certainly made by a sailor, if only from the minuteness of the details. The three drawings which Commander Carlini gave us are among our most authentic documents. They have been traced by the same hand and their resemblance proves that the artist knew quite empirically what he was drawing.

They probably date from 88 or 89 B.C. and are later than the two sackings of Delos. The owners of these noble houses must have fled or been carried off into slavery for their stuccoes to have been ruined in such an interesting manner. To the French school at Athens reverts the small naval triumph of having provided the research workers at last with a drawing of a trireme from the hand of a sailor, drawn moreover with an artistry worthy of a master. They are butterflies of the sea which decorate the wall, almost taking flight in their eagerness. Had we been left with nothing else to appreciate the marine of antiquity, this would have sufficed to have raised it to a very high level (30).

As I always thought when I examined the triremes drawn by Admiral Serres or the replica built by Dupuy de Lôme, the Greek vessel was much more alive and streamlined; none of those rectilinear methods of a reflective school (which falsified intuition) were imposed on naval design, when their prototypes, the birds and the fishes, were so full of curves. At Delos, the precious marine animal which a sailor artist drew with such patience and love on the high walls has nothing of this disturbing coldness. It has taken the shape which would give it a speedy flight. It is modelled on the waves.

At this period the beak, the *embolon* (30a), is shortened, while the ship itself is lengthened. The beak is now primarily designed for ramming and it looks from its mounting as though the supports are strong enough to stand the shock. Above it, two little armoured beams, the *pre-embolon* (c), whose aim was to shatter the upperworks while the lower beak burrowed into the fragile hull...A reduced *stolos*, less fantastic and perhaps an official design although related to those primitive designs which bore this erect horn a thousand years before....An open deck with gratings probably ran the length of the ship covering the rowers. In the stern a poop, which is seen to be lightly defended. . . . And finally an *aphlaston* (d), complex and free, with nothing about it of that funereal *palmetta* the Romans, in

common with our engineers, would fix like a meagre little
cockade on their poops. .... The gangway is horizontal, supported by its outermost sling. One can almost make out a spare
rudder lying against the rails like a raised duck's foot. It is prob-

34. Greek Cargo Ship, 500 B.C.

able that at this period a single tiller sufficed now that the
waterlines had become the last word in subtlety. Various insignia were placed along the beautiful hull, and just above the
aphlaston one can see the *stylis* (*h*), a very rare double *stylis*. This
was the equivalent of the flag staff and was to some extent
sacred. The trireme must be more than 120 feet long. One cannot guess from this drawing the number of oars, for it was un-
completed, but on the neighbouring sketch, which is of a
bireme, one sees how the artist, an artisan, has repented. He has
added four oars after making his strokes and finally counting
them; four oars with lighter shading slipped in among the
others, to salve the conscience of an honest mariner. This drawing, with the two tiers, would give the bireme a hundred oars.

Naturally the mast was stepped further forward and when the
sails were filled, with eased sheets, they must have given a
greater thrust and allowed easy steering.

As for the trading ship, we find very few reproductions. They
were always the same and were of little interest to designers: a

child will always draw a warship with its guns, for the mind is always intrigued by destructive powers.

We are right in thinking that the cargo boat had to sacrifice everything to its burden and to compete with the huge sides and the thick hulls of the Phoenicians. A very accurate model has been discovered and the contrast with the nimble craft which could come alongside clearly shows its special purpose. The Roman ships, in any case, will give us more abundant details (35).

Obviously I have only given a very brief outline of the ships of antiquity. One should distrust those hidebound classifications which the scholar, with his taste for generalisation, instinctively demands. I should not have dared to put forward ideas of which I was not more or less convinced; but I am well aware how much I have omitted. Forty years ago, one merely had to sail down the northern coast of France from Dunkirk to Brest to meet with almost as many types of ships as there were harbours, and yet we were already approaching the age of uniformity. In a period when communications were slower, when each trading station preserved its own customs and nationality, we had to expect a great deal of variety. In fact, in view of the extent of our ignorance, I sometimes feel that we know nothing. We have one single right: to enjoy aesthetically and philosophically the fine, intelligent types we have come across. Only in this way can we escape from that feeling of deception which must result from these poor studies if they are intended to be empirical.

*   *   *

But the greatest glory of the Greeks was the blow delivered to Xerxes, which on September 27th, 480 B.C., saved the antique world, together with Mediterranean civilisation, for several more centuries. In the history of the world, in its essential history, there are five great naval battles which were more important than all the battles on land, and which decided its shape and its spirit: Salamis, Actium, Lepanto, the defeat of the Spanish Armada and Trafalgar.

The mighty Asiatic avalanche was unleashed. The son of Darius conducted his Alexandrine conquest and everything bent before his might. Three million stinking, sweating, bloody, roisterous men marching towards the west. . . . Asia Minor had been overrun; her subjected princes and peoples had been incorporated in the invading flood and were hastening towards Attica, divine white Attica, the bright pearl of the Aegean.

On the Bosphorus, Xerxes caused the sea to be lashed when it refused to obey him. A bridge over a mile long was built for his hordes to cross. His fleets were swelled by Phoenician and Ionian vessels and had risen to more than a thousand warships without counting the auxiliaries, supply ships, traders and transport. Leonidas had just died at Thermopylae and Athens was still a smoking ruin. There remained Themistocles, Aristides and the triremes.

These men and these weapons, one against five, were to win a brilliant victory in which will-power, implacable leadership, courage and patriotic exaltation would make up for tonnage and triumph over numbers, weight and disorder.

Themistocles said it was ridiculous and shameful to abandon Attica and the arsenal of Eleusis. These comprised their last strength. Eurybiades, the Admiral in command, wanted to retire to Corinth and the arrogance of the young Themistocles aroused his anger. He raised his baton: 'Strike me,' the other cried, 'and you can listen afterwards.' The heavily built Spartan listened in surprise. . . . Themistocles convinced him. They would fight in the waters of Salamis under the eyes of Athene, in the reflection of the temples.

Xerxes also held his council of war. There was a certain grandeur about him and Greek irony seems to have distorted his figure. All his commanders were of the opinion that they should attack and profit by their superiority of numbers—all of them except Artemisia, Queen of Halicarnassus: 'The Greeks,' she said, 'are better sailors than you and their ships are better than yours.' The young King of Kalymnos smiled. He despised women and thought that she was afraid, but this particular sea queen was not one to be intimidated. 'You'll see!' she snarled threateningly.

At this moment a spy reported that the Greeks were about to split up and that the Persians must hurry up and take them in their nest. The man had been won over by Themistocles who in this way played his last trump. Xerxes set course for the famous bay.

Themistocles lined up his three hundred and eighty triremes. He waited for the north-west wind which he knew ought to spring up at midday. The Persian army beat up slowly towards the end of the Gulf, towards the *cul-de-sac* where they counted upon destroying the light ships of the enemy. Xerxes was carried ashore, his throne, under its purple canopy, visible from all sides. His vessels advanced into a narrow channel, where it was impossible to deploy, to the accompaniment of the roars of the galley slaves. The violet sea was covered with barbarian ships, ships that were already weary, dirty and hairy, loaded to the rails with huge baggage for the voyage and provisions and plunder from the conquest, making them heavy and leaden. The Greek ships were mere fighting units, stripped bare and ready for action: light, manœuvrable, manned, not by heavy, drunken corsairs, by panicky, irresolute sea-rovers, but by clear-thinking citizens firmly resolved to win, whose reactions had the speed of mathematical calculations. The triremes, too, were all of a kind, nearly all of them new since they had been built at the same time for this ultimate conflict.

Thus, at midday, when the breeze sprang up, the famous red and yellow triremes took wing exactly like ospreys, in a great flutter of sails, of tackle, of cedar and cypress hulls, diving on the breathless rabble with talons bared. Athens forward!

The Persians, with the wind in their teeth, made no headway; the Ionians on the right wing, the Phoenicians on the left. The clash took place off the Isle of Lipso where Xerxes had disembarked three thousand crack soldiers. At the first shock, many of the Ionians—their fidelity had been in doubt—made for the shore. Themistocles hurled his fleet at the Phoenicians, despatching his reserve division, forty carefully selected ships, to take them in the rear. The Phoenicians fought savagely but had to yield at last and to fall back before the Greek onslaught. The Queen of Halicarnassus fought at the head of her eight warships, plated with bronze scales. Xerxes remarked, 'Today the women are acting like men, and the men . . .' for he suddenly saw the Ionians deserting and putting about and the Phoenician sailors slowing down in their exhaustion. The

Ionians fled! Artemisia, beside herself with rage, hoisted the Greek flag and bore down on the galley of the good-looking, effeminate Prince of Kalymnos. She sank it. Having thus changed sides and assuaged her hatred, she sailed eastwards, a torch at her tall masthead flaming red in the darkness.

Aristides attacked Lipso and the mercenaries beneath the eyes of the despairing Xerxes, who could do nothing to rescue his troops since the rout had set in all over the sea. The ger-falcons, Themistocles' triremes, charged repeatedly, in a war-like intoxication which did not abate as darkness fell, piercing and sinking everything afloat, everything that fled. Men with large eyes and slanting lids, Syrians or Mongols with huge beards in ringlets and hair like cats, sank at their oars, spilled their innards on slippery decks, sizzled in the flames. The nimble Greeks searched them, opened them, eviscerated them, set them on fire. The immense Persian convoy dispersed, wavered, sank, pursued by the implacable triremes.

On his hillock, the King of Kings was no longer there to watch the agony of his Grand Fleet. He could have re-formed and continued the battle, but the contrast was too great and the initial shock had been too brutal. He was covered with humiliation. This Prince suddenly renounced the Empire of the world. He returned to his lands in the East, leaving Mardonius with three hundred thousand dispirited men to save his face. The gods had spoken through the exploits of the Greeks. This was the great Attic consecration.

35. Roman Ship, A.D. 200

CHAPTER V

Rome

ROME was never a maritime nation. She applied to the navy the method and tenacity which had brought about her success. She found herself forced to possess a fleet to maintain her victorious colonial policy, and succeeded, because she was constrained to do so, exercising at sea a superiority similar to that which she held on the mainland. Rome was able to give the world the *pax romana* of the sea, but at what a price! She paid for it in fruitless efforts, in fantastic defeats such as people experience who persist in pursuing a task for which they are unsuited, a task which worries or bores them. The caprice of the waves disturbed the solidity and the heaviness of the Romans. Here foresight was of no avail. When it was a question of despatching a legion through Gaul as far as Brittany, by Jupiter, they merely had to divide the distance in miles by twenty, which gave them the number of days required for

the journey; but with the sea there could be none of this honest
pedestrian accountancy. Meticulous application and regularity
were unable to subdue the unruly ways of the sea. They had to
recognise Neptune as the last remaining independent monarch,
with the right of rebellion against the Roman Empire.

This was so opposed to their nature that the Romans loathed
ships. An admiral never gained the prestige of a general; the
admiral remained an artist and that was all. Had it not been for
the national needs, the Senate, with the disdain that destroyers
reserve for creative artists, would have been capable of nomi-
nating a Greek to the command of its ships.

Furthermore, at the outset, the Romans found themselves
too harassed by their weighty continental wars to bother about
the sea. They only began to concern themselves with ships when
they came up against the power of Carthage. We know with
what vehemence men like Cato reacted against Carthage,
which, without receiving the credit for it, introduced them to
the sea.

*　　*　　*

The Phoenician colony had expanded to an extent it is difficult to gauge, for the Romans, who destroyed it so utterly that
not even ruins remained, were not inclined to minimize their
victory after so many grievous conflicts. Their writers attributed to Carthage 700,000 inhabitants in the city and 300
vassal towns. This might possibly be ten times more than her
true strength. The figures in antiquity are perhaps the most
deceptive in all history. As soon as they begin to reckon, one
must no longer believe them—at the very moment they seem to
be trying to be accurate. However, the exaggeration of the
Punic armies and fleets indicates at least that their resources
largely exceeded the average armament of the period. These
figures were born of fear and the emphasis was inspired by
terror. The Carthaginian city was important because Xerxes
himself sought an alliance with her to attack the Greek colonies,
and the Carthaginians are reputed to have massed 5,000 warships and cargo vessels against Sicily.

This conflict entailed a considerable improvement of general
material and the navy played its part. Dionysius of Syracuse

built quinqueremes—galleys with five rows of oars. His arsenal could house 160 in dry-dock sheds, two in each shed. The ram, in the year 400 B.C., became the normal weapon; the hulls permitted it. But Dionysius was a Greek, a man from a refined and facile civilisation. Rome was far removed from this.

*　　　*　　　*

Appius, surnamed *Caudex*, was the first Roman general to command a fleet. *Caudex* means 'tree trunk' and it is quite possible that historians are right when they maintain that he earned this title from the rafts, the primitive vessels with which he managed to transport his troops across the Straits of Messina. It was obviously a most rudimentary and simple type when we think that the raft, as we have already mentioned, had already been perfected.

But chance and the marine deities went over to the enemy and favoured the audacious as they always do. The Romans captured a Punic ship which had run aground. They flung themselves upon it like ants with all they possessed in the way of engineers and practical men. They copied it so well that within two months—and this shows that the type must have been clumsy and reduced in size—they built a squadron of 160 vessels equalling in number Dionysius' elegant triremes.

They were infuriating and yet absurd: while their naval counterfeiters were exerting themselves to the utmost, these excellent Quirites, without losing a moment, did not fear to train their future sailors, but they trained them on *terra firma* since they did not possess even a tub. They taught the oarsmen who were soon to be on the waves to row on the sand. As one can imagine, the result was disastrous. An appalling muddle and an indescribable defeat—the whole 160 sent to the bottom!

After this appeared the only Roman invention in the naval field—the *corvus* (36). The Romans deliberately renounced all progress and all real naval manoeuvres. They would turn sea combat into a battle of infantry. Therefore they had to hook the enemy first, to hold him closely and firmly and then to launch the legionaries. The *corvus*, which helped them to achieve this, was a mobile drawbridge (*a*) turning on a central pivot (*d*). Moreover it was armed with grappling irons and beaks—

hence the name of 'crow'—which clung to the enemy rails, joining the two ships together. Across it went the cohorts and in the ensuing battle they were of course favoured by their dis-

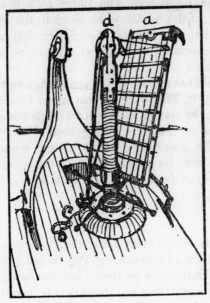

36. The *Corvus*

ciplined courage and science and even by their weapons. The Carthaginians were overwhelmed. In fact, Roman tactics were reduced to boarding.

Rome bestowed great honours upon Duilius, the inventor of the 'crow'. In addition to the rostral column (37) dedicated to him, which came to light in the sixteenth century and which ultimately inspired the Parisian lamp posts, he was escorted

37. The Rostral Column

home with torches and flutes whenever he went to dine in town. Perhaps the famous engineer began to hope that some resounding disaster would deprive him of his occasionally embarrassing escort. It soon happened. The storm took it upon itself to remind Rome of the humility she owed to the sea. She lost so many ships that the Senate, completely disgusted, officially forbade any extension of the fleet. It was reduced to a few coastguard vessels.

But this could not suffice. Reluctantly, they had to begin once more to build, to sink, even to win naval battles. Polybius is very emphatic: he assures us that not a single plank remained in Rome because so much building took place. At last they succeeded. The unintelligent will always triumph over the intelligent because they have the necessary obstinacy to give them simplicity. Obstinacy is the most ambitious of all the faults.

*   *   *

The Romans copied everything: the Punic vessel, the Rhodian *nef*, the Athenian trireme, the Phoenician galleon, even the *liburna* of the Dalmatian pirates. They increased each type in weight and caricatured it, but they knew how to build first-class fleets with medium ships, thanks to their spirit of logic and order. Even though jostled by the sea, they managed to establish themselves.

The difference, which is surprising, cannot escape the most inattentive eye. With the Romans, the boat immediately became monumental, strongly built and immediately lost its birdlike qualities (38). The documents are as abundant as they are tiresome. The light *aphlaston*, the fibrils, the wing-quills which quiver at the stern of Hellenistic ships have been replaced by the heavier, more regular *aplustris*, the stiff and clumsy *palmetta*, which immediately emerged from the stylus of an official designer. The bows curved into a thick butt embellished with great reinforced mouldings. The small cruel beak of the Athenian trireme was exchanged for a long ostentatious nose, laden with ornaments, as though the most beautiful adornment of an oared ship were not bareness, lightness and perfect finish. The Roman rowers had to drag heavy hulks of deadwood. The Roman ship was mass-produced like the American car. Compared with the Greek ship, it was a limousine from Detroit as opposed to a French Citröen. Everything was rounded and flabby. Even the men, who were in fact so tough, seemed to become molly-coddles. The *aplustris* soon became a shelter where the men could take cover.

38. Large Roman Bireme, 150 B.C.

They had abandoned the upper deck; this in any case had been very quickly dropped by the Greeks, as we saw on the *graffiti* from Delos. Pictures from Roman times corroborate the abandonment of this weighty platform which had to be replaced by better housing for the crews within the actual flanks of the galley, thus leaving the decks clear for action. The Venetian galleass would not lose sight of this.

But Roman aggressiveness accorded ill with Attic simplicity and heroic nudity. The Roman infantryman was carapaced like a crab (38) and he fought as a besieger. Towers of imitation stone (38), as heavy as they are ugly, appear rapidly on Roman biremes. It is obvious that these conquerors pursued their inclinations to the limit and chose to triumph by building ships irresistible through their weight rather than their speed. Clearly, if they finally caught the marine gazelles which they pursued so doggedly, if they managed to stroke them with their triple spur, nothing could have remained of the fragile and delicate craft, however welljointed they may have been. The Roman ship on its own could not accomplish very much, but a hundred Roman ships scouring the sea could give chase to their swift prey. On their sails they painted the she-wolf suckling the two young bandits; they hoisted a helmet as an emblem at the masthead. Weighed down by their armour, the Romans tilled the waves behind stout parapets (38a, a) which gave leverage to their oars. On these parapets the legionaries stood, ready for battle, with their short swords (still used today by the Cherkesses) designed for hand-to-hand fighting where they can cut as well as they can bludgeon.

*   *   *

To sum up, the Romans contributed to the marine world very little that was specifically their own. There were the navies of conquered races, some of whose intrepid sailors were used with the Roman genius for exploitation, particularly with regard to the merchant fleet. Rome modified the type from taste and pride and entrusted it to those who could use it better than she. We still possess numerous pictures of merchant vessels (39). We know that when short of corn the city organised transport fleets of uniform and standard type and this custom set the fashion. They all resembled one another. We even find a Phoenician ship of the decline fitted out in the Roman manner. Phoenicia still continued to play its role. Just as the Dutch were to do later, the Phoenicians had become world rovers, rovers who no longer worked for their own nation but for their banking accounts.

The huge hull was reinforced and consolidated. Stem and stern posts were subjected to the prevailing taste for research and easy construction. They became over-elaborate and exaggerated. The stern bent back in the hardly agreeable shape of a swan's neck and beak, or that of a duck, a form which had been too long employed in the baths (39a). The bows are difficult to explain, unless the little seat in the form of a chariot box was a kind of half-top to replace the stem where, in the old days, the Phoenician leadsman perched like an acrobat. Comfort appeared with the roof which sheltered the passengers (*c*).

39. Roman-Phoenician Cargo Vessel

Journeys were in fact very long. We have a detailed account of the voyage made by St. Paul when he pleaded his civic status: '*Civis romanus sum!*' What power in this appeal to the Praetor of Caesarea! Paul was put aboard at Joppa to be judged at Rome and his voyage has been carved in a bas-relief (of course this little merchant ship has nothing to do with the revered scribe of Tarsus). Paul insisted that he had already suffered shipwreck three times and since he does not appear to have been a globe-trotter, this throws a melancholy light upon the disadvantages of Roman packets.

The ship was not, however, a small example of the type, for it carried 276 passengers. They took 14 days in a storm to cover the distance between Crete and Malta with a dangerous passage through the Syrtes, which remained, as they were to do for a long time, mysterious and dangerous waters. The Apostle's fourth shipwreck now occurred. They stayed three months at Malta because no ships sailed during the winter; thus the

Dioscuri, which they boarded at last, bound for Italy, dared not risk putting to sea before the fine weather, even to cover so short a distance. Having left Phoenicia, then, about September 10th, having braved the equinox and its cutting north wind, St. Paul only arrived in Rome in February.

On the whole of this crossing, described in detail in the *Acts of the Apostles*, there is no mention of oars. This confirms the almost exclusive use of sail for merchantmen. Sculptured evidence does not even show any oarports on cargo vessels (39). The human mode of propulsion, the oar, was a costly agent reserved for the navy. Actually the trader must have been composite and able to muster a few oars aboard to leave a becalmed roadstead or to carry out a manœuvre, as was the case with all Mediterranean sailing coasters fifty years ago; but the *Acts* speak very clearly of the boat on a davit, of anchors and rigging.

*　　*　　*

Furthermore, the mechanics of sail had made considerable progress. The mast had been given regular shrouds reinforced by 'heart-blocks' such as we use today for standing rigging. The shrouds had ratlines which allowed access to the masthead. Some masts even had wooden ladders which made them look like giant thorns. The mast, when it was a single one, was stepped forward, as is only proper. The sail was still a broad squaresail reinforced by strips of cloth. It furled easily, as can be seen on the ship known as St. Paul's ship, with the lines known as 'extinguishers' (brails) which, hauling up the sail to the yard, actually extinguished it.

But the most remarkable and the most nautical feature was a new invention, the Greek *artemon* (39*b*), a mast like a mizzen stepped forward, carrying a small sail, which would one day become a magnificent bowsprit, the pride of the old sailing ships, prolonging the length of the ships by a third. The modern name means nothing; the mizzen of our period, on the contrary, is stepped aft. It is curious to follow naval terms down the ages and to see the way they have changed.

This bowsprit is still immature and its angle indeterminate. Even its fixation seems uncertain. I think that a modern maker of models would be wrong to secure it by a stay to the Roman figure-head. It does not carry the famous jib which appears only in the eighteenth century (about 1760) to give the ship one of its most intelligent aids. No, our Roman *artemon* carries only a puny sail of no great proportions but which was already an important step forward, a kind of lofty spritsail whose effect, working like a lever arm, must have been very vigorous. When they sailed with the wind aft, the sail, well sheeted in, acted as a weathercock and to a large extent prevented the changes of course which are so easy at this speed. On departure, it must have helped the boat considerably to catch the wind. This was already an indication of the semi-abandonment of the oar. At anchor a ship always lies head to wind. When dropped astern, this kind of spritsail topsail caught the least puff and it fell off before the wind.

This invention was used more in the merchant ships than in the warships. The shock of the ram must have proved fatal to it. This was not, however, a complete deterrent. We have seen in the fourteenth century ships equipped with a ram and a bowsprit of 90 feet, a bowsprit, moreover, upon which the whole rigging depended. These are mysteries of the maritime genius, but it would seem in the last analysis that the development of the forward crosier which characterises the Roman ship has its explanation in the protection given to the mizzen. If we examine the medallions conscientiously, it seems that the mast hardly protrudes beyond the upperworks and thus benefits by its solidity.

*　　*　　*

We are assured that the Roman ships carried in the stern an altar for sacrifices to the marine Gods; that anyone who clung to this altar found sanctuary. A white flag hung near the altar and this is perhaps the origin of the Ensign. The Roman construction, rudimentary at first, eventually became sure and even beautiful, but only at the very end, when these conquerors realised that certain of their victims were not necessarily helots. The galley recovered from the Lake of Nemi proves the quality at last reached by the Roman shipbuilders. It exceeds by 200 feet anything that we have built in the nature of an oared vessel in modern times. It is nothing more than a pontoon designed for dalliance, a floating casino, a kind of flower boat, or it might have been a floating altar. For Caligula, who had it built, probably only the first hypothesis is valid. However, the lines are superb in tension, trim and rotundity. In this case, where they might have created the most ignoble hull, the Roman engineers managed to give it a shape which sacrificed neither speed nor lightness.

The ornamentation, too, was inspired by Greece and carried out by Greek workers, reaching a perfection of treatment which is almost moving in its simple robustness. The wolves' heads which bite the mooring rings were brought from Attica. There is a certain genius in knowing how to recognise the genius of other nations, and how rare this is!

In this way, during the last centuries of her grandeur, Rome —who was the forerunner of the most beautiful Mediterranean fleet, that of Byzantium—was to ensure once more the destiny of the world, at Actium, in a naval combat without precedent.

The Mediterranean in 31 B.C. once more conquered the Nile, the Red Sea and the Indian Ocean. This was a strange epoch of Roman power, during which its masters shared the jurisdiction of the known world: Octavius, on one hand, ruling Europe and Anthony, on the other, ruling Asia. Valorous Anthony, of a different stamp to his Imperial colleague, lived a life of bloodshed and ardour. His passion for Cleopatra had become the frenzy of love to which he sacrificed himself entirely. What reward would she give him? Anthony proclaimed the two sons she had borne him Kings of Rome. He made Cleopatra the ruler of Cyprus, Cilicia, Cocele-Syria, Arabia and Judaea. He dreamed of making her the Empress of the world.

Rome could not tolerate these encroachments. Octavius, whose sister Anthony had abandoned, took up arms against the Eastern despot. Anthony replied and his armies and navies were vastly superior to those of Rome: Asia brought him its human masses and its inexhaustible wealth. The Antonine army should have sufficed to give its master victory, but destiny decreed that he should entrust his fate to the sea. Yes, this fortunate general, whose vigour and intelligence were incomparable, entrusted himself to wooden walls only to be betrayed. It is true that he had brought a woman into it; his veterans were indignant and disconsolate. One of his oldest centurions, who had covered himself with glory, pleaded with him in the following words: 'The land is our element. Give us the land.'

But Anthony would not listen.

The concentration of the fleet took place off the west coast of Morea in the Gulf of Arta. The opposing armies were massed on either side of the Gulf, hoping perhaps for a sea battle. Octavius, cruising along the coast, commanded a less powerful, less well-armed but rather lighter and most Themistoclean navy, in which the *liburna* predominated. Anthony was in command of veritable battle-ships, but instead of patriotic and eager crews he used mercenaries.

Very wisely, he had ordered his commanders to take the defensive. This offered him the greatest chance of success with the least risk. His floating fortresses, laden with men and legionaries, could withstand all assaults.

However, the courage—or the frenzy—of his sailors decided otherwise and as Octavius, or rather his Admiral Agrippa, remained undecided, the Orientals bore down on him. The Romans fled, putting about in order to disrupt the battle order of the attackers, who were the heavier. In the open sea, the manœuvrability of the *liburnae* regained them their advantage. Soon Octavius gave the signal to pounce on the enemy. Going about, they went into the attack.

In the conflict that followed, no quarter was given. At the outset the battle was uncertain, for the strength and weight of the Orientals made them tough even when singled out by several light ships. The rams struck. The mortars spat flames and smoke. The *balistae* roared, the great pikes stabbed, but the invulnerable warships took the blows and supported each other. They had to be separated again, so Agrippa tried to turn the left wing of the Orientals under Publicola. The latter in turn deployed his ships and dispersed in order to follow the movement and to parry it. Perhaps it was thought that he had capitulated. The crucial moment arrived. Suddenly they saw the finest, best-armed ships, the Queen of Egypt's 70 quadriremes, hoist their sails—so they were abandoning the combat. The Queen of Egypt was fleeing.

The Orientals continued, nevertheless, to let themselves be

73

hacked to pieces without blenching until the moment when, caught in a furious *bora* squall—that tornado which still ravages the Adriatic—split up, dismantled and torn to pieces, they had to admit defeat.

But they had fought without a general. Anthony, love-sick Anthony, shame upon him, had fled when he saw the Queen flee. He had jumped into a canoe and boarded the Egyptian vessel. Anthony, the intrepid, allowed his men to perish without him. However, at the moment of boarding, when the Queen raised the flap of her tent on the poop to let him in, the great Roman was suddenly aware of his infamy. He turned on his heel, made for the *stolos*, and stood there in the bows, crushed and rigid as though turned to stone, his hands to his ears, staring blankly out on the sinister southern horizon.

Three hundred ships surrendered to Octavius; 5,000 men had been killed aboard. The sea disgorged oars encrusted with mother-of-pearl, balusters, flags embroidered in silver and ivory. Huge purpurine sails made rose-coloured bubbles on the waves and silken cables floated like the tentacles of pale octopuses. The land army waited, already conquered, and a week later gave up the struggle.

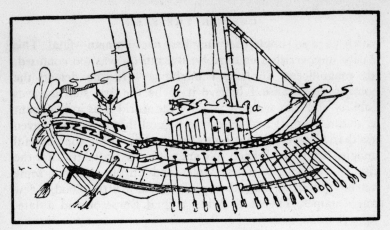

40. Large Dromond

CHAPTER VI

Byzantium

THE modern world and in particular France, is notoriously detached from the Byzantine epoch. No one bothers any more with Mediterranean history after the foundation of the second capital on the dazzling shores of the Bosphorus. For our students, the ancient world ends with the twelfth Caesar and for our men of taste, our sensitive scholars, Byzantium only acquired a new interest by calling itself Stambul; by becoming a dream country where the cultured and the idle found something to move them. Thanks to a naval officer of genius, Pierre Loti, whom it is fashionable to despise today, the connoisseurs of the nineteenth century discovered there the magic of the Orient and Turkey instead of exotic Christian splendours.

It is true that the glory of Byzantium occurs in chronology at a moment of weariness. After an overdose of so much sensitivity and all that Roman life, we need a rest and we are inclined to say of this agony: 'Come then death!' For we remain, whether we like it or not, imbued with Rome. Fundamentally, every Frenchman unconsciously admires, approves and relishes Roman state control and all that it represents in the way of the absolute, of system and of centralisation. Above all, our principle of clarity and of order attracts us to these concepts

75

which were so simple that they became inhuman—fatal. This clarity impoverishes us terribly. Byzantium was too confused, too magnificent. In fact, I might say—I, who defend the bourgeoisie because I believe it to be the first step towards nobility and that without nobility the world is as insignificant as an ant heap—I am inclined to suggest that Byzantium, even less than Greece, was not bourgeois enough to fire the peaceful imagination of the French. We are not in the least Attic. For the city of the *Basileis*, a few violet and purple shadows, some marble glittering beneath a perfect sun, a little blood, a few tragic names, Theodora, Arius, a final Emperor and a date, 1453 . . . that is all.

And yet the Eastern Empire lasted *eleven hundred years*.

*   *   *

The Byzantine marine has suffered from this indifference. Little is known of it and it has been accorded only a very mild importance. Even the keenness of archaeologists wilts here and each one utters his own explanations and hypotheses without the normal assurance of scholars. And yet Byzantium was the mother of all modern fleets if we postulate that Attica was the grandmother. It was at Byzantium that the traditions of ship-building were preserved and finally developed. Our Middle Ages were still at school while Byzantium flourished. We always forget that 300 miles away from a territory overrun by the Barbarians, whose Charlemagne would be a Dahomeyan Emperor, existed a civilised country which by some miracle had escaped the degradation of the west. It has been said that the Byzantine marine was a continuation of the Roman and made no other contribution. This is a blatant generalisation, although a very convenient one to excuse a lack of curiosity. But be re-assured, I am not proposing to make a regular refutation. I merely wish to point out a few characteristics which will suffice for those eager minds I wish to reach.

Byzantium was obliged to be a maritime nation. She armed herself heavily, with moments of laxity—to be found throughout her whole policy—particularly disastrous to fleets, which demand continuity. Her empire was essentially maritime. She possessed two vast basins and required a powerful water police, while at the same time she could not dispense with huge armies for defence or national conquest.

The crumbling of Roman power had caused piracy to be practised along the whole southern Mediterranean coast and the growing might of the Saracens depended upon this piracy

41. Dromond, A.D. 850

and gave it official blessing. The Byzantine navy therefore devoted a great part of its activities to reducing these sea rovers. It is logical to think that her fleets were formed more of light cruisers than heavy men-of-war. The advantage possessed by the Mediterranean corsair was his individuality. Each small potentate of a pirate town was a Grand Sultan in his own estimation and forgot any suzerainty except at a moment when a regroupment could prove useful to him. He submitted to this very rarely and when he did so it was a great opportunity for Christianity. Neither Lepanto nor Navarino would often be repeated. It was usually impossible to crush this rabble once and for all in the way this can be done in a war between two nations when the defeat of one will bring about peace. The navy which was to pursue these disorderly elements therefore had to be strong, fast and keen, in fact individual like the pirates themselves. It seems probable that this was achieved with the dromond, the *pamphylian* and the *galea*, the three types of Byzantine warship which must have replaced the *liburna* and which had increased power without losing too much lightness to act as independent units. These were the forerunners of the *chelander* or *selander*, which eventually developed into a mixed type. To this we must add the *cat*, a small reconnaissance ship. It appears from the documentation available that the dromond was related to the ship of the line. We know that there were small and big dromonds (40, 41)—in any case the name has escaped the general contempt and has retained a certain prestige. The dromond is associated with the splendours of Byzantium, which for some reason we so easily imagine to be trashy, possibly because they were above all very brilliant, over-loaded with colours and because we French are fundamentally black and white artists—at least we were when we had talent and did not tend to over-decoration.

The noble dromond seems to have been essentially a ship with at least two rows of oars. It would be pedantic to offer any precise length to the foot. To give some idea of it and to reassure the timid, let us be content to say that it was a large ship of about 150 feet. It had two decks which did not prevent it from lying fairly low in the water. Its line was conditioned by the narrowness congenital to an oared vessel, i.e. an eighth of its length from the spur to the *aplustris*, which was far more decorative and refined than the Roman *palmetta*. One of the main differences between the dromond and the *pamphylian* (42) was that the former had fighting towers. We saw the beginnings of these under the Romans. Here the bow and stern were armed and, occasionally, the waist, where a sort of citadel was built (40a). This central keep, this miniature castle, would disappear, only to return with the modern battleship, but the two others became the castles, those bastilles which remained in naval language even when the superstructures were absorbed under the name of fore and aftercastles.

* * *

In fact the dromond was the first stage of an evolution which would end with the dreadnought. It was provided with plates and metal defences, as the texts prove, but its novelty resided in its ability to attack from a distance in spite of its ram. The ram remained the final method of combat, of course, and this was very intelligent: how many times did the eighteenth-century navy, for example, let slip the opportunity and allow a badly damaged enemy ship to get away because it did not dare to risk this decisive encounter. But the dromond seems to have been armed to conquer without necessarily coming to grips. It had its archers, of course, as did all the ships of antiquity, but it also carried important war machines, mounted perhaps on the towers if they were not too heavy: *balistae* (40*b*) catapults, which gunpowder rendered obsolete and even ridiculous, some of which, however, flung half a ton of lead 750 yards. The final establishment of long-distance weapons seems to be an improvement—if I may be excused the term—due to the Byzantine

42. *Pamphylian*, A.D. 850

sailors. Now long-distance effectiveness must be taken into account and it is no longer possible to rely solely on boarding, which was the ultimate Roman goal. This remains the essential modern condition. Modern naval warfare is based on maintaining the greatest possible distance between the two adversaries.

The *chelander-pamphylian* (42) could have been a dromond reduced in size, usually carrying a single row of oars. Pure supposition? Not quite. The ship called the *selander*, which in the Middle Ages plied between France and Jaffa, also carried a single row of oars. Moreover, Venice, which more than any other city was subjected to Byzantine influence, also equipped unireme *pamphylians*. Venice, whose luxury and grandeur were of the Byzantine order, the only European civilisation capable of giving us some idea of Byzantium, copied the Greek Empire. Does not the galleass remind us of the dromond?

The *pamphylian* (42) corresponds to the light cruiser, while the *galea* recalls the frigate of the sailing squadron: a ship a little more powerful than the *cat* but whose role was to convey information to the fleet rather than to fight, although if it came to an engagement it was not devoid of armament and could play its part. From this *galea* evolved the more modern galley, a word which conjures up so many pictures, from Gehenna to luxury, from naked suffering to sensual ease. Was the galley marked by the absence of castles on deck, by having on the poop a kind of light shelter which gave us the round-house of the seventeenth century? It would be foolish to be dogmatic for the types are too variable and too far removed from modern standardisation. I shall merely remark that the Byzantine galley appears very over-decorated and particularly luxurious. Some of their sterns are covered with cloth of gold, brocade and silk embroideries which, in the grand manner, were allowed to trail in the water.

But a more important modification was introduced—the lateen sail, which should by rights be called the 'Byzantine'. This light, admirable wing was to remain the typical Mediterranean sail. It would be years before it succumbed to the western sail, square in form—a decline which only became official at the end of the nineteenth century. In our days the triangular lateen sail has come into fashion again and is used for racing yachts.

We have seen so far all the ships of antiquity hoisting a square sail, except in the over-heated imagination of naval experts and sailors. It was the most simple sail and it was simplified once more. We know that the Phoenician sail carried a yard and a boom, thus making it possible to sail near the wind and even allowing beating to windward. The boom was suppressed to bring the centre of effort forward before daring to alter the position of the mast. Huge bubbles of canvas drew and raised Athenian triremes to the limit of their sheets. The trireme was preceded by a bellying cloud, a pale cumulus.

*   *   *

Here we come to the question of efficiency. The *antenna* and the lateen sail, the yard and its triangle of canvas made the greatest use of the wind. The lateen yard was lashed to the mast by its lower third. It was mobile, balanced, or nearly so, by the difference of canvas surface and the weight of the boom. Rope arms could 'pack' it, that is to say, bring it almost parallel to the mast or set it at a convenient angle.

The advantages are considerable, particularly for oared ships. First of all, the diminution of the mast by two thirds. This 'tree', as the 'Mokos' would say, is replaced aloft by the upper part of the *antenna* itself. With sail hauled up, the mast remains reduced; the *antenna* comes very low and the lack of balance is less, as well as the wind resistance. Now the Byzantine navy had to face pirate ships from the Archipelago and its shores, had to pursue them into their lairs, into shallow creeks, sheltered roadsteads and ravine-like narrows. By 'peaking' the *antenna* the ship received and made use of the least puff of wind which the neighbouring heights would have masked. Finally came the question of efficiency. The Byzantine sailors seem immediately to have hit upon a use of sail which brought fortune to the Mediterranean. This had taken thousands of years to discover (except in China) after the instinct which had inspired it had been shamefully despised. The lateen sail was, in fact, in ancient days, the *bête noire* of the famous 'sheet eaters', the western sailors who put to sea in weather when the people of the south remained peacefully in harbour. The men of the north were inhuman enough; it earned them a hardening of heart and boredom in activity. . . . But let that pass.

We know today that the luff of the sail is the place where propulsive action is the strongest. Overnight all the pleasure yachts adopted the lateen and the 'Marconi rig', a long triangle which lifts the peak a third higher than the total length of the small craft it propels. One of my friends told me how amused he was when, with his new sail, in the Solent, he outstripped the best racing yachts beneath the outraged eyes of the tradition-loving British. With half the amount of canvas one can achieve the same speed. A moderate wind drives you along like a stiff breeze. What an economy in weight and manpower!

The people of the Mediterranean, however, eventually became ashamed of their lateen sail. When they passed Gibraltar they immediately changed over to square rig to be up to date. But today the ghosts of the old Algerian pirates must smile in that purgatory where divine justice keeps them—which is probably not too severe since it is divine. The Barbary pirates were right when they scudded, *antennæ* aloft, making their bird-keels shake, those feluccas, those settees which M. de Tourville himself could not catch.

*   *   *

However, it was another invention which distinguished the Byzantine navy. We have no specific details, but all the same it cannot be refuted. Greek fire!

We should like to fake the documents to avenge modern science, but they are too numerous to suppress. It has been maintained that Greek fire was only the use of gunpowder before the charming official invention of the monk Schwartz. Nothing doing! This is too facile a solution. Greek fire was liquid and an explosive at the same time, a liquid that could burn on the water and which the waves would not put out. It could only be doused with sand, vinegar or urine. (We quote the latter because of its ammoniacal effect.) And it exploded. It was loaded in pots which were the absolute equivalent of shells. Even today the receptacles, the grenades in which it was transported when it was used at a distance, are still being dug up.

It was Greek fire that delayed the progress of Islam and once more temporarily saved Christian civilisation by allowing it to develop sufficiently to benefit by the heritage of Byzantium. Had the city fallen in 953, for example, history would have taken quite another course. The Byzantine ships triumphed for a very long time against all assaults thanks to this monster, this jealously-guarded secret which they made fight for them. One of the most terrible actions in which it was used annihilated the ships of Prince Igor—that Prince Igor who for the modern reader is only an operatic character who usually reminds us of Chaliapin. This Russian with 10,000 ships full of armoured savages attacked the dromonds of the *Basileus* who, without waiting for the Reds to approach, opened fire. Nothing remained of them. Despite their armour, the Russians leaped into the sea to avoid the gleaming darts, the horrible tongues of flame directed at them.

On account of its buoyancy and resistance to water, one might think that petrol or spirit entered into its composition but it also contained some sort of explosive.

*   *   *

This method of warfare is described in as great detail as in the manuals of the perfect naval gunner. Exhaustive accounts are given of the celebrated *siphons*, which must not be taken in the scientific sense—a tube with two unequal branches which functions by utilising atmospheric pressure—but on the contrary, in the popular sense, rather like the soda water siphon, like a beak with two open ends which distributes a fierce jet. The dromond carried in the bows a bronze *protomé*, a roaring lion's head; from this mouth emerged long, pliant, jointed metal tubes, each one covering a certain direction. From these, probably by means of a pressure apparatus, liquid fire was squirted at great speed, on the principle of a flame-thrower. The mouths of these siphons, where the jet was lit, were provided with inflammatory material and oakum. The soldiers themselves used Greek fire from kind of individual guns. The catapults slung it a great distance in the form of projectiles which ignited in the air or burst on landing.

The fray became more and more atrocious. The Moors charged like lost children in this sickening atmosphere, in this incredible smoke. Today we know only too well what sediment fills the air after an oil fire. The burning of the oil tanks at Rouen covered the whole of Normandy as far as Cherbourg in 1940.

This must have been the reason for the armour plating (40c) I have mentioned even on the ships of the attackers. An all-metal hull would have become obligatory had the Greek fire not disappeared so rapidly. The men of the period should have covered their wooden hulls, where they came in contact with the fire running over the waves, with lead and copper. But they still used untanned leather, new skins, and piled on the deck heaps of sand which were just as ineffective as they have proved in the attics of modern buildings.

*　　*　　*

The fleet despatched against Crete is said to have comprised 2,000 ships equipped with these terrible siphons; an obvious exaggeration but a good indication of the enormous size of the Byzantine fleets. Let us admit 200 vessels, each with a crew of 170, and we already have a marine force of 34,000 fighting men. But ten times this number—and, in addition, the devastating effect of the unknown weapon of war!

Perhaps even more surprising than its discovery is the mystery surrounding this Greek fire. Once the Christian Empire fell, this terrible device was hardly ever used again. The *Basileis* guarded the secret and transmitted it from father to son as they would have done a State secret. They pronounced a curse on anyone who should discover or reveal it. However, the great city on the Bosphorus fell in spite of its waves of fire. It disappeared in spite of its drongairs and grand dukes, its admirals and dromonds, its *pamphylians* with their heads of beasts.

On the other hand, it was Byzantium which, after obtaining it from the Chinese through the medium of the Arabs, introduced the compass to European ships and, from a nautical point of view, one must admit that this too was quite a consideration.

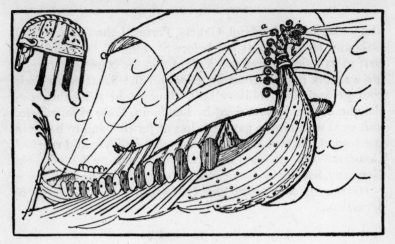

43. *Drakkar*, A.D. 950

CHAPTER VII

The Vikings

THE Byzantines were familiar with these blond giants with
hair like silk. Scandinavian mercenaries served in every
army and the Varangians, the warriors from the north,
formed the most trustworthy and terrible part of the guard
whose duty it was to protect the *Basileus*. Already the acclima-
tised Normans of Sicily were alternately friends and foes of the
Byzantines and made their courage respected. But the great
encounters took place between the navies. As in the case of
everything concerning Byzantium, what little is known is
irrefutable. In 1102 Eric the Saint, King of Denmark, was also
anxious to play his part in the Crusade and left his Kingdom.
He crossed Russia, which at the time had been formed by the
eastern emigration of the Vikings, and rejoined his fleet at
Byzantium. He died exhausted by the warm climate, like a
transplanted Polar bear. He succumbed despite his tremendous
robustness, and his wife Botilde, who had taken his place, died
at Jerusalem on the Mount of Olives.

In 1106 Sigurd King of Norway, embarked at Bergen after
four years of preparation. He was in command of 60 vessels
and his journey lasted another four years with various stages

and winterings in England, Galicia, Portugal, the Balearics and Calabria. He arrived at last before St. John of Acre and took part in its relief. Sigurd was a giant and the colossal stature of his warriors had as great an effect on the Saracens as their courage and their military skill. None could resist their on-slaught. Sigurd was received by Baudouin, King of Jerusalem, and went with him to gather palms at Jericho, and to bathe in the Jordan. He took Sidon, ran aground off Tyre and reached Constantinople at last, from where he returned home, via Germany, leaving his commanders to bring back the fleet.

He was named Sigurd the Hierosolymitan, the pilgrim of Jerusalem.

* * *

The naval and warlike ardour of the Vikings lasted long after they were installed in their kingdoms, but now it was no longer a question of organised and general piracy. The Vikings became, to a great extent, individual corsairs.

One must not try to discover if by the term 'Vikings' are meant Norwegians, Swedes or Danes. The childish, unbelievable controversies of the greatest Nordic scholars have this much to be said for them: they have proved the mixture of all these nationalities in the Norman pirates from the eighth to the eleventh centuries. The Vikings were Scandinavians and that must suffice.

But in order to understand their exoduses and the end of these journeys, we must recall the special conditions of their homelands. To begin with, they had a very great number of children. Marriages *more danico*, in other words polygamy, resulted in a wild crop of children which made family life difficult. Added to this, military defeats sent them into exile. These people, who were always at war, tended towards a single leader, towards the formation of nationalities and States which absorbed the petty chieftains; the latter, unwilling to endure even a vassalage, preferred to emigrate and they emigrated on the sea. When the Vikings had consolidated their invasion and were relatively accepted, they were absorbed. At the same time, the Christian faith brought with it a rather precarious monogamy, but wide-spread enough to limit the number of births.

And what emigrants they were! Endowed with a vigour which kept them inexorably in the thrall of adventure, the chiefs who made their way to the west were conquerors rather than vanquished. I must confess that this Viking epic, which delights us by its violence and success, would have seemed extremely disagreeable at the time. 'They were carefree robbers and unpunished murderers,' people of good sense will say, but I shall reply: 'Above all they were heroes.' They harboured such a disdain for death, such a complete indifference for everything apart from valour and action, combined with so lucid an intelligence in their frenzy for conquest, that from our very heredity we cannot help being drawn along in their wake, and we feel far more Norman than Neustrian. They put to sea intoxicated by the unknown, determined to carve out a land for themselves since theirs had been taken from them. They could do this only by risking their bodies against other bodies, by matching their strength against another strength. They were not equipped with those devilish weapons which make a battle a diversion for those who start it and a butchery for the enemy. They fought almost naked, proud of their wounds and scars.

One must recognise them as a race superior to those they conquered. The results are there: with them was born a sort of *pax romana*, but more limited and more alive. Legislators, dispensers of justice, magnificent sailors and engineers. . . .

They carried their depredations across the world, but also their genius. Everything has been said about their European conquests, while the others are less known. However, in 861 Naddohoh discovered Iceland and emigration began in 874. In 982 Eric the Red, looking for land to the west, discovered Greenland and later his sons and sons-in-law settled in America. There is no possible doubt of this today. The Dighton Rock in Massachusetts was discovered in 1680 bearing this runic inscription: 'CXXXI men of the north occupied this country with Thorfinn.' This Thorfinn was the eighth descendant of Regnard Lodbrog and with him we enter historical times. Furthermore, in 1867 a Nordic tomb was discovered on the Potomac. The runes when deciphered read as follows: 'Here lies Syasi the Fair-haired, from Eastern Iceland, widow of Koldr and sister of Thorga by her father, aged 25. May God be merciful to her. 1051.' (There is some controversy today, based on philology, as to the authenticity of the inscriptions. Does not this seem rather fragile? Let the sceptics first explain to us the object of such a well-documented hoax.)

Finally, my friend the Marquis de St. Pierre, from whom I have obtained these details, assures me that in the archives of the Vatican may be found a complete list of the bishops of Greenland from 1121 to 1418, bishops in whose dioceses were American territories—among others Vinland, with its religious capital on the shores of Mount Bay. The Papal accounts record American gifts from 1276 to 1309. It is very odd that Colombus remains in our history books as the only discoverer of a continent on which the Normans set foot 500 years before him.

* * *

What type of vessel would allow such exploits? A ship which, with the trireme, was the most hotly discussed, most laden with hypotheses and reconstructions and which eventually gave the most sensational lie to archaeological pride! For after people had pontificated and estimated, one, then two and eventually as many as thirty were discovered, all of them entirely different from the sketches of the scholars. They differed, too, from the description of Tacitus, who assured us that they were exactly alike in bow and stern and that thus they acquired a great military value since they could go ahead or astern without having to manœuvre. It is certain that the old historian possessed only second-hand information about the boats. We must admit, of course, that we have found no Scandinavian vessels of his period. Let us add that in the reign of Severus, the Byzantines also built 'amphisdromonds'. It is easy to see that the Nordic ship, designed to sail in the fjords and narrow channels, would obtain a real advantage from this type of construction. Furthermore, rather than dismiss entirely the description of Tacitus, let us say in mitigation that even if, with the exception of the launches, the vessels discovered have a very definite direction, their bow and stern are similar enough for him to have made a mistake. The earliest discovery dates from the middle of the seventeenth century and little attention was paid to it. In the nineteenth century archaeology took possession of it: the *drakkar* of Nydam, preserved at Kiel in 1853, was dated from the third century A.D. Roman coins from A.D. 89 to 217 were found in it. But two new discoveries brought to light the most precious monuments of maritime art: that of Gokstad in 1880 and that of Oseberg in 1904 ... one from the ninth century, and the other slightly older, with the remnants of a third *drakkar* or serpent ship, that of Tune. These three ships, brought together beneath the same roof in the form of a T, are the pride of the Oslo Archaeological Museum.

The number of boats discovered in the barrows or the peat bogs increases year by year. Perhaps we possess one or two in Normandy beneath some unexcavated tumulus.

These unparalleled finds are reserved to Viking countries, except for one at Sutton Hoo, near York, in 1939: an almost intact serpent ship containing the most wonderful ancient jewellery that has yet been discovered. The preservation of these monuments is due to two facts, one geographical and one social. The peat bog brought about the immersion-burial of the ship abandoned in its quagmires; but the second reason for preservation is typical and stresses the characteristics of this eminently maritime nation. Each petty naval chieftain did not hesitate to call himself 'King of the Sea', and admittedly he had acquired his sceptre by an energy and an art worthy of the sharp-pointed crown. The attachment of this king to his frail and sensitive palace, to his ship, was so great that he could not imagine any other coffin. He would rest on the planks which had enabled him to conquer the waves. Thus the vessel was dragged ashore, the dead king was laid on it after being provided with everything necessary for so long a journey; the immense sepulchre was covered with stones in the form of a vault and then with soil (44*a*). This formed a gigantic tomb above the dead sailor's head and the mound, its dome rising to the grey sky, recalled the valour of the one who was now about to sail the eternal seas. On other occasions the vessel was burnt —iron rivets and forged chains have been discovered—and on yet others the chief and his ship, after it had been set on fire, were abandoned to the waves.

*   *   *

And what is the nature of these ships which have been excavated? They are among the most perfect that have ever been designed and carried out by master carpenters (44, 45). One might have guessed it without being a soothsayer. To have

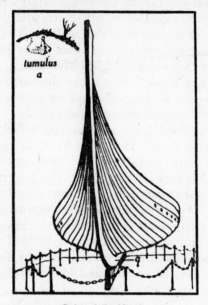

44. Gokstad *Drakkar* Stern

succeeded in what they attempted, the Vikings must have been equipped with an incomparable vessel. Hatshepsut's ship, the Delos triremes and the serpent ship are the most beautiful types of vessel that will be met with until modern times.

Long, powerful lines, strikingly almond-shaped, very remarkable too by the brusque and decisive elevation of the bows and stern (44): the bows immediately offer a volume of resistance and buoyancy to the water; the same applies to the stern, which does not sink too far at the moment the *drakkar* rises to a sea. . . . When there is a following wind, the stern provides protection from the waves. Primarily light, the Scandinavian vessel is reduced to the main essentials. The whole craft is composed of slender sides, rising from a narrow keel. It is solid, inasmuch as it benefits from the spring of very long strakes whose elasticity reinforces and tautens the structure, and because it has a royal sheer: this sheer is the natural result of the long plank to which one wants to give simultaneously a curved and oblique shape. Take a slat, twist it, and you will understand immediately.

Furthermore, it is clinker and not carvel built. Each strake overlaps the one below and is secured to it, thus doubling the overall strength.

The *drakkar* was designed for oars but could carry a sail and could probably even beat to windward. It was only a fifth of the length in the beam, whereas the galley reached an eighth, but the *drakkar* made up for this by seaworthiness and very delicate lines. Finally, it was flexible and flexibility has always remained one of the great imponderables of shipbuilding. The planking below the waterline is not nailed; it is lashed to the frames.

But the most significant features are the stem and stern posts. The stern is merely a tall curve, sometimes incised, rising like a tail above the waves. The bow carries some monstrous figure, some reptile head (43*b*, 46*b*) which gave the vessel the name of serpent ship. The head rears, watches, seeks and threatens. These figureheads are obviously artistic and they complete the vessel with grandeur and precision; but it is not too much to believe that the Vikings were also seeking a warlike end and wanted to inspire dread. Ancient terrors were evoked: the arrival of marine monsters, those enormous beasts of prehistoric times. When the red and black or green and blue *drakkar* appeared between the crests, hoisting its mask of fury above the foam, lashing its caudal fin, burnished shields gleaming like serpent's scales (43), part of the task was accomplished: the bowels of the enemy turned to water.

*   *   *

The craft is so perfect that the eye never tires of following its curves. One is amazed at the line of the hull, starting with a considerable beam and gradually tapering off to end in this plume-like stem, just as one can never get used to seeing delicate feet below a pair of wide hips. The line is so perfect that the least imaginative person must be impressed.

This admiration increases as we examine the vitals of the

drakkar which are the last word in delicacy. Starting from the straight line of the keel they gradually assume an oval form and bulging flanks. For a lover of ships, this is the great art: for him a craft is to be admired from aft. Moreover, speed resides to a great extent in the successful line. In certain boats like this, it approaches a living form. The transition is invisible. The sensation of bellying yields continually to that of tapering, and yet the plastic miracle has taken place. One has left the rod, the ruler, the keel, and one arrives at the sphere without one's eye being offended by the least sign of broken continuity. As a personal recollection, may I be allowed to say that I have built about a thousand ships in wood, and that I have never remained indifferent to this enchanting progression, to these curves and hollows. I awaited them as I began the model as the reward of my handiwork.

For the first time in fact we find the keel (44q), that superb dorsal spine of a ship. Everything is based on this solid, firm and unshakeable axis, while around it the contours undulate. The keel is a very effective element of strength, but, furthermore, it adds to the understanding of a ship that intellectual conviction which the column brings to architecture on land.

* * *

Some of the *drakkars* had permanent decks; the more elaborate of them had a system of movable panels fitted in the beams, those cross-thwarts which hold the craft together. The panel functioned like the lid of a snuff box. It was by the removal of these panels that room was found for the rowers. They sat on the beams, which formed their benches. The largest of these vessels yet discovered reached a length of 75 feet, but in the state of perfection in which we see them it is certain that ships almost double this size would have presented no difficulty to the shipwrights and it would not be too ridiculous to admit the dimensions given them by the poets in the great maritime sagas.

The hull ends with the penultimate strake perforated to allow the passage of the oars, making a series of ports, the great peculiarity and characteristic of Viking construction. These ports are round holes with a narrow diagonal slot (45a) which

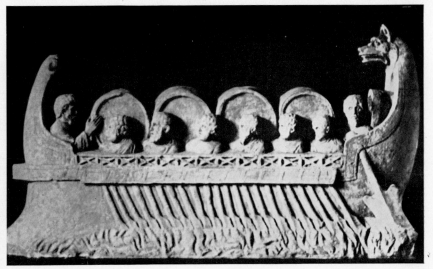

(a)

ROMAN BARQUE

Bas-relief detail. *Musée de Saint-Germain-en-Laye*

(b)

ROMAN GALLEY, DECKED AND ARMED
WITH A FORECASTLE

Bas-relief from the Vatican

PLATE IV

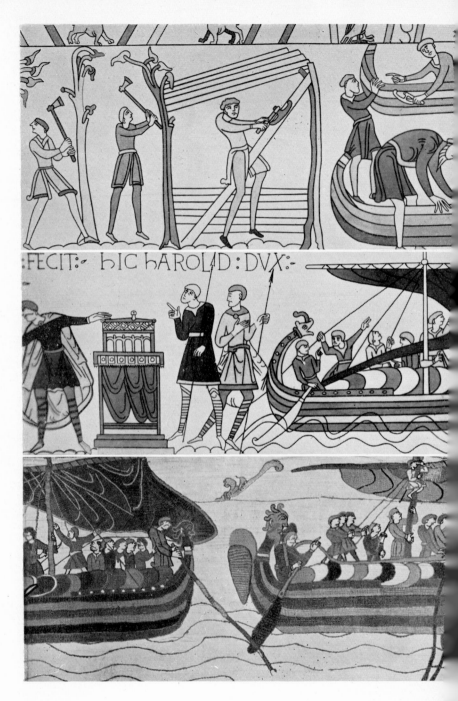

:FECIT:- ᚻIC ᚻAROLD:DVX:-

THE FLEET OF THE NORMAN C
THE SHIPS AT SEA. ᴛ

From

PLATE V

Photo Flammarion

. THE BUILDING OF THE SHIPS.
ARRIVING IN PORT.

apestry

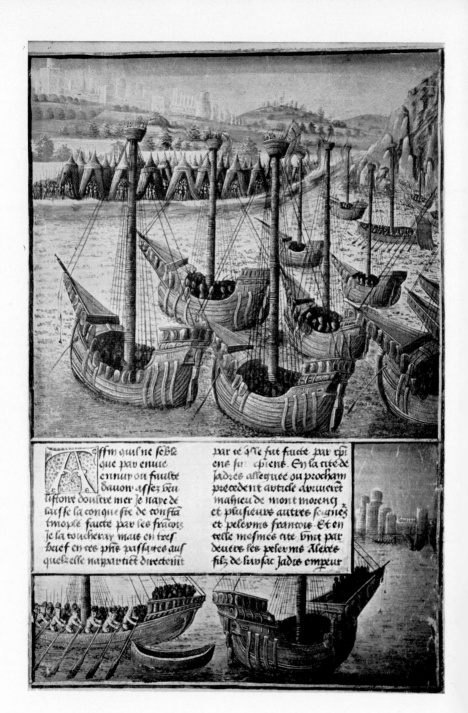

SHIPS ON THEIR WAY TO THE HOLY LAND

Voyages d'Outre-Mer by Sébastien Mamerot.
Fifteenth century miniature. *Bibliothèque Nationale*

PLATE VI

allows the blade of the oar to pass through. In this way the oar is held firm with nothing to obstruct it. An *oculus* closed the little port when the ship was under sail.

*   *   *

Above the gunwale rose the line of shields after the style of the *pavesade* which had been used for so many centuries.

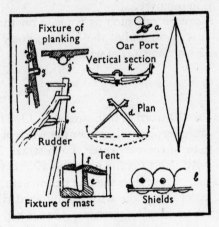

45. Details of the *Drakkar*

They were absolutely flush and centred by a metal *umbo* so that they could slide in a slight rack mounted on battens (45*b*) which held them by the lower fifth of their circumference. The insides of these bucklers were always painted white and they were reversed to indicate peaceful intentions; but the outsides were vividly coloured, each of them different and in regular contrast —a yellow, a black, a red and a black—like the skin of a serpent.

The rudder (45*c*) was fixed on the starboard quarter; this strange predilection for the right which obsesses us—except in politics. This steering oar is of delicate, almost scientific construction, ingenious in any case. Fixed at two points by a ring and spindle, at first sight it seems condemned to complete immobility. It appears to be nailed half way up to a projection of some kind, but this nail is only a whalebone which holds it fast and acts as a pivot. The Viking rudder can only work

93

effectively in semi-rotation; it therefore maintains its directive function by its pressure against flowing water.

A tent supported by two jointed poles with ornamented heads (45*d*) protects the sailors during the night or shelters the watches when they are off duty. From the centre of the tent, amidships, rises the mast, whose step (45*e*) is a stout oak block, and the mast hole has a hinge (45*f*) allowing the mast to be lowered as in the seventeenth-century galleys when hove to. A winch helps this manœuvre.

The sail is a square sail such as we saw on the triremes of Themistocles. It is possible that the Vikings knew of the block and tackle or at least some sort of windlass.

* * *

This craft is the last word in technical skill. One might almost say that the Nordic serpent ships were the work of the cabinet-maker rather than of the carpenter. Each strake is finished as if it were the only one to count; regular rivets, with washers made of cow's hair, brace it to the one below with an even grip and the juncture of the strake with the inboard rib shows skill and an even greater conscientiousness. One is reminded of the details of Egyptian construction given by Herodotus. Inside the strake is a rectangular wooden bracket fitting into a mortice in the frame (45*g*), which is bound either by tree roots or whalebone passing through corresponding holes.

The reason for this difficult and complicated construction is hard to understand. We may suppose that by restricting to the utmost the use of heavy metal, the *drakkar* was given a buoyancy which did not merely come from the air inboard. Even if it were holed, it would still have floated and saved the men clinging to it. But perhaps these intuitive sailors sought a flexibility which they deemed useful and whose effects we have not sufficiently studied at sea. Certain very speedy canoes from the Polynesian islands are remarkable for a flexibility which makes them almost undulate. Is it possible that the elasticity of the craft would have the same effect as a tyre on the potholes in the road, partially absorbing the shock without impairing speed?

A feature of these ships was their violent colour. In their

present state, as they come out of the soil or the peat, they have been subjected to a blackish carbonisation. Their perfect construction, on the other hand, would encourage us today to leave them in their natural state, the better to enjoy the uncompromising, conscientious workmanship. But this respect for a difficult task was scorned in an age when man took a pride in putting the best work into his most commonplace tools. Just as in our cathedrals they nonchalantly painted the astonishing work of the sculptor, with no regard for its form, so the *drakkars* were extremely garish and brightly coloured. Each strake, each plank must have been of a different colour, as can be seen in the Bayeux tapestry, and the poets tell us that the kings bestowed gifts of painted sails. Some of them go so far as to speak of *drakkars* entirely covered with gold. What a sight among the cold blue of the fjords, the icy reflections and the wisps of fog. Even the Arabs were impressed: 'The boats of the men from the north glide across the sea like flocks of scarlet birds.' I have stressed this a little because the present-day tendency is to see old ships with a lack-lustre eye, rather in the Dutch manner.

*   *   *

The most sensational and valuable discovery in this field was the Oseberg serpent ship. Here we were able to perceive the wealth of sculptured ornament carried by the *drakkar*. In addition to this there were other details of the greatest interest. On the stem and stern posts and on the exposed frames appeared hollow, wild and complicated sculptures, highly stylised and clearly inspired by Byzantine distortion: they were true bas-reliefs, with none of those childish incisions and brutal knife-cuts, and instead of making the vessel heavier might almost have lightened it.

This wealth of beasts, flowers and convolutions terminates in a very beautiful figurehead which, for some reason, was never fully restored. Probably the debris could not be used and was replaced by a simple, bare spiral which reproduces its shape only schematically. It is the head of an eared serpent biting its neck as it twists in a kind of tragic convulsion of rage. Apart from the decorative effect, the realism of the movement is in itself very strange and beautiful.

95

It has been established that this processional ship, extremely flat-bottomed and obviously designed to sail on calm waters, belonged to Queen Asa, one of those Amazons whose boundless courage was described in the sagas. But perhaps in real life she was merely a tender, hesitant and gentle woman, very

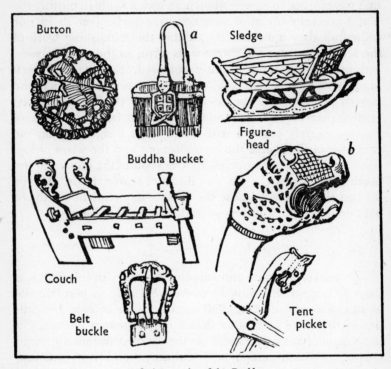

Button   *a*   Sledge

Buddha Bucket

Figure-head   *b*

Couch

Belt buckle

Tent picket

46. Accessories of the *Drakkar*

beloved or very powerful; for nothing was spared in the way of solace for her years in limbo, so that in the manner of the Egyptian burial chambers we have caught a slight glimpse of her life in her death.

Beds, chariots, coffers were discovered and embroideries where the task begun would never be completed (46). The preservation was surprising thanks to the peat turves which formed an hermetic lid above the stones.

Queen Asa wanted to take her personal cavalry with her to the grave. The skeletons of fifteen horses were dug up; her kennels with the bones of four dogs; her cattle-shed with the remains of two bulls. The stomach of one had remained intact and enabled us to discover its last meal: bracken, honeysuckle, juniper and reeds—her death occurred, then, in autumn. But Queen Asa was also followed into death by her faithful maid. Other bones are mingled with hers in the mortuary chamber at the foot of the mast. The hand of the Queen is believed to have been identified: it is the one with the fingers hacked off by thieves who, a few years after her burial, violated the great tomb and must have found the jewels on her hand. But that was all: in order to make no distinction and also to celebrate the devotion of her faithful companion, both of them enjoy royal honours.

However, among all these relics by far the most suggestive is the so-called bucket of the Buddhas (46a), a laminated oak bucket bound with bands of copper, wider at the bottom than at the top, a real combat tub with a handle; and, as clamps for this handle, two Buddhas, cross-legged in the Hindu manner. On their chests can be seen an enamel shield bearing the swastika, repeated four times.

It is believed that this was made in Dublin during the second half of the ninth century, but the influence involved is a very intriguing problem; it fires the imagination to the strangest conjectures. Hindu models must have inspired it. Articles were copied which had crossed the Indian Ocean, sailed through the Red Sea or down the Euphrates, been transported across the Isthmus or brought by the Aleppo caravans; then, carried by Mediterranean sailors in search of tin or amber, had finally reached the large island of Erin.

In any case, the Oriental influence cannot be contested. Have we in these ornaments which decorated the Viking ships a proof that we are correct in invoking Byzantium? The pre-Roman capitals reproduce the same charming distortions, the same luxuriant freedom with an outstanding feeling for the grotesque, but the construction follows a Mediterranean, if not specifically Phoenician pattern.

From a ship with a horse's head, from a ship with symmetrical and very clearly defined stem and stern posts, one can with a stroke of the pencil make the serpent ship as it stands before our eyes today. The oval, almond-shaped form itself is abnormal and is probably born of admiration or surprise. It would have been more logical to reproduce the bodies of sea-birds, since here they could not have started their navigation on a fascine: the Nordic countries did not possess those huge mangroves which were so prolific in warm waters. Everything indicates unbroken relations between the Baltic and the sunny south, even to the armour. Certain helmets of Viking warriors (43c) resemble those of the hoplites and even appear to be vaguely Mycenaean. I know that there are few ways of protecting the head and face, but when the form of the decoration is reproduced one is justified in seeing some connection.

*   *   *

To be sane and logical, nothing proves that because we have excavated seven or eight we are in possession of all the Nordic types. We must admit the information to be found in the sagas. Since they are so accurate when they portray the *drakkars* we have found, why should they be false when they describe those we do not yet know? Let us admit then that in Scandinavia there could have been ships protected by bronze plates and completely armoured: ships with rams, belts and wales of iron. Logically again we must presuppose vessels quite different from those we know to have been in current use. In the Gokstad serpent ship we have a warship plainly aggressive and designed for sea-going purposes, but was this the invasion ship? I have my own ideas about the Viking invasions and I am inclined to think that numerically they were much less abundant than we have been told; that the ubiquity of the attacks exaggerated their effects in the eyes of the terrified victims. But finally there were the emigrations of several thousand men and women at a time. These aggressive waves postulate a naval organisation, in other words, cargo ships and transports. We cannot doubt that the warriors were superior in audacity and military knowledge but there was also the question of their weapons, baggage and families. To what extent does this increase the size of the proud, razor-sharp ship of Gokstad which seems hardly to rest on the water (44)?

*   *   *

We can obtain some idea of these heavy craft from the ships which William the Conqueror assembled for his great conquest in 1066 (47), the last and most famous of the Viking invasions. It is certain that the Normans did not employ other ship-wrights than those who had first earned for them their fortunes —the Scandinavians or, in default of these, shipbuilders

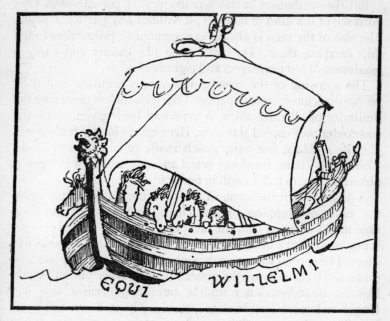

47. Norman Transport Ship

instructed by them. William, like his predecessors, remained in touch with the Vikings. He was apparently so closely allied to the Danes that he diverted them to England to create a second front at the very moment his own fleet was ready.

The naval occasion undertaken by William was analogous to the one the less fortunate Napoleon tried to realise from Boulogne. All the Nordic yards worked at full speed. One can assume that the Viking vessels came to increase the number; how otherwise could he have gathered together such a fleet in five months? How could he have built it or found sufficient seasoned wood? William's armada consisted of 696 actual warships, and a sum total of 3,000 craft charged with the transportation of 50,000 men and 6,000 horses across the Channel.

We are familiar with these ships from the priceless document known as 'the tapestry of Queen Matilda', which, incidentally, was not embroidered by the Queen but came from an Irish convent. It remains, however, the most reliable testimony of the period, one of the few that cannot be contradicted.

But the symbolism in this tapestry is very considerable. One must see in it a kind of hieroglyph without any particular scale. The size of the men is always exaggerated in proportion to the ship carrying them. The craft seem like canoes and carry a maximum of ten passengers and eight horses.

The drawing of the vessels, however, is accurate and their proportions have been respected. One feels this on observing the similarity of all these ships. A type had been given which the embroideresses copied slavishly. Here we no longer find spoons like the *drakkars*, but vats, vessels made to carry heavy loads. This is the Viking transport vessel and one must not imagine a distortion due to lack of skill in embroidering.

A Viking ship: the same silhouette though slightly plumper; the same overlapping planks, clearly indicated by shading. One might even say that the inexperience of the embroideresses is one more mark of sincerity. They represent these planks like slices. The special steering oar is mounted in the same place and is identical; the sails are the same. The shields are placed exactly like the Scandinavian roundels, but here, because they are longer and more oval in shape, they are lying down and over-lap. The colour contrasts are observed in the manner of the Gokstad ship. The only real difference is within board; the warriors' heads only just appear over the gunwales while the horses are visible only from the neck upwards. From this one point can be fixed—the depth of the deck, at least four foot six below the rail. We therefore have a picture of double-purpose ships, for transport and warfare at the same time.

The importance given to the figurehead on the tapestry should not be a matter for surprise; this always happens with an amateur. The old sailor who builds a model of the ship in which he has sailed for ten years and which he adores, will always triple the size of the siren reclining at the bow. She seems to him to be larger because he knows her better and pays more attention to her. However, here we have a variation of the *drakkar* type; the monstrous figurehead has been transformed and lost its formidable character. Perhaps it has become mere decoration and will soon become just humorous (48*a*). To begin with, not all the ships possess figureheads, even if they have the mortice on the stem and stern posts (48*b*) into which

48. Detachable Figurehead (*a*)
Figurehead of *The Mora*, William the Conqueror's Flagship(*b*) right

they can be fitted. There had been no time to attend to such details when they were building this type of ship so fast. This mortice tells us that the figurehead has become detachable; that it has also appeared at the stern and this possibility of change gives strange results. Some mariners have placed the figure in reverse. They could also put it on sideways, giving a very jaunty effect. The crew were no doubt delighted to see the lions, dragons and basilisks putting their tongues out at them.

The Mora, William's ship, is larger than all the others. This is hardly visible on the tapestry but we learn it from the texts. *The Mora*, we are told, presented to the Conqueror by the Duchess Matilda, surpassed in size and strength all the other vessels. This was apparent when William, having waited until after the equinox, gave orders to set sail. *The Mora* outstripped all the rest of the fleet. Only the Normans dared to leave by night. William hoisted his flag at the masthead and the sail was loosed before a southerly wind. The long wait to which the

Bastard had to subject his ships shows that oars could not suffice for this rather long crossing, since his excuse to the troops, which was considered justifiable, was always the persistence of unfavourable winds In fact it is possible that William was waiting for news of the Danish invasion he must have premeditated, but everyone agreed that with a head wind the crossing could not be attempted. *The Mora* flew at the main the standard sent by the Pope, which later became the Flag of St. George, and at the stern she carried the first figurehead we meet with (48*b*).

A conclusion which might have been foreseen occurred next morning. At dawn the Duke of Normandy found himself on an empty ocean. As far as his eyes could see, nothing but white horses. For a moment he must have thought that all this feverish haste, this immense effort which had lasted nine months, had been merely a nightmare that had lasted longer than normal dreams. However, a sailor sent to the masthead soon announced that he could see something astern on the southern horizon, and a little later appeared a forest of masts: the 3,000 *drakkars*.

49. The *Montjoye*, A.D. 1250

CHAPTER VIII

The Crusades

THERE has been a tendency in relatively modern times to separate European shipping into two branches and to make a clear-cut distinction between ocean-going ships and Mediterranean ships, chiefly due to the lateen rig and the more frequent use of galleys in the south. A seaman of course would have recognised, by a quick glance out to sea, the part of the maritime world in which he found himself but he would have needed to examine a fairly large number of ships, and their rigging in particular, for it seems probable that a basic identity existed very early and that, from the fourteenth century onwards, there was practically no difference in the hulls. There were also galleys in the Channel and *nefs* in the Mediterranean. The imitative instinct of sailors immediately took advantage of the various improvements they found in the regions they frequented. The interest in following the marine through the countries and down the ages arises precisely from these influences, from this incessant improvement thanks to which the ship became the emblem of a growing civilisation.

The maritime preponderance shifted to the north, but very slowly, so imperceptibly in fact that British supremacy finally appeared as a transitory anomaly which, however, ultimately had to be accepted. We may take it that improvements in the North came, above all, from the *drakkar*, but with all due deference to Viking pride, would they not have been even more remarkable had they taken more into account the progress made in the Mediterranean, where cities like Byzantium, Venice, Genoa and Marseilles preserved the ancient tradition?

For centuries yet, the great traffic and massive craft belonged to the Latin sea, and the Crusades extended to its limits a naval activity which already surpassed all others.

* * *

The Crusades lasted a very long time even after the official set-back to the eighth European expedition, which ended with the death of St. Louis on his bed of ashes at Tunis. They were continued by the Knights of St. John of Jerusalem who, abandoning Cyprus, fell back on Rhodes and then on Malta, where they became sea-borne crusaders, still chasing the Infidel; continued also by the great fleets equipped against the Turk or the Barbary pirate; by the battle of Lepanto; by the bombardments of Algiers by the galliots of Petit-Renaud and Duquesne; and by the decree of the last King of France, Charles X, who in 1830 ultimately reduced the Saracen navy and brought about the eclipse of the Crescent. One might even say that it needed the First World War for Jerusalem to be returned to the Christians and to realise the Crusaders' vow of the eleventh century.

But it is even more difficult, in our simplistic age, to imagine the immense naval movements caused by the Crusades. With the contemporary means at their disposal, embarking, transporting and disembarking armies with all they needed in the way of horses, weapons, machines and provisions already seems a prodigious undertaking. Furthermore this was not all. To the soldiers must be added the incredible host of pilgrims. There were as many civilians as warriors and it could well be that the great pilgrim transports with Mecca as their destination were only small compared with the faithful who, from the first Crusade onwards, wanted to visit Jerusalem, to pray there and some of whom, as a supreme goal, wanted to die there. We have already seen that St. Paul's ship carried 300 passengers and the figure may surprise us. But we are accurately informed as to the capacities of the Marseilles *nefs*, thanks to the contracts which have survived, and this time we are forced to admit that, averaging at least 500 tons burden, they frequently carried 1,000 people. A thousand people—like a trans-Atlantic liner!

The famous Jal, the first nautical archaeologist, who having been a sailor added his sense of the sea and its necessities to his criticism, devoted himself to the study of these real packet steamers. A curiously picturesque figure, red-faced, short-sighted and deaf, as bad a story-teller as he was a distinguished philosopher, and valuing his tales above all else, he had his works printed by order of the King, although he was both a sectarian and republican. A dreamer and a painstaking scholar, he turned directly to anyone who could give him the best information, not to the literary men, but to the accountants. Jal published the results of his researches in several of his essays and his deductions are difficult to attack. Possibly he was too meticulous and complacent in his desire to magnify his discoveries and the efforts they demanded. He remained little known and famous only amongst specialists, for the details he brought to light are not designed to fire the popular imagination. For details of the shipping of the last centuries of the Middle Ages one relied and one still relies on pictures linking the antique galley and the *drakkar*, when these were actually so very different both in appearance and in power. Furthermore, it needs a certain courage to follow this antiquarian step by step and word by word in his flights. But it pays well to do so and one comes away with a series of surprising images of these wooden whales (49), these enormous hulls with crazy sails, loaded to the scuppers with enthusiastic men—pious, fili-bustering, spitting, vomiting—beneath a bright blue sky, on an indigo sea.

*   *   *

St. Louis was obliged to ask for ships from all the maritime cities of the west and the Levant. We have records of his transactions with Venice and Genoa, which provided a number of craft for a fleet such as had never been seen before.

The Venetian tenders are particularly valuable. They never matured but *la Serenissima* proposed fifteen ships and, to show what she could do, specified three different types to be delivered. Fortunately she has described these for us in great detail: the *Roche-Forte*, the *Sainte Marie* and the *St. Nicholas*. Here I must emphasise that it is not a question of legend but of figures and measurements. Had one been able to find anything similar for the navy of antiquity how much ink, saliva and bile would have been spared.

The result of it all was a very strange craft, to judge by its mass, height and, in particular, its beam. Thus the *Roche-Forte* afloat measured 95 feet from bow to stern and her greatest beam reached nearly 43 feet. Yes, nearly the half. This is the indigestible pill one has to swallow, particularly as it is corroborated by the dimensions given for the two others and again by the breadth near the bow and stern, which hardly taper and which give them a shape not unlike that of a dab, a plaice or a ray. I have never come across any proportions to compare with them. They conflict so much with what is known to us that this is probably the reason for our lack of understanding for the *nefs* of St. Louis.

They are absolute buckets, barrels! One realises perfectly well that oars will serve no purpose here or at most only as a last resource to bring the vessel to her moorings—every mariner who signed on agreed to pull if necessary. We must remember that the ratio of beam to length in the galley was one to eight; it is obvious then that it was absolutely necessary to wait for the wind to propel the *nef*, which was a hippopotamus. However, we are finally convinced that these vessels were good and solid craft, slow and heavy but reliable, and that our incredulity comes from not having been able to follow their development.

Nevertheless such must have been the actual proportions of these merchant ships. The Phoenicians may perhaps have dared to build hulls of this breadth, but their monuments never tried to reproduce them or, if they did, they were always in profile. No medals were struck for the happy arrival of a convoy of cotton bales or vegetable oils. The Queens of Egypt recorded their commercial victories but these were made with warships and they were conquests of perfumes.

In height—moon-sheered from the keel to the after-castle—they were more than 40 feet. One can judge the mass, then, with a draught of 18 feet, when the triremes of Themistocles had a draught of only 5½ feet. However, the silhouette

50. The Gallery and the *Paradisa*, A.D. 1250

was broken, for the waist was not higher than 30 feet from the keel to the rail and it comprised three-quarters of the vessel's length. The remainder, which towered above it, was reserved to the *paradisa*, fore and aft, built on their half-decks, quarter-decks and forecastle decks (50). These structures overhung outboard, and forward—as Joinville remarks in his tale, which is a masterpiece of simplicity, freshness and accuracy—could be seen 'the beakhead of the *nef*' which gave the vessel a very noticeable prolongation (50*b*). This might appear to fine down the extraordinary obesity but did not diminish the waterline, the flatiron on which the *nef* perched, resisting with impunity the anger of the tallest waves. There was no danger of her being swallowed up by the sea; she merely smoothed it out.

*   *   *

The inboard arrangement was very precise and also very curious. There was a deck over the hold, the modern lower deck, nearly 12 feet from the keelson below. Six feet above this there was another complete deck, then a half-deck which was called the gallery (50c), the main street of vessels until 1840. On each side of the *nef* were boxes from bow to stern, above which one passed to go from one end of the vessel to the other. These bridges formed the fore and aft gangways in the old ships, but here, arranged and split into compartments, they became the private suites for rich passengers, similar to our deck cabins. Finally, above this, came the gunwale or *pavesade* on which hung the shields and bucklers of the nobility. This was usually crenellated—a bulwark against the sea and a protection in battle.

This emplacement, which, with the breadth of beam, was the characteristic of the *nef*, formed an enclosed rectangular court-yard of a very special aspect, lined on each side with narrow cabins and ornamented at both ends by the pilasters and arches of the luxury quarters. We must not forget that the people of this age had built that jewel the Sainte Chapelle; they were therefore sensitive to the ethereal yet solid decoration around them.

From these pens, which obviously housed the gentry, every-one appeared at the same moment at the slightest incident. Cabin doors banged, a crowd streamed out onto the deck, into that courtyard where everyone talked, gesticulated, larked and played. There were violent colours on the walls in this age when the barbaric stripes of their temples indicated the need for bright hues. Brilliant or simple costumes, but striking. . . . Occasionally, perhaps, the long blue cloak of the Crusaders, worn during the voyage, for coolness, directly over the shirt, without cuirass or chain mail and which, like the sails, bore a red cross. . . . The linen bellied over the great muscles of these men who had been educated exclusively for battle, trained solely for combat, tender gladiators who loved as well as died nobly. Here, in the idle hours and by her mere proximity, woman—every woman—won a new crown. How they gloated over the Queen's maids of honour on their return journey, which would last for six weeks between Cyprus and Hyères. There were 800 aboard!

It is certain and very much in accordance with Mediterranean custom that in the sunny hours the mariners stretched a sail over this hollow gallery, filling it with cool, dappled shade. Dinner must have been served beneath these tents. The King was enthroned at one end, towards the stern, thoughtful and smiling, a prey to his dreams and eating without too much thought for the food and drink. Around the King, his brothers and his seneschals, among them the gentle Count of Anjou, who was an expert at shooting cherrystones with a catapult of his own invention. On board this *Monnoie* or *Montjoye*, there was great hilarity even when the saintly King was at prayers. In the Levantine marine *'faire une Montjoye'* is still synonymous with an exceptional carousal, in memory of a truly regal voyage.

Only one thing could make the King scowl: blasphemy. According to the ancient laws, the blasphemer was condemned to have his tongue pierced with a red-hot iron. The King, who was more gentle but still a strong man, merely had the culprit towed in the launch, to be either grilled or soaked.

But in stormy weather the fine 'gallery' became a most uncomfortable swimming pool.

The end rooms were called the *paradisa*—parade rooms, Jal assures us rather unconvincingly. The *Roche-Forte* had two of these, one forward and the other aft, if we stick to the height given, and not two superimposed. They formed two large saloons where the passengers took refuge when it rained. Possibly, too, they were the luxury apartments with windows looking out on the sea. Joinville confirms this by telling us that one day the Queen set fire to one of her curtains and threw it out through the window; had this window opened on to the deck, this would not have helped matters very much. In any case it is probable that on the return journey the Queen lived aloft in one of the poops which formed the fourth and fifth storeys of the *nef* and which could evidently be removed, for Joinville reports that during a storm off Cyprus the Queen's bedroom was dismantled. This superstructure in a high wind tended to make the ship list dangerously.

Finally, a combat gallery ran around these poops, forming an overhanging and protruding balcony (50*b*).

Did all this rise vertically? I do not think so, in spite of Jal's opinion. Verticality was not the way of sailors, nor even of the contemporary masons, who gave some 'batter' and slope even to towers. I think that the naval architects must have been preoccupied with the weight of the ship under way as well as the effect of the waves on perpendicular shoring. It is probable that these castles were slightly oblique and raked. The combat gallery seems to prove this and to be designed to provide the overhang necessary for fighting.

Finally, as regards looks, one must above all take into account the sheer and the general curves of the whole edifice which gave it an agreeable appearance as well as great solidity, and which were so familiar to the peoples of the Mediterranean. Thus, this mastodon of the seas, lengthened by salients, curved and reinforced by wales which exaggerated its bulge, managed to take on a nautical look (49).

* * *

On the other hand, in the question of the masts and the yards, we come up against the most painful data—painful by reason of their obvious lack of proportion and their audacity.

The *nef* was also rigged with lateen sails, but what sails! The foremast, known in those days as the 'misaine', was the tallest and from the step to the top (fighting top) equalled the whole length of the ship. This has always been respected, even in three-deckers. It was stepped, according to a persistent custom, in the gripe, a huge beam which began the curve of the stem. Thus in the *Roche-Forte* it rose 60 feet above the gallery. The 'master tree', which later would be the mainmast, was 6 feet shorter and was at the most about 30 feet abaft the 'misaine'. Both of them had fighting tops, semi-crow's-nests like deep baskets, *abaft* the masts. When Jal portrayed them like circular baskets surrounding the mast, he forgot that with the manœuvring of lateen sails the forward projection would have been impossible. When the *antenna* was shifted from one side to the other, following the breeze to receive its full effect, the huge yard had to pass before the mast. It was made to jump on the front of the tree and this manœuvre—already so tricky—which ultimately condemned the lateen yard, would have been interfered with by any protuberance of the crow's-nest.

The proximity of these masts produced a remarkably cumbersome silhouette which became almost extravagant when the *antennæ* were rigged. It must be remembered that an *antenna* always has to be twice the length of the mast carrying it and this ratio was maintained until the end of lateen sails. The fore *antenna* of the *Roche-Forte* actually measured 96 feet equipped with its *spigone*, its little jutting end, and the other was 84 feet. One can imagine the extraordinary area of the canvas.

*   *   *

This was such a strange anomaly that it gave me food for considerable thought. I have often wondered if the Mediterranean peoples did not discover one of the most modern effects of the wind acting on oblique and close-hauled sails, as in the case of contiguous staysails: the so-called funnel effect which greatly increases the propelling power of the sails. Today, racing sails are set like this. A staysail, which has become very large, is hoisted far abaft the mast. In any case I have found out by trying it on a model that ships rigged in this way were best able to catch the wind. They achieved this, in spite of their fat bellies, because of the depth of their draught which made the keel drift to leeward. They were even close-winded ships, thanks to their aftercastle, which acted like the tail of a weathercock. All the 'experts' have attributed the discovery of this new nautical possibility to the great Genoese admiral Doria in the sixteenth century. However, the Mediterranean *nef* of the twelfth and thirteenth centuries—not the ocean-going *nef* with its big square sail—seems to have been created to use this rig alone. A ship like the *Roche-Forte* must have been much more seaworthy than we believe and could sail near enough to the wind to take full advantage of it. A last consideration: the prevailing winds in the Mediterranean are the dry winds, the sirocco and the mistral, southerly and northerly respectively. A cross wind or wind on the beam was therefore normal when sailing the length of this inland sea. A stern wind in any case must have been despised. Lateen sails are the most pitiful engines in a following wind. The sailing ship in the south had made the progress which was still awaited in the north and the *nef*, with its load of warriors, priests and ladies, sailed along well, cleaving the waves under these incredible 120 foot lateens.

*   *   *

But we are forgetting the strangest feature of all. Not only did the *nef* carry the Knights but it also transported their horses.

51. Trap Door for Embarking Cavalry. *Vissier*, A.D. 1250

Yes, each *nef* had its stable which had been built to this end and moreover built very intelligently. Of course special stable-boats were chartered, the famous *vissiers*, but Joinville states categorically that the *nef* embarked cavalry—*their* cavalry: the knights perhaps refused to be separated from their steeds, their most reliable comrades, their *alter ego*. Joinville is writing about Aigues-Mortes—not Marseilles, for only the fighting galleys could make their way up the Crau, the paunches of the *nefs* keeping them in the maritime harbour: 'On this day we went aboard our *nefs*, opened the door in the nose (51) and took on all our horses that we were to transport overseas.'

So even in St. Louis' ship there was a stable, and its stench must have risen through the hatches to the promenade deck, mingling with the nard, musk and benjamin used by the ladies of the Court. And there were at least fifty horses on the big *nefs*, no doubt about this. How and where? Did they embark the beasts by a crane and a double girth? The oxen were raised by their horns, but what of these noble horses? Did they hang like a wretched sack of withers and legs? No: these people were too practical and too kind. Joinville lets us into the secret. He mentions the big door of the *nef* and here we have the ingenious solution.

The *nefs* actually possessed a loading port of vast dimensions, a huge door (hence the *huissiers* or *vissiers* from the French word *huis*, a door) on a level with the lower deck, probably forward but on the quarter in the drawing (51). The weight was displaced aft and the bow rose above the landing stage. They only had to place a large gangplank and the chargers entered a rather ill-lit stable. 'Then', Joinville adds, 'the door was reclosed and well sealed as one closes up a tunnel, because when the *nef* was at sea the whole door was in the water.' They carefully caulked the great port and, with the vessel brought once more on an even keel, the horses had nothing more to do except to die nobly.

Authentic documents show that they did not have very much room. From the Marseilles registers Jal found that they were given only three hands'-breadths, that is to say three feet, while the modern horseboxes in ships are nearly four feet wide. In the ancient manner, however, the horse was suspended by its girths to the ceiling of the stable, not very high because to begin with the ceilings would not allow it. Its hooves had to brush the ground. This is still done today in very bad weather to prevent horses getting cast or breaking their pasterns, but here it was the permanent arrangement. The horses had no firm footing on the floor and when the knights, who, like the squires of olden days, could not dispense with a little visit to the stables, went down to the lower deck they were reminded to a certain extent of the adventure upon which they had embarked. They saw 30 or 40 horses swaying rhythmically with the movement of the ship. The horses were chivvied to give them some exercise and this put the Crusaders in good spirits. In this semi-darkness it must have been a strange and noisy sight: the clatterings of hooves, furious neighings, coarse laughter, the crack of whips and the leaps to safety of these sailing horsemen.

They arrived at Cyprus at last on the 26th December, after a 40-day crossing.

*   *   *

Despite the storm, which had been murderous, when the King left for Egypt he was still at the head of 1,800 ships, *nefs*, *busses* or *selanders* and galleys. I have not yet mentioned the round ship. The *buss* was the smallest example. Henry Doria's *selander* carried a crew of only 26 men whereas the *Roche-Forte* needed 110. Is one to conclude that this ship was both a warship and a transport? It is of much finer proportions. The ratio of beam to length was one to three like the finest modern sailing vessels, which do not exceed one to four. The masts were much shorter and suggest that oars may have been used on the way. As to the *galea*, it was the ancient galley, accoutred in the fashion of Byzantium and essentially military. I shall close with Joinville's description of the *galea sottile* which belonged to his handsome cousin, Count Gaultier of Jaffa.

I have given a modern text in order not to tire the reader with archaisms:

'To port' (they disembarked on the beaches at Damietta) 'the Count of Jaffa, who was the cousin of Count de Mont-béliard of the Joinville family, drew alongside. It was he who beached most nobly for his galley arrived painted within and without with his escutcheons, which are *or* with a hooked cross. There were 300 rowers, wearing a huge buckler with the Count's armorials and on each buckler flew a pennon embroidered with gold. As they made for the shore, the galley seemed to fly over the water under the power of the oars and thunder seemed to fall from the heavens, so great was the noise of the flapping pennons, the cymbals, the drums and the Saracen horns. As soon as it had come as close inshore as possible, he and his Knights, exceedingly well-armed and equipped, leaped from the galley and came over to join us'.

Joinville himself had only managed to embark 'with eight of my horses on a little *nef* which Madame de Bayruth had given me'. As the King had refused to give him a galley, Joinville was forced to make his landing in a small boat in which they were all nearly drowned.

We know that St. Louis jumped into the water in his impatience to get ashore and into the fray. Courage made him do this but it was also due to poverty. The King had bought so many knights that he could not afford the luxury of disembarkation galleys whose shallow draught allowed them to beach directly on the sand. The rich men thus stepped directly ashore while the King and a number of his knights were obliged to jump into the water where many of them perished.

The vessel on which the saintly King embarked in 1270 for the last Crusade bore—already—the name the *Paradis*.

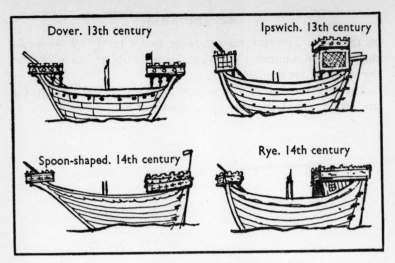

52. Types of Nordic Vessels

CHAPTER IX

The North

IN the north vessels were to increase in size and be perfected on lines parallel to their development in the south, where conditions were very different. In northern waters, tricky problems which never affected the shipping of antiquity would have to be solved.

Everyone knows that the Mediterranean is not an easy sea; the volubility of the southerners has stressed this to the point where one forgets the terrible hindrances the navigator found on the coasts of the Atlantic and in particular in the Channel. The tides alone would have sufficed to upset all the concepts of antiquity. In the north one could never be sure of a channel, either in depth of water or in the currents, without being obliged to take into account not only the time but the month and the strength and direction of the wind! The ancient ship, of course, sailed beyond the Pillars of Hercules but only in exceptional cases, such sorties always being looked upon as great exploits. One remembers the amusing account of Alexander arriving at the mouth of the Indus. The Greeks thought they were lost when the tide came in; they saw themselves as the victims of an unparalleled disaster—which occurred twice in twenty-four hours.

Doubtless, for the men of the north sailing in the Mediterranean was a yachting party compared with the dangers confronting them in their fog-bound seas, the treacherous shallows and the long dark nights spent, without heed for the uncertainty and the darkness, at the mercy of the waves.

At first the development of the ship of the north in size and shape was quite individual, slow and modest. It was behind the southern ship as regards speed, convenience and tonnage. It had to adapt itself to the hard conditions that ruled. Then came a gradual emancipation and emulation: it submitted to southern influences in so far as they could be reconciled with its essential needs. This second period lasted until the fifteenth century. After this date, on the other hand, having finally acquired an increasing reputation in the difficult art of navigation thanks to the boldness and skill of the men who sailed in it, its turn would come to take the lead.

The point of departure was, therefore, the ship which was used in the Norman conquest and whose characteristics I have already mentioned. These ships were a development of the *drakkar*, but heavier, loftier and widened craft. In order to understand them completely, however, we must note other influences and see, under Viking direction, an autochthonous influence. The shipwrights must have taken into account a pre-existent marine which had proved itself in the waters it frequented. The Vikings were far too intelligent sailors to deny the value of experience in the type of sea which would be met with.

We can safely presume that some Celtic type must still have been used along the coasts, even if it were only a fishing boat, a boat which probably derived from the famous *gaulus* mentioned by Caesar which gave him such serious trouble in the Gulf of Morbihan. He could only conquer the Veneti thanks to the defection of the wind. Caesar does not conceal the threat represented by these tall, stout, heavy ships; the *ponto*, a Gallic ship which figures on the Althiburus mosaic, strangely resembles William the Conqueror's craft. Moreover, the northern ship impressed the Latins so much that in the thirteenth century there existed in the waters of the Levant a large cargo boat known as the *berton*, or *breton*, and behind the medieval ships one can catch a glimpse of heavy shadows. For two centuries, in fact, Anglo-Norman shipping does not appear to have departed to any extent from a heavy type very far removed from Viking slenderness. William's ships, in the light of later developments, may not have been built merely as transports for this special expedition, but may have been a current type of warship. Had they been only for temporary use they *would not have continued to build them after the Conquest* (53).

*　　*　　*

And this they undoubtedly did. We possess precious documents in the Seals of the English or French maritime towns—particularly English towns, for France was a long way from individual creation in the realm of shipbuilding on account of its geographical position on two seas.

The ships on the Hythe seal of the twelfth and thirteenth centuries closely resemble the ships on the Bayeux tapestry. They seem to be merely a tracing when one looks at the hull. There are the same thick strakes, obviously of heavy oak from the north, from which there often oozes below the paint that 'tan', the bitter blood of the tree; the same rectangular, barge-like distension, the height of the planking allowing only the heads of the horses to appear. One thing is lacking—figures at the bow and stern: those luxurious monstrosities have left their mortices for ever—at least on the Channel shores. A Danish fresco, however, the Skamstrup paintings, still shows us vessels with gentle, mocking dragons putting out long, straight tongues like cigars. So at last, homely and friendly faces appeared in the place of those which had once inspired so much terror.

Additions to the William-ship to give a warlike touch were the superstructures, the towers and brattices placed fore and aft. These were most strongly developed at the stern: an indication of the importance the sterncastle would eventually assume (53). These English seals are very intriguing for lovers of ships, for they portray the prototypes of those fine raised edifices which would one day sail from the same ports.

The combat towers are usually only light structures supported by stanchions. The texts assure us that the Vikings built similar edifices and this is quite logical. The reason perhaps that we have not found any on these vessels is because they were erected only for combat. The Vikings were too nautically minded to encumber their craft in this manner and make them heavy at sea.

We have here a structure completely *sui generis*, entirely native in its fundamental robustness. It is probable that these ships served alike for war or trade. Their capacity and defence against the waves favoured the carrying of merchandise; and to make them fit for combat they merely had to erect castles for their warriors. For a long time this would be the advantage of the *nef* and one can see in it a reason for its ultimate preponderance. We find here the influence of commercial realism, of the common sense of the Hanseatic towns whose business was extremely active. Gone is that Viking lyricism which inspired those great conquerors of the sea to defy the waves. The nautical intoxication of the Viking has today become a commonplace, but this does not prevent it from remaining one of the greatest physical and intellectual stimulants the world has ever known; the north still echoes with it for anyone who cares to listen. However, in the ships of the twelfth century we must admit it did not seem to play a part at all. They could take aboard a heavy burden of merchandise; they provided shelter from the sea: a certain comfort ensued very far removed from the heroic bareness of the *drakkars*. They were cargo boats.

* * *

We see these stout vessels growing larger and more serviceable. The Hastings seal shows an already more scientific arrangement around the stem and stern posts, which the sides now join, incorporating them in the general construction in a manner that forecasts the shape of the modern ship. The Rye seal, for the first time, displays brattices forming part of the hull —of the upperworks. The Dam seal—still thirteenth century— portrays a ship with castles still separated from the hull but which is remarkably modern; a stern for the first time entirely different from the bow—the stern of the Norwegian vessel. This stern even carries a rudder hung amidships, the *bayonne* type (53a). Forward, extending to a point, the strakes assume at last that curve a nautical eye always appreciates and which later will become the cutwater.

Later, the castle becomes definitely incorporated in the hull. With the taste for comfort, it became a sort of sloping roof. The quarters of the Mediterranean *nef*, the *paradisa* I mentioned in my chapter on the Crusades, are clearly indicated. They are still clumsy but formal, while the bows are laden with the pointed construction which will become the beakhead of the *carrack*.

The Rye seal (52) appended to a fifteenth century charter, must have been taken from a far more ancient matrix; it also shows that the aftercastle is still increasing in size and solidity. We can see the doubling joining it to the body of the ship. The vessel tends to take on the spoonshape, with the bow for handle: this is a shape which all the *nefs* retained for nearly 200 years. We have arrived in fact at the vessel which developed so much slower in the north than in the Mediterranean, where the great traditions were preserved. I have the impression—despite the more or less badly-translated documents—that in the Channel the capacity hardly exceeded 200-250 tons burden and this was already quite substantial. I admit that elsewhere when I myself have quoted huge Mediterranean tonnages of 1,000, 2,000 and 4,000 tons, it was only out of loyalty to my predecessors and the experts and that fundamentally I remain sceptical about these figures. A sailing vessel of 2,000 tons was a whole world in itself! In any case, due to the difficulties of navigation encountered in the north, great load-carrying would appear only with modern ships. Until the fifteenth century the small boat, the Newfoundland schooner type, rather more distended, almost fantastically heavy, but restrained, was the order of the day.

In fact, so faithful are the painters to the same forms during the same periods, that one comes to think that uniformity reigned. A huge, pot-bellied hull (53), with a stern gallery and rails for soldiers or passengers; on the sternpost, its bore sliding below the planking, a long-shaped rudder (*a*) of considerable proportions because of the width of the stern. . . . The variations are reserved for the bows, sometimes a third higher than the stern and giving a curious impression of a raised neck with the small castle forming the head, sometimes the same height as the stern, but always tapering to a point. No more oarports as in the earlier types. The oar is still used to get out of a tight spot, but it was employed too rarely to necessitate special arrange-ments. At most one can ascribe to the need for the oar the rather low waist.

*   *   *

It was towards the end of the fifteenth century, as far as I can see, that European ships took the shape of the fish. Let me

53. *Nef* at the beginning of the Fifteenth Century

explain. For the plan of the water line which should one imitate, the fish or the seabird? The seabird would seem the most logical because it is not entirely immersed. It has a hull and a superstructure, but it is broadest at the stern. China opted for the bird: her ships glide whereas ours cleave, since we have placed the centre of gravity forward and depressed the hulls by loading them with ballast to ensure seaworthiness.

And this, which seems a trifle, is of major importance. The whole of shipbuilding hinges upon it. Even today we still do not know which is preferable scientifically. Some American sailing ships, with the main breadth right aft, have achieved un-paralleled passages....

It is possible that, at the outset, the form we adopted was not completely premeditated, even if at a later date it was studied and deliberately discussed. It must have been favoured by the use of a central rudder, which demanded a tapered stern to allow the maximum effect. Let us pause for a moment to consider the curious anomaly which will remain for centuries: the stern, whose lines had become so constricted, giving so little buoyancy, was loaded with structures.

*   *   *

For three centuries the method of using sail in the north hardly changed. The barbarous solution of the mainmast amidships, with a single square sail, was retained. Probably from love of order, symmetry and solidity, they clutched like grim death on to this central mast which, for a ship with only one mast, became ridiculous. When the boat was completely lenticular, the idea of a central mast in this long ellipse was natural. The shrouds were sufficiently splayed and the stay was at a sufficiently wide angle to give good support. The mast stood up better to the forces acting on it. Later it is certain that the weighty foremasts, heavily raked, put a great strain on the keels. It is curious, however, for until the fifteenth century the northerners knew virtually only how to go before the wind, and it is precisely with a stern wind, in order to avoid pitching and a zigzag course, that it is useful to have the point of traction as far forward as possible.

However, they clung to the central position. They made up for this by the incredible fullness given to the main course. A large part of the canvas was not used for propulsion and only served to move the point of traction further forward. The part of the sail rendered almost horizontal by the bellying had no other effect.

It was not romanticism which made the artists of the period blow up their enormous hempen lungs to bursting point; it was compulsion. With this liberty given to the sail, I think that a mathematician would find the centre of effort, the crux of the wind, in the same place as in modern sailing ships, about a third the way aft from the bows.

But in those days the sail was so long that it greatly exceeded its normal depth. However, they did their best to make it handy in order to use it even in the stiffest breeze. They employed two methods, of which only the second was to remain: the laced bonnet and the reef. Both of these can be seen clearly in the paintings of the period and they must have made a great impression on the imaginations of the artists. A strange thing, however, that they should pay such attention to particular details. In my youth there was not a child who did not add lifeboats suspended on davits to his drawings of ships. Well, no engraver of olden times ever forgot either the reefs or the bonnet. The bonnet was a strip of canvas laced, from eyelet to eyelet, to the sail itself, adding to its depth. The reefs were brails solidly fixed to each face of canvas, in stages. By hauling on each of them, one shortened the sail which was made fast to the yard. In the old days the reefs were taken in below and this has survived in our fishing boats.

The ratlines, those ladders which joined the shrouds, first appeared at about this period. In the south we have found them more often in the shape of a rope ladder fixed abaft the mast, but in the north we have to wait until the sixteenth century. The artists would no more have failed to draw them than would children, who never forget them. All the topmen had to climb with the aid of their arms and legs. This was quite natural, actually, for the masts were not very high and these men, who were for the most part agile peasants, thought nothing of climbing a tree. I have never seen these ladders clearly portrayed in the north prior to the famous stained-glass window in the Bourges Museum which figures Jacques Coeur's ship.

The galley never carried ratlines, probably because of the mobility of the shrouds which were cast off to leeward so that the lateen sail would set better. I have no idea how the sailor on watch reached the top cage of the galley. No one and nothing has ever been able to tell me; neither the scholars nor the models of the period. The little boat in the Science Museum, with its rope ladder abaft the mast, reeks of the bazaar. One merely notices in the galleys a sort of fork with a block which could have served as a lift.

*   *   *

It is obvious that galleys were also used in the north. We

know that at Rouen and Harfleur there existed 'the galley dock'; that our princes and even the English kings employed Italian admirals and shipbuilders; that Richard Coeur de Lion was in command of a squadron of galleys; but we find no trace of them in northern sculpture before the sixteenth century. It is probable that the role of the ship propelled entirely by oars was very modest west of the Mediterranean and that the imagination of artists was hardly inspired by tugs or very small traders. Our illustrators show only *nefs* in the naval battles of the north, although occasionally they slip in a few charming rowing yawls with sumptuous tents in their sterns.

The great hulls have very little decoration. They are usually of natural wood with a protective coat of heavy brown varnish. The famous *White Ship*, in which, on the 25th November, 1120, at Barfleur, the King of England's son and so many of the flower of French nobility were drowned, must have been far more dazzling and have retained the brilliant luxury of the Viking ships, each strake of which had its own colour.

Our *nefs* had only their flags hanging on the bulwarks to make them gay. Occasionally the *nef* seems to have had its arms or particular emblem—a more important pennon which gave it a discreet luxury. The capital ships also carried sails painted either in the national colours or the colours of the Grand Admiral. A light decoration, carved rather than sculptured, sometimes adorned the stern bulwarks and was repeated on the tops when there were no escutcheons. The overall effect was very sober. As a mark of ownership, the Royal arms were in the centre of the stern balcony and heralded the special importance this place would assume from the emblems which decorated it. It would later be the place for the ensign.

In the Mediterranean, at the beginning of the fifteenth century, we meet with a devotional figure on the stern, a Virgin or a Saint. The custom would spread gradually to the north. No figurehead on the bow before 1450-1480; a light decoration adorns the two handrails which mark the limits of the triangle.

*   *   *

At this point in the development of rigging, a little problem arose: the influence of the northern *nefs* on the Mediterranean craft and the regression of the latter. The crude but solid shipping of the north, with its rudimentary solutions in the matter of sail, impressed its characteristics on the southerners, who abandoned their admirable lateen sails and adopted the great square form, which gave a weak return and limited them to going before the wind. In 1480 uniformity was achieved. Carpaccio shows us northern rigging on Venetian vessels. Even though the tales assure us that the *nefs* still carried triangular sails, we do not possess a single document to prove it. There was one slight difference; in the north the shrouds were made fast outboard and in the south, inboard.

We come at last to the disposition of sail that held good on all the seas: to the three-master (1400?). The three-master—it actually had four if we include the bowsprit, which did not count—would reign a long time. The mainmast had become incredibly massive and tall, abnormal and disturbing; one would have thought that a gust of wind would have capsized the pumpkin into which it was stuck. The topsail appeared. This small trapezoid sail, supported by a spar almost invisible in comparison with the other, was carried at the top of the obelisk mast, the factory-chimney mast. This spar was half the length of the main yard. In the bows, almost on the beakhead, was a smaller mast which became the foremast, carrying a sail whose size varied between a third and more often a quarter of that of the mainsail. From the bow rose a raked spar which supported the topmast and which also carried a sail, the spritsail. Finally, in the stern, there was a sail with *antenna* carried on the mast which, after many vicissitudes, became the classic mizzen mast. This sail was the concession made by the north and the last vestige of the southern *nefs*. Lovers of ships will look affectionately at this last lateen sail of our ships and it seems that even the navy had an almost fetishistic respect for it. It lasted throughout the age of sail. Borne at the stern at the end of the fifteenth century, it survived in its derivative but recognisable form as a gaff spanker until the twentieth century. The ships of Louis XIV would cut off its forward extremity—the triangle of sail which projected beyond the mast—but they would keep the *antenna*; Louis XV's sailors, in turn, would cut off the fore end of the yard whose after end then formed the gaff and we come to the famous brigantine, which in 1790 was equipped with a spanker boom, so characteristic of all the great sailing ships. It looks like the caudal fin of the ship.

We see how the vessel has thus become complicated and refined. In the mainsail it possesses an instrument of propulsion and in the foremast, the mizzen, the bowsprit and spritsail, manœuvring devices. Was it in order to obtain manœuvrability that the Mediterranean peoples abandoned their native rig? It is possible that with the increase in size of hull and tonnage the Latins found themselves forced to sacrifice speed to manœuvrability.

One other detail which confirms my intuition: it is very probable that the fifteenth century was the first to be faced with important tonnage and that for these burdens the lateen sail proved too fragile and too difficult to handle.

The *nefs* must have had to remain far longer in the Atlantic than in the Mediterranean, particularly when commerce with the Hanseatic towns and the British Isles had become so great.

It is a well-established fact that the Latin ships set square sails when they passed the Pillars of Hercules. From there to rigging *nefs* with this destination in view was only a matter of commercial common sense. Two rigs would have been very costly and even if the *nef* lost time between Gibraltar and Venice, it was less costly and this, after all, was the main consideration.

I must stress this matter of size and tonnage, the almost certain cause of the abandonment of the lateen sail. As a proof of this we must examine the ships of Columbus. For the terrifying journey, the *Santa Maria* and the *Pinta* were converted to square sails while the small *Niña* retained her three lateens, which, in a ship of that size, were easy to handle even in the Atlantic.

54. Barbary Coast Galley, Seventeenth Century

CHAPTER X

The Mediterranean
Wasps' Nest

THE ARABS

MARITIME activity in the Mediterranean was incessant, varied, episodic or general; extraordinarily complicated, a mixture of commerce and war, of greed and sacrifice, obscured by petty national rivalries which were as active as they were narrow. The northern and southern shores drew closer, became involved in official or private warfare, in declared or treacherous skirmishes; those of the west and east, in pitched battles and carefully prepared forays. To harry the Turk became a frenzy which took hold of the Christian and for centuries caused any voyage by sea to be looked upon as an expedition. Every commercial privateer became a war leader. Even in peace-time the Mediterranean boiled beneath sharp keels and gunfire.

In the other camp the enthusiasm was no less keen. Their reply to 'accursed infidel' and 'bloody renegade' was 'Christian dog'. It was more a religious quarrel than a national fray. The renegades, whom the Moors themselves despised because they had abandoned the religion of their ancestors, pushed cruelty to the extreme. Exiles from honour, they very soon became the worst of all. Their sin acted as a spur.

On the one side Islam, on the other Venice, Genoa, the Knights of Malta, Pisa, Spain and even Portugal, who chased back to their lairs the corsairs who attacked them on the high seas. The fleets of what we should call today the Great Powers rarely counted as much as those of the maritime cities. Even the Pope was involved and the Powers had too many fronts to defend: French support, for example, could never be compared with that of Venice.

But, fundamentally, the same applied to the Mohammedan adversary and the arena was curiously symmetrical. That the Moslems constituted a sort of piratical hegemony which the Christians bravely attacked, was due to individual efforts, to the naval fertility of the small coastal states and the corsair cities. The men of Barbary, Turks and Arabs, all joined in the same action, but without any great political ties. There were corsairs of Asia Minor, of Cairo, Alexandria, Tripoli, Tunis and Algiers. Above them soared the Commander of the Faithful after the collapse of the Greek Empire, but he acted more in an honorary capacity than as an organiser. The decline of Rome had delivered the sea once more to the sea-rovers of the south. From every creek, from every roadstead, these incomparable sailors set their course northwards. At each end a great State encouraged the combatants, but the wasps' nests remained face to face.

*　　*　　*

To obtain a true idea of the Barbary pirates, they must be considered as the natural heirs of the Phoenicians. Like them, these Arabs had very few ties with the land. They had acquired some land thanks to those prodigious tides of invasion which followed the death of their Prophet and led them in three waves to the battlefield of Poitiers, while eastwards they sailed as far as India and China. These nomads suddenly became sailors, taking the place, with incredible speed, of the nations they had conquered. Their commerce was on the sea exactly as it had been for the men of Tyre or Joppa. They became the brokers of the African, Asiatic and even the European world. How did these military conquerors suddenly become such superb sailors, whose quality made suppression so difficult that it was 1,100 years before sea travel could be considered completely safe? The Mediterranean has, of course, become perfectly safe today, but what about the Red Sea, the Persian Gulf and the Indian Ocean? Trade there is not altogether without risk. I could even show that there remains a little of the old pirate yeast in *Mare Nostrum*: the 'rackets' there are easier and more scientific than elsewhere. The 'Moko' retains a superiority in cunning which the men of the west are quite right to fear and the Arab is still a fast, expert and unscrupulous sailor.

The Arab appeared as the commercial successor of those Assyrio-Phoenicians whose political and geographical place he took, reigning on the shores of Asia Minor with a capital at Baghdad, close to the site of ancient Babylon.

* * *

Opinions on Arab civilisation are very divergent. For some, the Arabs were geniuses in invention, intuition and assimilation. I am inclined to share this view merely from a consideration of the way they adapted themselves to the ship when previously they had crossed nothing but sand: and even if they had only used the 'Ship of the Desert', the camel, this would be a poor enough metaphor to quote in explanation.

Others, and these are very numerous, are inclined to underestimate the faculties of this little-known nation and to look upon the Arabs merely as monkeys capable of perseverance and application. People say that, fundamentally, Andalusian civilisation gained nothing from the dark-skinned conquerors but everything from the exploitation of the ancient Roman culture which had transformed their country. I have the feeling —although I hesitate to oppose such an expert as Charles Maurras—that these critics are carried away by racial exaggeration, by a pro-Latin sentiment which incites them to contempt. They remain Romans and everyone who is not *civis Romanus* is for them almost a barbarian. Other defamators have been spurred, unwittingly, by religious rancour—a resentment which, together with political hatred, is the hardest to efface.

If the Arabs copied the Romans, the Byzantines and the Greeks, they did so with particular genius, a mixture of very individual ardour and dreams, poetry and patience, which seems to be their own prerogative among all the racial qualities. As to their general intelligence, it is very difficult to over-estimate these masters who gave so much to the European world, if only in the field of mathematics; they brought refinements to algebra even if they did not invent it; their language is one of the richest in the world, possessing a suppleness, wealth and clarity which give food for thought. The French vocabulary may contain 300,000 words? The Arabs claim 2,000,000!

We still admire their calendar, and an Arab astrolabe compels your admiration. The complication of the designs shows clearly what science had become customary for their sea captains, the *raïs*. My grandfather, the Admiral, enjoyed taking his latitude from these beautifully contrived instruments—beautiful also to the eye for Arab art was at a peak of perfection. Many of these astrolabes disappeared in the turbulent period following the French Revolution when ignorant oafs considered themselves entitled to despise the entire past; but I belong to the school of the old naval officers whose tales of buying these astrolabes for 10 francs in all the second-hand shops of the Levant fill me with envy. This is another proof of how much they were in current use. We should not forget the chronometers sent by the Commander of the Faithful to Charlemagne.

We must not swim against the stream and insist that Europe was the most scientific, the most civilised and the most intelligent. It is a strange thing: we have to age in order to arrive at the point, which we have almost all reached, of considering that this European supremacy is a stifling, chauvinistic vanity. I think that we still have to reconstruct the *real* history of the Arabs in its entirety: the history of its magnificent, cruel and gentle Emirs, heroes on land and sea; of its sublime women, who are to the Ouled Naïls of today what the Queens of France were to our peasant women; of its pedigree horses, whose ancestry went back to the time of Christ; of their vessels which preserved their mastery of the seas until they lost it to the hard and calculating men of the north.

*　　*　　*

The men of Barbary, and when we use this term in France it is to denote certain followers of Mahomet, also built huge ships in order to have an instrument of warfare capable of opposing those directed against them. Their intelligence probably rebelled. A new weapon is always necessary to win a battle. Who ever would have thought that an aeroplane could sink cruisers? The vainglorious Caliphs of Baghdad also built powerful hulls during their struggle with Byzantium.

Everyone knows, from Gaston Paris, the astonishing ship which Richard Coeur de Lion attacked on the 7th June, 1191, when this marine monster tried to relieve St. John of Acre. The Arab vessel carried 1,500 fighting men, led by seven Emirs. It was sheathed entirely with yellow and green leather like a crocodile from Memphis. The whole English fleet, mainly composed of galleys, sailed round it in vain and attacked it. It defended itself by hurling at the English glass shells containing Greek fire—evidently the Byzantine secret had leaked out. The English could not board it, and sank it by ramming. Richard's galleys were probably of the Roman type for in the north we knew nothing of the ram: the formidable Arab ship was only a dromond.

We still quote today an enormous ship which Pedro of Aragon captured from the Moors and used at the siege of Algeciras in 1342. It was called an *uxel* or the *Uxel*, or perhaps this was the name of a type. We know its dimensions, about 150 feet long, 30 feet wide and 14 feet deep. It could carry 50 horses and its beam, a fifth of its length, makes us think that it normally used oars. Was this already a prototype of those galleasses which the Venetians and the Genoese used so successfully?

In any case, at the outset of the Mediterranean fray, after the collapse of the *pax romana*, ships of large tonnage were preferred. The commercial nations increased the size of their merchant vessels to protect the cargo from pirate attacks. A powerful vessel can also carry a large crew and weapons. Ships up to 4,000 tons burden were built: we must admit that this is an astonishing figure. Ship owners who had not armed their ships were subject to considerable fines.

* * *

But the Arabs were never very enthusiastic about the heavy northern hulls. During the last period of their success they employed tall ships, but without holding them in great esteem. A curious example of their contempt can be found with regard to the frigate *El Merikana* (*The American*), a 40-gun ship which they bought at Baltimore in 1798. They sold her while she was brand new; the famous Hamidu, a great corsair said: 'She's worth absolutely nothing.'

Doubtless French ship construction was safe and cautious but it was too much in the spirit of a *paterfamilias* who provides for everything. The square rig was a model of prudence: masts that could always be repaired, in three sections; well-kept yards; countless shrouds and blocks; topmasts with a crow's nest. But the propulsion given to the ship was heavy and sluggish. Lateen rig, with its *antennæ*, was to free propulsion what the aeroplane cylinder is to the steam piston: it reduces the weight per horsepower although the engine itself is less robust. The sailing ship of Europe was a carriage for very rich and intelligent old gentlemen; the Arab ship, a vehicle for hot-headed youths.

* * *

All the typical Mohammedan ships could use oars. They stuck to this principle because, above all, they desired mobility. The doldrums? 'Not a bit of it; the big Christians can twiddle their thumbs while we can pull on our oars and capture them.' Tacking in channels with a head wind? None of these zigzags for them. They made far too great use of the creeks and navigable channels of the islands they frequented and all this dodging about lost too much time.

Their ships developed from the galley, with very prolonged waterlines offset by the slope of the hull. The midship frame of the Barbary craft was in the form of a basket, the submerged hull being flush with the part above the water. This meant that they could carry sail well to windward without falling off or luffing when they heeled too much.

They replaced the weight of ballast by their broadening lines and their sheer. Certain sections of their xebecs are almost incomprehensible to someone familiar with European sections: they are helmets turned upside down (57a).

They used the method of construction which they retain today and which ensures lightness above all—a construction on moulds. We know how our shipwrights build; first of all, a skeleton with the ribs, which are the timbers and the frame, fastened to the spine, which is the keel. The Arab proceeded in a different fashion. He laid down his stem, sternpost, keel and the main beam amidships; upon them he bent his sides and bound them, taking the utmost advantage of the elasticity of

55. Large Brigantine, A.D. 1660

the planking. Once the sides had taken shape, he bound them once more and reinforced them withinboard by means of supple slats. One can see how this decreased weight and increased pliancy. Sometimes they sewed the sides together. However, one can imagine how handicapped they were by this fragility, particularly when it came to cannon balls. In fact it was the broadside which defeated them. But with the lateen rig, these ultra-light hulls seemed to leave the water and to be borne away on wings.

In this manner they conceived the brigantine (55) and the pink (56) which reached 300 tons burden. The pink was the ship which most resembled the sixteenth-century galley, and it still existed 50 years ago. It is slightly higher, without protruding *apostis*, with a beakhead, a spur which was never used for ramming but simply to make fast the foresail and give it some

K   133

appearance. It is remarkable for a rather important construction aft: a covered cabin, a small poop which distinguishes it at once from Algerian ships. It is the heaviest of these vessels, carrying three masts for lateen sails. The foremast raked forward and the sail served as a jib. Later this ship became trader and was square rigged after passing Gibraltar.

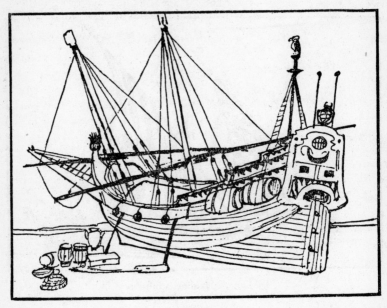

56. Pink

The brigantine had nothing in common with the little ship which bore this name in the seventeenth century and was the fashion particularly among the filibusters of the West Indies and the Brotherhood of the Coast. It was still merely a ship with lateen sails and oars. Its height and a more accentuated sheer made it more seaworthy than the galley. The captain of a brigantine relied entirely on his speed.

* * *

Next came the felucca (58) and the xebec (57), the tiger and tigress of the Mediterranean jungle, the king and queen of the chase and the attack, sufficiently powerful and invariably light.

If a xebec or a felucca flying the green flag was sighted off Messina, all traffic was suspended. Three cannon shots were fired to give warning that the sea was *brutto*: a general flight followed, even of ships of 1,000 tons burden. They took refuge wherever they could from these pirates whose displacement did not reach 50 tons.

The xebec (59) was the most handsome of these little Mediterranean craft. She was soon adopted by the men who used this sea and who wanted to go fast and to good purpose. From afar she looked the lightest of sea-birds, with her curlew beak and interminable tail which fined down her beam and her solid sides. She seemed to depend entirely upon her three lateens, but on closer inspection one could see the oarports between her guns. This type reached such perfection and elegance that under Louis XIV the French sailors copied it, making it slightly heavier but entrusting it to the best of their young men for pursuit and counter-attack. In the eighteenth century to have been in command of a xebec was the finest recommendation in Toulon naval circles; but the type was so perfect that our shipwrights gave up copying it and bought it ready made.

The felucca was only a small galley reduced to 30 men, but remarkable for its spritsail rig, like the *speronare* which the Maltese alone continued to use.

Below, quite at the bottom of the scale, came the frigate and the settee. The frigate gave its name to the loveliest of all European sailing ships. It was the most popular and best known to men and poets alike without bearing the slightest resemblance to the Arab frigate except in its relatively small size. The Latin frigate did not exceed 45 feet and carried two triangular sails and light oars. The same applied to the settee which sometimes sported only one sail and in warfare became the 'hit and run' bandit, the cheap criminal, the jackal.

*   *   *

The Grand Turk was the man who normally fitted out galleys, while later the Dey of Algiers followed suit. This was expensive and the galley, as it had developed, demanded State subsidy. The Ottoman galleys (60) were similar to the Christian except in a few points, which hardly changed their silhouette, such as being higher out of the water and stouter in build; in decoration too, the crescent being the chief motif. Captives were usually employed as rowers, and this did not help the Turks at Lepanto. The Arabs were good oarsmen, but their bad character was a disadvantage and the Ottomans preferred the melancholy passiveness of the Christians.

Rowers were always the first to be selected from among the captives. By comparison, these galley slaves were better treated on the Algerian benches than on those of the Christian galleys. Their work was better paid and in spite of everything the Turk seemed to remember that he was using prisoners of war. Punishments, of course, bore the stamp of African cruelty. In cases of mutiny, their eyes were put out, or one or both ears were cut off.

A strong man fetched between £8 and £12 in our present-day money and was therefore far less expensive than a horse at current prices. The captives provided them with all their servants and even their pleasures. Educated men could not find a master among the still savage Algerians, but in Asia Minor jobs were easily found for them. Musicians were very much in demand. A young woman with all her teeth fetched a good price and if she were young and pretty the bidding in the slave market became very keen. Eventually she was always sent to the great female slave markets in Constantinople or Smyrna, where she could easily fetch more than a strong man. Some of them went into the Imperial harem and, through a woman like Validé, from a noble French house, the Sultans have French blood in their veins. But the old women, alas, were drowned in a sack off Aljifna Island. However, in 1581 two well-bred Spanish matrons, captured on a Cartagena galley, found a buyer for 14 *baseta réals*, which today would be worth about 3d.

* * *

The corsairs very swiftly grew used to trafficking in human flesh and the petty lords in particular preferred this to attacking ships. A frigate with 12 benches, carrying about 30 men, would steal silently by night into some little lost creek. Before dawn it set sail again after carrying off every living thing in the neighbourhood. No ship could follow it. This was why the coasts remained uninhabited for so long. The Moors revived the Viking menace.

But other profits accrued from which the Turks were not the only ones to benefit. The European cargoes brought by them to Algiers or Tripoli found Christian buyers who had brokers in all the pirates' nests. They bought for a song what had cost so much and it was not rare to see Arab ships flying a French flag bringing back to Marseilles cargoes which had left Genoa a month before.

His Most Christian Majesty made a pact with the Algerian pirates: he was perhaps not very proud of it although he hoped to limit the evil. The French Consul gave them safe conduct until France herself stirred up the wasps' nest with a few well-placed cannon shots. However, the Dey once sent back her Consul in pieces after binding him to the muzzle of the main gun of the forward battery of a galley and firing him. This atrocity took place in 1683 from a culverin which was later called *La Consulaire*. Oddly enough we possess two specimens of this gun, one in the port of Brest, set up in 1830 on a column, and the other in the Musée de la Marine in Paris, No. 1913.

The ceaseless activity of the Barbary coast pirates was the cause of incredible family upsets. Many are the comic or tragic situations owed to them by our old playwrights! A child would disappear with its faithful nurse; women were widowed, pleasantly or unpleasantly, or committed bigamy when they thought they were widows. Poor Régnard, with the Marseilles beauty he wanted to marry, learned just before the wedding that the monks had found the husband alive and kicking in an African gaol. He must have cursed the magnanimous action of these good fathers, who constituted a sort of *Bureau de Change* in the pirate centres.

One might also say that these charitable institutions helped to prolong piracy. Captives no longer resisted, for there was always the hope of being ransomed, and resistance was more dangerous!

*   *   *

Three men rose to great fame as pirates and were considered the kings of the sea. They inspired terror but also admiration.

They were representative of these heroic bandits: Dragut, Uluch and finally the great Barbarossa, the second Dey of Algiers. From the sixteenth to the nineteenth centuries their memory haunts all the tales of the south.

57. Xebec, Eighteenth Century

Dragut, who on account of his beauty caught the eye of one of the *raïs*, a notorious pederast, received in return for his favours a 100-ton *fuste*, a type of xebec. He drew attention to himself immediately by his skill, courage and treachery. Captured once by the great Andrea Doria, he was put at the oar on a Genoese galley without shedding any of the natural dignity of the Moor, who seems indifferent to any strokes of misfortune. Barbarossa, who loved him, ransomed him for a

58. Felucca, Seventeenth Century

very small sum, but the terms included Dragut's promise to spare Genoa. Three days after his liberation, Dragut returned to ravage the outskirts of the marble city. Doria gave chase and missed him in extraordinary circumstances which show the tenacity, vigour and resolution of these savage *raïs*.

He held him finally imprisoned in a narrow creek. Dragut, realising that he was caught and to delay the issue, disembarked

59. Xebec

his artillery and defended the channel. Certain of success and not wishing to take risks, Doria sent in his fire ships. At dawn the Genoese admiral saw the redoubt abandoned, discounted his success and entered the creek. Nothing but burnt capstans and huge stains on the ground. . . . During the night the pirate, after collecting 500 natives, had crossed the isthmus to rejoin his squadron, dragging and pushing the ships on rollers for a distance of three leagues.

Later, whenever Dragut's name was mentioned, the great admiral touched his three-cornered hat.

Uluch was reported to be a Calabrian and Brantôme assures us that during the Italian wars he saw the birthplace and the relations whom the corsair sometimes visited. He intended to become a monk but, captured by the pirates, he renounced his faith. 'I think he took to the turban to hide his tonsure,' says Brantôme. He was a great sea captain, more classic than Dragut and capable of leading a fleet. At the battle of Lepanto, he alone brought back his squadron intact and reported the defeat to the Grand Turk with no heed for the rage which usually fell upon those who announced bad news. He was victorious in a warlike exploit which made him even more famous— the capture of la Goulette, near Tunis.

But Barbarossa was as well known as the Emperor Charles V. With his brother he had become Regent of Algiers with the idea of making it a personal kingdom. He did the same at Tunis which the Emperor managed to wrest from him but without being able to capture him. Right under Charles V's beard, he succeeded in putting out to sea with the galleys he had hidden in some creek, to deliver a furious attack on the Christian rein-

60. Turkish Galley

forcements, to return to Algiers, ravaging the Balearics on the way and, as though the Mediterranean belonged to him, to take all his prizes with him to pay homage to the Grand Turk at Constantinople. There he demanded support from his liege lord. It was granted and he started again, more powerful and more intrepid than ever.

Legend maintained for a long time that he was a Frenchman. He actually served France faithfully and with devotion at the request of Francis I. He spent an entire winter at Toulon during the first evacuation when the whole of the French population was removed. There he led a life of fantastic debauch, as much from personal taste as at the behest of the men in charge of the King's affairs. Actually, he was the son of a Greek renegade and an Andalusian woman, in fact, a European. His nickname, Barbarossa, was better known than his Ottoman name of Khair-ed-din, 'the defender of religion,' a surname given him by Soliman II, perhaps to hide his birth. He enjoyed 62 years of naval conquest. When he decided to retire, he brought back to Constantinople from what he announced to be his last campaign, 18 prizes with 7,000 captives.

Then came a break which completes the portrait of this incredible figure. He went into absolute retirement. No more

140

Barbarossa, no more Khair-ed-din; there only remained Azor, the poetic name of his childhood. In 1544 he bought a pretty little property on the banks of the Bosphorus, a house with a flower and vegetable garden, where he died peacefully tending his peonies and pruning his trees. Voltaire had him in mind when he created *Candide*.

61. Galleass, Sixteenth Century

VENICE AND GENOA

THE Venetian and Genoese navies were more important as
State navies than as partisan fleets and seem disproportionate
to the territories owned by these cities. Both Venice and Genoa
lent their aid to nations a hundred times larger than themselves
and no naval occasions took place without their being invited
to participate.

Venice was essentially a maritime city. Her crown, the little
pointed bonnet worn by the Doge, was the simple cap of a
fisherman from Torcello or Chioggia. No other nation has ever
possessed such a cult or a love of the sea; the ruler married it on
Ascension Day and despite all the literature surrounding this
ceremony, the gesture still causes surprise.

On a gilded ship with scarlet velvet trappings, the Doge went
to throw his nuptial ring to the waves, proclaiming: 'I espouse
you, oh sea, in sign of your perpetual domination.' The Inquisi-
tion could do nothing against this almost pagan ceremony:
it had been instituted by a Pope. The first ring to be cast into
the waters was engraved with the barque and the drag-net: this
was the ring of Alexander III, whom the Venetians welcomed,
defended and restored to the throne in spite of Frederick
Barbarossa, whom they defeated in 1177. An inscription in the
Vatican preserves the memory of this aid and the feat of arms.

Proud Urban VIII caused it to be removed. The Venetians, furious at seeing the triumph of their Ziani forgotten, protested so vigorously that Innocent X restored the plaque. This caused great amusement and Pasquino wrote: *Quod Urbanus inurbaniter deleverat, Innocentus, innocenter, restituit.* 'What Urban lacking in urbanity deleted, Innocent in his innocence restored. . . .'

Insular Venice at the far end of the Adriatic annexed this sea as a roadstead for her commerce and defence. The first Arab reverses were inflicted by Venice when she imposed peace on her maritime corridor. She returned blow for blow, never wearying. The Genoese and the Greeks felt the strength of her rancour and the obstinacy of her desires. It was not for nothing that the map of Venice so closely resembled a ram's head. Venice held up her head to the very last and for more than a thousand years.

She achieved the most brilliant naval triumphs. She besieged Constantinople and took it with the help of the French, but her fleet played the principal part. In 1203 the Venetians provided 110 light vessels, 70 round and 60 long ships, out of the Confederate fleet of 300. A giant vessel dominated the whole fleet: she was so gigantic in fact that she was called *Il Mundo*. On the 7th July they attacked the port in two waves, the first with the knights in flat-bottomed boats, accompanied by their steeds caparisoned with taffeta and fringes. Other craft, laden with archers for defence, circled round them. Then, astern, came the galleys, each towing a *nef*. This is curiously reminiscent of the attacks on the Crimea, when steamships towed the big three-deckers.

They arrived at the harbour chain, which—a very strange detail—a vessel managed to cut with gigantic scissors, forged to this end.

On the 17th July they launched the assault. The huge Venetian *nefs* drew close, rising as high as the walls, thanks to the erection on their decks of towers covered with new skins to counter the Greek fire. They dropped moveable bridges, *corvi*, onto the battlements. Old Doge Dandolo led the attack: he was nearly 98. This magnificent nonagenarian typified Venice. He went into the attack like a lion. For 30 years this man whom the Emperor Manuel had half-blinded had nursed a fierce hatred against Byzantium. When in the following year, on the 12th April, he had to capture the town a second time and the Empire was dismembered, Dandolo could justly call himself lord of a quarter of the Roman Empire. He was the founder of an illustrious dynasty. In the old days one used to say 'as noble as a Dandolo or a Montmorency'.

*   *   *

But the Venetians were in turn conquered by Byzantium. The only point of contact Latin imagination still possesses with the great Greek capital is through Venice. And yet today this Byzantine influence has been weakened by age and the fading of the colours. There remains St. Mark's, a brazier of violent hues, of gilt mosaics, inlays, enamels and rare marbles; and, throughout the city, something especially rich and ornate, which has remained like delicious bad taste in everything Venice produces. Yes, in everything she touches, whether it be houses with painted façades, apartments decorated with absurd and elaborate stuccoes, woodwork (even of doors) encrusted with mother-of-pearl, furniture of tortured and exasperating opulence, but exquisite all the same, in its wealth, the glorious extravagance of effort and material. What an epoch when compared with our constipated simplicity. The materials, the brocatelles, the lamps, the glass, the ironwork from Venice are a riot of colour and ornate opulence. Her school of painting astounded the Italians. Her masters, from Bellini, through Titian to Tiepolo, with their lust for life, laid low the somewhat bloodless and severe Italian artists. A woman of Palma Vecchio is no longer the chattering Italian with the black mantle and swarthy limbs, but some indolent and intriguing maiden from Trebizond or Armenia with a smooth, soft skin. Venice arouses a Frenchman to enthusiasm, to passion. He has reached the Orient without transition, that fabulous Orient to which Byzantium could have opened European eyes.

*   *   *

Intransigence was the predominant quality of the Venetians: a curious anomaly when we consider their sensuality. They were never flabby despite their appetite for pleasure and their taste for luxury. This uncompromising attitude could, on occasion, degenerate into a mania, and the hatred which inspired their 300-year quarrel with Genoa is a melancholy example. These two Christian cities ravaged each other for centuries instead of joining forces against the Arabs. The Venetians won the final battle but both their ferocity and their exhaustion were extraordinary. In 1383, to avenge a defeat, they despatched a fleet of sixty galleys against Genoa. On the day of battle they fastened fifty together with unbreakable chains so that no one should even be tempted to flee as King John I of Bohemia and his knights had done at Crécy. They advanced against the enemy in a gradual mass movement which nothing could resist. It was more than a fleet; it was an advancing island laden with thunderbolts. They avenged their lost glory.

Until 1453 they fought like mad dogs, but with the capture of Constantinople the Christian nations felt the fierce blast of the cannon ball. It was too late. Everyone turned towards the Turk. Who knows what would have happened had this Balkan question not raised its insoluble complications? What would have happened to Europe?

The Venetian navy made a last effort in an unsuccessful defence of Candia: two years of epic struggles in which our poor Roi des Halles, Beaufort-Apollo, perished mysteriously. But, exhausting herself, Venice wore down the Turk: it was the end of the great Ottoman fleets and of Turkish activity. The Venetians had repulsed fifty-six assaults, consumed 30,317 barrels of gunpowder. The cost in lead alone had been 18,044,957 *livres*. Venice perished on the corpse of her enemy.

*   *   *

Genoa seems to have been much more western. She has always retained something of Rome in her outward calm and a sort of dignity comparable with her stylised terraced town; a moderation which excluded neither ardour nor violence, quite in the Roman manner. Her products were also sumptuous and she created with opulence. We still admire her velvets and her gilded, embossed leather. She made contact with the east but without succumbing to an intoxication such as inflamed the Venetian spirit.

The whole of her strength lay on the waves. Genoa fought unceasingly against the Saracens and the first great battle she fought with them, in 806, allowed her to annexe a little island whose name was to become famous, Corsica. Later she continued to fight at least to the same extent as Venice and with an astonishing naval wealth when one considers the poor country lying behind her ports. She equipped a fleet of 620 galleys against Pisa and aroused great anxiety in the Greek Empire by conquering Mytilene and Galata, at the very entrance to the Golden Horn. She reigned on the Black Sea and this maritime hegemony was the main cause of the hatred of the Venetians.

It was against Pisa that Genoa became skilled in war, this time in a struggle against constant provocation. Pisa had for centuries possessed a strong navy but had not the resources of her northern rival. From 1120 to 1290 the Pisans attacked but they were always beaten in the end; in fact a caustic saying of the day ran: 'If you want to see Pisa, go to Genoa.' But the Pisans always returned to the fray. This tenacity in counterattack, these savage reprisals, would have been almost humorous had not tragedy been so near. Barely a year passed without a naval battle.

At last, when the Pisans were utterly exhausted, without however admitting defeat, the dispute came to an end and Genoa became involved with Spain and Venice. For centuries she remained the friend of France.

There are many great names to be found in Genoa. A certain Christopher Columbus must be counted a Genoese citizen despite great controversy, and later the 'marble city' could claim a certain Buonaparte—a name necessary to history, but which had a sinister ring for the world.

But it was above all the families which counted in Genoa. An oligarchy and a republic like Venice, she owed to this form of government her surprising triumphs and the resilience of her policy. An oligarchy is probably one of the least damaging forms of power, thanks to the emulation it fosters in descendants, the respect it inspires and the careers it favours and exploits. In any case it tends towards grandeur. In addition to the Boccanere, the Fregose and the Adorni, Genoa was almost the only power in the world to have a family of hereditary successful admirals, the Dorias, whose galleys, covered with red crosses, brought constant glory to the flag of St. George, the patron saint of their city before being adopted by England. From the twelfth century until the close of the Republic, the Dorias ruled the sea.

The most renowned was the great Andrea, a long-bearded magician, a thoughtful man who cast a spell on the waves in his famous galley with four rowers to each bench—four oars to a port. Andrea Doria was the only 'Sea General' whom Barbarossa avoided.

Let us examine this family a little more closely—this naval genealogical tree, this branch of coral: Andrea, the Admiral-issimo, waged war with four vice-admirals, his four nephews; Giovanni-Andrea Doria, his favourite, Filipino Doria, who won the battle of Naples, Antonio and Giovannino. I do not think that in modern times there has ever been such a powerful family on the seas. Their race belongs to the history of sail.

Andrea Doria wanted to rescue Francis I by sea after the battle of Pavia, when he was being taken to Spain. The King of France dissuaded him, knowing that at the first attack he would have been put to death. Later, during the siege of Naples, the break came. With appalling irresponsibility, Francis I appointed La Rochefoucauld to replace Doria. La Rochefoucauld could not distinguish a pink from a frigate: moreover, he annoyed the Admiral on a question of money concerning the ransoms of the prisoners. Doria abandoned the French cause and went over to the Emperor. At one blow France lost the mastery of the sea, the realm of Naples and re-conquered Italy: a whole century of French achievement was wiped out.

* * *

Venice seems to have set the fashion in shipbuilding for all these regions, even rivalling the Greek Empire. She perfected the *nef* and the galley—particularly the galley, for it is possible that the *nef* with the square sail, which everywhere replaced the *nef* with lateen sails, may have been a retrogression.

La Serenissima achieved great perfection of method. Her arsenal organised piece-work in a completely modern fashion, but with slightly more order. Each part of the ship had its own workshop and this made possible an entirely new tempo, of which the following is an example: when in 1380 the Genoese took Malamocco, naturally a *casus belli*, the Venetians were able to commission 38 galleys in two days. In 1571 Venice employed 16,000 artisans, working night and day shifts. They invented the galleass which in its time was the 'dreadnought' of the Mediterranean. They perfected the galley and every navy copied their famous 32 benches.

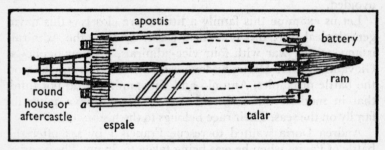

62. Plan of a Galley

Once more we find the galley (62), which would hardly undergo any further changes until the end and which was essentially the same as the original. The Greek trireme has been flattened out, has no spur; the dromond has been lowered. The length is 120 feet. The castles are now reserved for the stern, where there is still a defensive structure though it is more a protection against the sun and the rain than a fighting rembate. In the fifteenth century galleys, however, we still meet with small edifices on the deck without being able to see clearly how they could be reconciled with the general disposition of the galley slaves. They look more like roofs than towers and no place seems to have been reserved for the engines of war.

A very great difference marks the fifteenth century—the forward battery. Artillery also conquered the galley, but it was a very reduced and specialised artillery. Guns to the maximum number of seven were placed in the bows; in the centre was an enormous mortar—more powerful and of bigger calibre in the Christian than in the Ottoman galleys, for Barbarossa lengthened his fire, saying that it was more useful to have a long arm than a stout fist.

Another very important modification as regards looks is the increase, the protrusion of the *apostes* (62a, *a*), the kind of fins we saw on the pedestal of the Victory of Samothrace, which are now extended and form a sort of rectangular box, an almost horizontal lid, the *talar*, placed over the hull itself. The vessel is now clearly designed to carry galley slaves. In plan the galley of modern times is very simple: a long, floating spindle on which is laid a rectangle, covering four-fifths of its length, with only the bows and the stern of the vessel protruding, the prow and poop *palmettæ*.

The bows have lost their underwater spur. Forward of the battery is a sharp elongation but this is above the water. We can see that in the galleys of the fifteenth and sixteenth centuries the possibility of combat by shock was not entirely ruled out, for the projection is still strong enough and finishes in a diamond point: later it will have no other effect than to please the eye.

The stern, with its cross-beams and balusters, will form the round-house of the classic galleys. Forward of the round-house, which carries a lantern, is an empty deck space, 12 feet long, the *espale*, which serves as a quarter deck.

The rowers were installed below the *espale* as far as the battery. A cat-walk or gangway ran amidships from bow to stern. It is the spine of the galley, into which are dovetailed the ribs, the rowers' benches, very deflected in the fifteenth and sixteenth centuries, with two steps. The galley slaves were loosely chained by the leg. They climbed these steps as they followed the rotation of the oar, stepping backwards as the ship went forward: a brusque shock and a terrifying jerk, no longer the back-thrust of the oarsman but the body-blow of the galley slave. The palms and buttocks of the rowers became as hard as sharkskin. They were never allowed to wash for fear of splitting the callouses.

In the fifteenth century the *talar*, the great lid where the men rowed, was almost flat and gave the galley a very crude appearance. Towards the sixteenth century, however, they began to make the sides sheer and streamlined again until it became so elegant and supple a vessel that it can only be compared with a musical instrument, with a kind of lute, before which the most beautiful and refined tall ship takes on the appearance of a tub.

An important point of construction: I must apologise for the technical details. Until the seventeenth century the galleys were rowed *zenzile* fashion, that is to say rather in the tradition of antiquity, by groups of oars, or possibly in stages. Three oars were normally manned by three rowers seated on the same bench (33), a stout thwart deflected to allow the best use of each oar. In those admirable marine canvases by Carpaccio—for Venice also produced the best and most sincere marine painters —we can see this arrangement perfectly. The oars rest on the gunwale in groups of three. Andrea Doria's famous galley, which was wider and larger, as we have seen, carried four rowers on each bench.

Later, the *scaloccio* method of rowing became general. This, as everyone knows, is three or five rowers harnessed to the same oar, one oar per bench. This is very important and indicates the persistence of the ancient tradition as well as the virtuosity of the rowers.

The sixteenth century galley usually stepped only one mast, which stood forward, with a huge, double lateen sail. The mast ended with a rectangular box at the masthead which housed the wheels for hoisting the enormous yard.

This rectangular form was a peculiarity and reminds one of the construction of the Egyptian masts. Abaft the masthead was a kind of hod which replaced the top of the warships, the half-top from which we have the well-known word topman. It was narrow and seemed more for observation than for battle. This mast had no fixed yards and no stay. The rigging was completely mobile and on blocks for it had to be cast off to lee- ward to hoist the *antennæ* to the height required. The galley had no reefs to reduce the canvas; the sail was changed accord- ing to the weather. This was in order to obtain the maximum return, since a lateen sail had to be fully stretched in a perfect curve.

The rudder was a huge scimitar fixed to the sternpost, ex- tending far beyond the keel: an abnormal shape, although I have a small notebook with a picture of it, drawn by one of my young ancestors who was page to the Grand Master and who died on arrival in Malta about 1600. His effects were sent to his unfortunate parents in Normandy. His private sketchbook came back with three drawings of galleys equipped with this strange, exaggerated steering oar.

* * *

Battle tactics consisted mainly of boarding. The soldiers crowded on the gangway between the oars, and they were launched at the enemy's ship. First a volley was fired in a rather rudimentary way by the bow guns: the whole ship had to be aimed for the guns were fixed and could not swivel. The big bow gun on the gangway was lashed to a carriage without wheels mounted with a short breech tackle. Certain people think that in these heroic times the bow gun was fixed on a very strong inclined frame to take the recoil. The lighter pieces, placed on fixed stanchions, give support to this idea.

Luxury was greatly in evidence. In the stern was a very richly-decorated saddle-backed tent with sloping sides, probably of damask, brocade, or even of quilted embroidery. In certain of the very light galleys, which were only large launches, this tenting trailed extravagantly in the water as did the flags of the high ranking officers in the old days. A magnificence which inspired all the painters. . . .

These little galleys were sometimes very curiously contrived. The rowers were occasionally placed on planks outside the hull, on an exposed outrigger where they had hardly enough room to sit. Here they always rowed seated and their oars were so short that they seemed almost to be paddling.

Many explanations have been given for these *galee sottili* as opposed to the ordinary galleys. It seems that they merely wanted to differentiate between galleys with a rounded, and those with a tapered stern. All those of the eighteenth century were *sottile*. It is a pleasant description.

*   *   *

At the beginning of the sixteenth century the Venetian, Francesco Bressano, invented the galleass (61). By 1550 this ship had become very intelligent—for that matter are not ships always intelligent and invariably a triumphant solution of local or temporary difficulties? But this naval formula brought a satisfactory answer to problems which the galleys could not solve. The galleass combined seaworthiness, fighting manœuvrability, armament and protection. It may, as people maintain, have been a hybrid solution and therefore contemptible, but it proved itself by winning the battle of Lepanto and ensuring the

Venetian hegemony of the sea. The galley, despite its speed, was helpless in a heavy sea. It could not put to sea except between May and the 24th September. After the 1st October only a few foolhardy *nefs* appeared on the waters. The galley, moreover, seems to have been equipped with artillery only for the purpose of making a noise. The rowers were exposed to every attack. Admittedly the extraordinary sailors who manned them played the principal role but by common consent between adversaries certain exploits were never demanded of them.

Without lengthening the galley and not wishing to abandon the length of 120-50 feet around which the ship remained for so long, it was made more capacious, given greater draught and height. The large galley was born—the *galea grossa* or galleass. Its beam was a fifth instead of an eighth of the overall length. Additional depth allowed the construction of a stronghold forward, well armed with swivel guns. The arrow-head of the galley, the ornamental spur, was suppressed, to be replaced by an effective and terrible point—occasionally several such points —and, later, by a solid cut-water, designed to act with a crushing effect, which the momentum acquired by the heavy vessel made particularly terrifying. The stern and the sides were also armed with guns.

Above all, that modern invention the protected engine had been realised. The galley slaves no longer rowed in the open air; they were covered by a skylight deck whose heavy grating protected them from any oblique volley, halting the arrows and even the lead of the Barbary pirates. Furthermore, the fighting men, instead of hopping about among the oarsmen, now had a huge platform from which they dominated the enemy and his decks as the ancients had done.

Rowing during a battle was of a special nature. The rowers were yoked in both directions, some pulling and others pushing on the 50-foot oars. The galleass oar differed from that of the galley; it had a double grip, slots where the oarsmen could put their clenched fists, the oar itself being too large for them to grasp.

*   *   *

The writers of the period have not differentiated between these vessels and very often in the sixteenth century we should read galleass for galley, particularly when it is a question of long distance navigation and transport. The incessant cruises in the Mediterranean that Charles V undertook, with a passion his device, *Plus Oultre*, expressed so well, were certainly made in galleasses and not in galleys, which allowed of no comfort.

The galleasses were even used in the Atlantic for important journeys. One must mention the Duchesse de Longueville's voyage from Le Havre to Scotland in a galley whose rig had been changed from lateen to square sails. The transportation of Francis I to Spain after Pavia must have taken place in a *galea grossa*, a ship which Charles V, out of courtesy, had ordered to be painted entirely black, down to the rigging.

The perfecting of sail, combined with the difficulty of finding sufficient oarsmen, caused this naval type to be abandoned in the seventeenth century. But in Venice, as long as the galleasses lasted, they were entrusted to the nobility, who swore on their honour never to refuse battle even against twenty-five enemy galleys.

*　　*　　*

The *Bucentaure* (63), the famous ship in which the Doge married the sea, was a galleass transformed for the occasion. The combat deck which protected the oarsmen became a sumptuous promenade and reception deck enlarged by a balcony with arcades. The model in the Venice arsenal is one of the most beautiful and is as well known as the royal galley in the Louvre.

The sculpture on this vessel was rich and florid, positively dazzling. In the bows, a Doge seated beneath a canopy supported by recumbent Titans, preceded by the Lion of St. Mark invoking the sea. . . . Each corbel is a human figure and, on the poop, a spacious loggia protected the elected ruler of the naval city from the importunities of the crowd.

One sees how far the love of ornament could lead the Venetian designer—that ornament which men of ill-will have so despised. Obviously there could have been no question of going to war in a massive hull of gilded wood such as the *Bucentaure*.

But decoration and opulence are not incompatible with war. The splendour of a weapon bestows pride in that weapon and fine uniforms tend to promote courage, to produce in the men

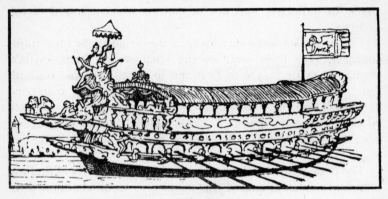

63. The *Bucentaure*

who wear them that exaltation, that heroic intoxication, which produces the absurd but sublime spirit of self-sacrifice.

Napoleon ordered the *Bucentaure* to be burnt, in order to extract a few pounds of gold from her fittings. . . .

*   *   *

Venice, thanks to her predilection for oars, has retained the famous gondola, just as the men of the Barbary coast bequeathed their handsome caiques to Constantinople.

The tempo of the barcarolle (the song of the gondolier) is one of the most difficult to acquire and it demands a very special technical skill. Some people maintain that this skill can never be acquired and that it has to be inherited. The gondola is too well known to need explanation. I shall merely draw attention to two less outstanding details; the median line is not straight but slightly curved to compensate for the weight of the boatman. The gondola has the shape of a banana. Its black colour was decreed by the Senate to prevent the ruin of the noble houses who vied with each other in the splendour of their boats. Only the Patriarch of Venice, provided he were a Cardinal, could enrich his *felze* with scarlet braid. In the old days only a foreign Ambassador could decorate his gondola; but . . . Jean-Jacques Rousseau glided on the Grand Canal between painted and gilded Hercules and beneath billows of brocatelle.

MALTA

THE Knights of Malta belong primarily to the heroic story of sail. They were the naval masters of Europe and their science inspired all the fleets of Christendom. A strange brotherhood, sometimes pious, sometimes less devout, but always composed of incomparable sailors very much in advance of their time—a brotherhood of almost fabulous heroes.

With a ridiculously restricted military equipment—shamefully restricted—showing the sordid and scandalous economy of the States which profited by their activities, the Knights of Malta policed the Mediterranean.

Their history should have been written in purple capitals on parchment of gold. I should have liked to relate it, not so pompously perhaps but with all the enormous respect and enthusiasm that I feel for this brotherhood. The Pays d'Ouche is famous for the six dignitaries of Malta which it produced in the seventeenth century, five of whom were my ancestors: I possess a small and exceedingly rare book, *Pour donner l'habit*, thanks to Commander de Bonneville-Chamblac, my grand-uncle. Even if the Bailli de Chambray, a local celebrity who gave his name to one of the towns of the Order, did not leave the service of the Faith, France employed famous Maltese in her navy, from Chevalier Paul, a Commander of the Order although a sailor, to Tourville and Suffren who, in the service of the king, still wore the famous eight-pointed cross.

* * *

The beginnings of the brotherhood by no means heralded the warrior exploits which would make the scarlet cassock so terrible. They are as little known as the Order of Malta itself, which has been subjected to gross misrepresentation. Originally these great seamen were only stretcher-bearers and hospitallers, animated, it is true, by a quite abnormal spirit of sacrifice but far removed from all militarism. Some Italians, jealous of the Greeks who had their own church in Jerusalem, obtained permission to found a chapel there in the Year of Grace 1048, before the first Crusade. Next they created a hospital to receive the pilgrims who were already pouring in, dying of fatigue and poverty. Their *Maison-Dieu* was dedicated to St. John the Baptist and these hospital orderlies formed a company half lay, half religious, observing the three vows of obedience, chastity and poverty, without being ordained but with complete devotion. The hospital, which was well endowed, devoted its wealth to material aid for the pilgrims and later extended the role of the hospitallers to the protection of travellers. They left all operations on land to the Templars in order to busy themselves with maritime rescue and defence against pirates or Mohammedan regulars. Thus we see them resolutely undertaking a mission of rescue and sacrifice which was to last 750 years. Whatever their rank and glory, they retained on their rolls their primitive titles, and the Grand-Masters, Grand-Priors and Commanders, despite their ducal crowns, always signed themselves as 'Hospitaller Brothers of St. John of Jerusalem'.

They accepted all those who longed to fight and serve on the seas; they became an international Order like the Templars, but within narrower limits. The latter spread out across Europe, whereas the Hospitallers lived in a community. The most varied nationalities met on the neutral territory of the Faith.

Their vicissitudes were numerous and severe. When Jerusalem fell once more into infidel hands, they made their way to the Phoenician coast; chased from there they regrouped in Cyprus, the kingdom of Henry de Lusignan. They fitted out vessels to escort the pilgrims and to harass the enemy. Since Cyprus did not come up to their expectations, they cast their eyes on Rhodes, which at that time belonged to the Saracens. The Grand-Master sought out the Eastern Emperor and requested him to guarantee them possession of the island of Rhodes if they could recapture it. Inspirited by the protection of the Virgin, they took it by assault on the day of the Assumption, 1309. After this victory they called themselves the Knights of Rhodes and held the island despite incessant attacks and almost perpetual sieges, which the Grand-Masters, from Gérard de Pins to Pierre d'Aubusson, were able to resist.

The reputation of the Knights was so well established that Camali the corsair, when attacking the island of Lego, raised the siege when he thought he saw them appear in the breach: the Governor, himself an 18-year-old Maltese, had disguised peasants, including women, in the black soutane with the white cross, the primitive garment of the Order.

They upset all the triumphs of the pagan Sultans. This weak force, by its valour, offset the mass victories won by the kings. They even captured the *Mograbine*, the 'Queen of the Sea', a colossal carrack that was the pride of the Prince of Egypt. She was a seven-decker with a bow rising 45 feet above the waves. Six men were needed to encompass the mainmast. She was manned by the Chevalier de Gastineau, Commander of Limoges.

*   *   *

After so many exploits, their most illustrious Grand-Master was forced to give up the island. He put up an epic resistance. Philippe de Villiers de l'Isle-Adam won a sorrowful and un-rivalled glory. The town was reduced to a pile of rubble and the ruins were alive with fierce, wounded men and blood-stained ghosts. The Knights held out for six months: they numbered 600 with 4,500 fighting troops. Facing them were 400 Ottoman ships, 140,000 men and 60,000 pioneers. They killed 40,000 Turks while the Christian nations, with the exception of France, who despatched Préjent de Bidoux to their aid, shame-fully let them perish. They even seemed to have been aban-doned by God, since Soliman entered Rhodes on the holy day of the Nativity. Marvelling at their courage, the Sultan granted them the most honourable conditions and Philippe de Villiers left Rhodes on New Year's night, 1523, with his 30 vessels and those inhabitants who wished to accompany him. Soliman allowed him to keep the huge carrack captured from the Egyptians.

Everything conspired against the Grand-Master: the winds, the sea and the plague. When, after six months, he finally appeared off Messina, the great Philippe no longer had a flag or a distinctive standard for his homeless wanderers. In this way 221 years of human and divine glory vanished. He hoisted a simple banner with the dead Christ in the arms of the Virgin. . . .

It fell upon Charles V to repair to some extent the wounds inflicted by Providence. On the 24th March, 1530, he ceded the island of Malta to the Hospitallers of St. John, together with that of Gozo, but rather shabbily threw in Tripoli so that the Knights should defend what he had already made up his mind to abandon. The grant was *in perpetuitatem*, in free and noble fief, with the single tribute of a yearly falcon to be delivered on All Saints' Day. I have quoted this clause because later, as though unwilling to stress this mark of their vassalage, the Knights paid the King of France in gerfalcons. These Maltese falcons were eagerly awaited by Louis XIII.

*　　*　　*

From now on they were called the Knights of Malta and they started on their perpetual travels. Their tenacity, skill and courage, their victories, restored all the lustre of the Order. Any nation in difficulties with the Turks or the Egyptians turned to them for aid, which was never refused. They never despaired, despite a train of harrowing misfortunes. On the way to Malta, amidst the great hardships suffered on his first voyage, Philippe de Villiers apparently had a premonition. The Knights had no time to settle down before they found themselves at the mercy of a great storm. On the 23rd September, 1549, during the autumnal equinox, at seven o'clock in the evening, Malta lost *all* its ships in the space of one hour, in harbour. A tidal wave broke them and flung them in pieces on the island.

The ensuing help was very touching. Philip II sent two powerful galleys. The Grand-Prior of France, François de Lorraine, came to the rescue with two magnificent galleys and a warship which he gave to the Order. Philippe Duroc brought a large galleon from Marseilles and all the Commanders of all the *langues* bled themselves dry, increasing their responsions and their tithes, until they were reduced to living on beans, so that the Faith should revive. 'The Faith': what a sign of grandeur, in a period when religion was of such importance, that only the Order of Malta should be given this qualification! Nevertheless, at the peak of their disaster, these fanatical warriors were still able to beat off Dragut who had attacked them.

The siege of the island, undertaken by Soliman II in 1565 in an attempt to renew the exploit of Rhodes, was a bloody reverse for the Ottoman power. Malta was attacked by 200 vessels equipped with a great weight of cannon; more than 50 bombards firing an 80-lb. cannon ball, whereas the largest of Louis XIV's guns were not more than forty-pounders. The majestic galleys of the two Turkish vice-admirals were covered with gold and sported three lanterns. Forty thousand men set sail, including 6,000 picked janissaries in leopard-skin bonnets— the leopard-skin bonnet which after numerous transformations would later become the helmet worn by the dragoons until 1916. Jean de la Valette, a Frenchman, successfully bore the weight of the attack for four months with 500 Knights and 5,000 men. Soliman raised the siege.

Mon siège est fait, an expression which denotes that one's mind is completely made up, recalls this famous victory. The historian of Malta, Abbé de Vertot, who had just written his own version of the exploits of the Knights, refused to modify his story in any way in spite of documents which were brought to him. 'Too late', he said, '*mon siège est fait.*'

*   *   *

The Knights of course used tall ships and the majority of the victories won by the Bailli de Chambray, drawings of which are still preserved in the castle of that name near Damville, in the Pays d'Ouche, depict round vessels. But, like the Venetians, the Maltese above all used the galley, as being more mobile and more practical, maintaining its glory well after the other navies.

The Maltese galley was much more delicate in its lines than the one used by the Barbary corsairs. It carried the almost scientific improvements which the Knights brought to the art of shipbuilding. Apart from the flag, it had a very special distinctive mark: it was painted throughout in the colours of the Order, with long alternating white bands and scarlet wales. As soon as the Moors caught sight of these colours in the distance, they fled. Moreover it was the custom even among the nations of Christendom, so jealous of their prerogatives, to make way for the galleys of the Faith. Perhaps this was inspired by a religious spirit: all the galleys of Malta, by Papal Bull, carried the Holy Sacrament. When they did not embark chaplains, the Captain took Communion in case of danger. For this reason, and because they could take Communion without fasting before battle, the Host in these galleys was called the *viaticum*.

The Maltese galley usually had 25 benches. At full complement she embarked 22 Knights of Malta, without counting the troops and the crew, composed largely of slaves, but with a proportion of *bonne-voglies*—volunteers who were far more numerous than in any other navy using oars, including that of the Popes. Certain wealthy young knights equipped these galleys at their own expense; young men who had become rich by some unforeseen circumstance, some prize or heritage, for all the knights were younger sons of the nobility and therefore, quite naturally, somewhat needy.

* * *

The Knights were the first to don a uniform for battle. Until the sixteenth century they wore a black doublet with the cross on one side; then, as soon as they were at sea, the celebrated cassock I have mentioned, which resembled a huge smock of black linen with an enormous white crucifix, a crucifix in the shape of a gibbet. Apparently the Maltese cross only appeared with the occupation of that island. The old documents from Rhodes still show the Knights with pennons bearing the Latin cross.

In the seventeenth century these mariner Knights fought in dark armour, wearing only a Venetian mantle, but less purple and more of a vermilion than dragon's-blood red, which was to herald the famous dolman. This was at first an over-vest, a sleeveless surcoat, and it was followed by the famous red habit which, under the blue sky and a bright sun, won a prestige almost as terrible as the old black Rhodian tunic.

The Knights Bailiff wore on the front of their cuirasses, glued to the iron, a broad eight-pointed cross ten inches wide, originally in white linen and later in enamel. This gave them the name of 'Grand Cross', a name which has spread to the highest dignitaries of the other orders. The Commanders wore one of six inches, usually hung from a black cord. On land, in over-vests, they displayed on their blue waistcoats an enamel cross surmounted with a Royal crown in glittering stones. The remainder were known as 'Knights of the Little Cross', or merely knights.

They were the last to wear full armour, ignoring the fashion which stripped the warrior, not through fear but through obedience. Athleticism, too, played a part: the young men exercised in heavy armour and by going into battle in light armour, they achieved a new agility. The crowning exploit of a young knight of the galleys was the 'flight of arms' which consisted in boarding the enemy in full armour with a huge broadsword and running the length of the cat-walk to the after-deck, scything everything as he went.

*   *   *

The following are a few lesser-known details about this extraordinary brotherhood. It bore the name of Republic and, under the orders of a Grand-Master, elected for life, recognised as spiritual sovereign the Pope, and as political sovereign the Viceroy of Naples. The Grand-Master was chosen from among the Knights of the Grand Cross after an election regulated by conditions so complicated as to make the most involved systems of franchise appear quite simple. As a matter of interest, here are a few of the stipulations. All the members of the Order were allowed a first vote on condition that they did not owe more than ten crowns to the 'Faith'. These were called the 'vocals'. Each *langue* voted separately to choose three electors of the second class, making twenty-four in all. The latter, after appointing a spokesman called 'the President of the Election', chose three new electors and retired.

This triumvirate chose a fourth elector and the four then elected a fifth and so on, up to thirteen in all. These, with the triumvirates, made sixteen, two for each *langue*, and they finally elected the Prince.

All this, however, was child's play compared with the election of the Doge of Venice.

The Order accepted brothers from all the Christian nations. They were divided into eight *langues* or national associations, representing: France, Provence, Auvergne, Italy, Aragon,

Castile, Germany and even England. The French Knights, with three *langues*, were the most numerous.

The Order was composed of three elements: the Knights of Justice or plain knights, nobles with eight quarterings, from mother, father, and ancestors, both male and female, of two generations, except in the case of the Germans who had to produce sixteen; then the chaplains or priests, over whom the others took precedence although they were not ordained. It was the duty of these chaplains to maintain the religious traditions of the Order. Finally the serving brethren—and this is not generally known—who, although not belonging to the nobility, fought in company with the Knights and who seldom left since some of them could rise to high posts in the Order.

The statute which made these brothers-in-arms the leading sailors of Europe insisted upon an education received entirely at the headquarters of the Order in Malta itself. The young man was sent there at the age of twenty as a professed knight, or more frequently, which gave better results, as page to the Grand-Master at the age of sixteen. He brought a little dowry with him, known as his 'passage money', in memory of the ancient transport of pilgrims to the Holy Land. Later, as a result of abuses, there were Knights minor. This by no means signifies, as is generally thought, that the quality of their families destined them by birth to enter the Order without ordeals, but that their parents obtained their immediate enrolment, to procure them the benefit of seniority, thanks to a larger dowry than the normal 'passage money', fixed at a minimum of 300 gold crowns.

The education at Malta was given by the very best teachers. Mathematics were held in high esteem, without, however, dominating all other studies. Each of these children made four 'caravans' of six months' war service at sea, without which they had no status. All the naval schools took the Order of Malta as their model.

*　　*　　*

In must have been very difficult to keep the peace in such a gathering of gentlemen, jealous of their honour and the glory of their nations. The Order quickly realised that there was no hope of this except in combat—combat which, under whatever pretext, could only be given to an infidel ship: there is no example of the Order having intervened in favour of a particular European sovereign. Thus, on the same bench, in the same ship, could be found a Spaniard, a Frenchman and a German, whose kings were at war with each other, but who were united with the same ardour against the Turk. Ashore, however, it was not humanly possible for the same rule to apply.

Thus, a careful segregation was organised. The knight ate in the *auberge* of his *langue*, a huge hostel of which the chief, the Pillar, was the oldest Grand Cross of his nation. These refectories were victualled at the expense of the Order.

It disposed of funds from the chase, the prizes belonging to the Faith and not to the man who captured them; from royally bestowed customs and administrative dues, but never from trade, which it was quite rightly considered might lower the moral integrity of the man who transacted it. Finally, the regular revenue came from the estates of the Order, from donations pouring in from all parts of Europe, some of which were long-standing contributions from pious people.

These estates were administered in each *langue* by three kinds of dignitary, who assumed the right usually by seniority and sometimes by election, and who took over the Grand-Priories, Bailiwicks and Commanderies from which came the famous titles of Grand-Prior, Bailiff and Commander.

Normally the Grand-Priors were resident. The Bailiffs occasionally went to sea. These two posts could only be held by Knights of the Grand Cross. The seven oldest Bailiffs, known as Conventuals, became Pillars of the *auberges*; seven because after the schism England formed only a nominal and traditional *langue*. The Commanders were resident only on retirement. All these titularies disposed of only a part of the revenues from the lands assigned to them; the rest, the responsions, were sent to Malta in the nature of a tithe. An interesting point: the Order, as a good and cautious landlord, would tolerate no negligence in administration. Before being given a more important command, the old sailor had to take an active part on his farms and prove that he had made improvements during his period of management.

* * *

These retreats for the Officers of the Scarlet Cassock were one of the most active causes of naval recruitment so far from the shore, particularly in France. That country was the richest in properties belonging to the Faith. In addition to six Grand Priories and three Bailiwicks, she possessed 271 Commanderies. They housed 280 sailors of all ratings, who lived there with their servants, their bodyguards and their pages, for all of whom the sea and its fortunes was the most desirable thing in life.

They arrived with a complete store of legends. Their tales and their behaviour deeply disturbed the spirits of those who listened to them open-mouthed. A Commandery and its out-buildings became a sort of naval centre with its own influence and its own language. One finds in the extreme north expressions and images which are entirely nautical and appropriate to the Mediterranean and quite unlike the jargon of the Atlantic. To mention two typical examples: I have heard a rafter called a 'bottom' and the 'bottom' was the keel of the galleys, the rafter, in fact, upon which it was mounted. On another occasion I heard a peasant talking about 'striking' (*désarborer*) the rails of his haycart, which would mean in the Levant that one was lowering one's mast.

Around the old sailor as he sat drinking his Cyprus wine, could be found a group of young simpletons, smitten with an immense sea-fever and a desire for heroics.

* * *

Napoleon, in his utter ruthlessness, captured the island in 1798 on his way to Egypt, and disbanded this naval Order with no heed for its glory and the services it had rendered. The Faith was reduced to two *langues*; Germany and Italy. Then at last it was transformed once more into an aristocratic and pious society, very deserving of interest, where one still finds the old ranks of the Order, but of which, alas, the members are the heirs and no longer the founders.

CHAPTER XI

Portugal

WE come now to the era of the great maritime discoveries. The English were very late in contributing to this epic; the promoters of colonisation were Spain and Portugal. The latter, in the fifteenth century, is strangely reminiscent of England and her empire of the nineteenth. Moreover, Portugal owes her survival to England and one can easily understand her fidelity to the British. It is true, also, that a part of her temperament—ardent, sprightly and resourceful—can be attributed to French influence, since the founder of the Lusitanian nation was a prince of the House of Bourbon, a fact we forget far more than do the Portuguese.

It was a happy kingdom, a fertile Spain without the desert grandeurs which give to the land of the Sierras its arid emaciation but also its intransigent aristocracy and its arrogance. Portugal offered the best harbours of the Iberian Peninsula. Her men were courageous and imaginative. Fate was kind to them and unkind to Spain. Twice the British ships came to her aid and saved her life, that little life which today is still precarious.

In 1147, after defeating five Moorish Kings, whose united escutcheons form the coat-of-arms of the kingdom, the Count of Portugal besieged Lisbon, then in the hands of the Saracens, with the intention of making it his capital. Things were going very badly when an unknown fleet appeared in the Tagus. Alfonso thought that this was the death blow. It turned out to be a triumph. Instead of the Moors he saw a British fleet —Crusaders on the way to Palestine whom the bad weather had driven into the Tagus. The Count went aboard: 'You have no need to sail so far if you want to kill infidels. We've got plenty of them here.' The Crusaders disembarked on the 28th June and captured Lisbon on the 25th October.

In 1190 Don Sanchez, Alfonso's heir, besieged, battered and harassed by the Miramolin of Africa, found luck repeating itself. At the direst moment of the siege some large vessels were seen approaching. The English once more and what English! Our Anglo-Norman Richard Coeur de Lion who flung himself into the fray with the enthusiasm of a great, confident, wild beast. Without the British navy there would have been no Portugal.

*　　*　　*

Then came the slow rise of this country to maritime power, of which it had learned to appreciate the value. After long struggles against the Moors and the Castilians, against a united Spain and her allies, after a number of successes and of reverses which did not, however, succeed in retarding her development, Portugal found herself by the fifteenth century in a flourishing naval position in advance of the other nations. Territorially hemmed in by Spain, she looked upon maritime adventure as the only reasonable means of expansion. Spain, in the course of building up her own unbalanced power, had left her only far-off countries. The vitality of Portugal drove her on, combined with a taste for trade and big business, as well as a moral element: faith. One must recognise these ingredients if one wishes to understand the primitive spirit of the Conquistador. The conversion of the pagans, discoveries in the name of Christ, stirred the heart at least as much as future riches inflamed the mind. Up to and including the fifteenth century a crusading spirit over-shadowed the desire for gain among the navigators. It must be noted, with all the respect felt for the English influence by any naval enthusiast, that it was England who perverted this initial tendency.

Furthermore, Portugal knew what it meant to have a prince infatuated with geography, an enthusiast and a dreamer, whose fervour, in common with all great apostolic movements, became eminently communicative: the Infante Duke Henry, son of John I of Portugal, upon whom history would confer the glorious title of Henry the Navigator. He was the moving spirit of the expeditions which brought honour to his country.

A strange and passionate man, a sort of patron saint of geo-

167

graphy and of the ship, eagerly seizing upon any improvement, interested in all science, he was haunted by plans and intuitions. As a Grand-Master of the Order of Christ, he devoted the treasure of his brotherhood to the search for new lands and possible converts. Literature has never exploited this princely, self-sacrificing figure who dominated a whole world of legend.

He lived in utter solitude at Sagres, at the very tip of the Peninsula, almost in the sea, on the ultimate slender promontory of Europe, just south of Cape Vincent.

One cannot follow without emotion the projections of this mind which gradually left the land, made its way to the west, or descended to the south; the arrows which darted out from Sagres grew longer and broader. 1410: Henry's first personal expedition. He descended to Cape Ganaro, to Bojador, 26° north. 1420: the arrow turns towards the vast west; Madeira is discovered and wins fame as an almost paradisial island. Tradition assures us that the Saint accompanied his ships (1433) when they rounded Cape Bojador, where the waters rush into 'deep places'. Pope Martin V marvelled at this and conferred upon Portugal the possession of all the lands beyond. In 1441 they passed Cape Blanc, 21° north, then Cape Verde, 15° north. Soon they descended as far as 2° below the equator. They discovered the Grain Coast, the Ivory Coast and the Slave Coast. They returned laden with wealth, bemused by Africa, full of magnificent stories and Henry the Navigator disappeared with a smile to meet death, who had been quite willing to wait until his plans had been accomplished.

But the kings of Portugal completed his dream. John II despatched his ships further to the south until, in 1487, Bartolomeo Diaz, sailing doggedly on, reached that massive point of Africa which he called *El Tormentoso*, the Cape of Storms, but which John II, on hearing his tale, re-christened the Cape of Good Hope: the hope of the Indies.

*   *   *

At this juncture Spain intervened in the age of discovery with Christopher Columbus. But Portugal did not give up. In 1497 came the voyage of Vasco da Gama. He is rather overshadowed by the glory of Columbus but he was no less great a man. With him sailed an illustrious passenger, old Diaz, the man who had discovered the Cape of Good Hope. By this small detail one can see the tenacity of these dreamers, since the veteran did not hesitate to place himself under the orders of a twenty-six-year-old captain, to serve him as pilot.

They arrived at the Cape of Storms and, overcoming their terror and a mutiny, rounded the famous Table Bay. Blown off course to the south, they ran into an iceberg, the first to be seen in the Antarctic. It seemed to follow them when, in their terror, they let their ship flee before the wind. They turned north, skirting the coast of East Africa. The crew believed they would soon see the Mediterranean again, and the skipper did not disillusion them. Near Melinda, where the bore made the water boil and foam, they observed the phenomenon of a milky sea. Then came the incredible change of course eastward, piloted by a maniac who could be leading them to their death. They covered 700 leagues in 21 days and, to their bewilderment, sighted land in Lat. 12° south, the coast of India at Calicut. A King in a robe of cotton embroidered with golden roses, a gold tiara on his head and bracelets of gold on his arms and legs, jewels on every finger, gave them a magnificent reception.

The route was open. Vasco da Gama returned to Lisbon after a voyage of 26 months.

The King next despatched Cabrera with 13 vessels which suffered great hardships but managed to reach the land of Hindustan. As they were late in returning, four more ships were sent. Finally, in 1502, the King asked Vasco da Gama to repeat his exploit. Da Gama embarked, this time on a warlike expedition. On the way he conquered Mozambique and Goa, territories in Africa and India which still belong to the Portuguese and which it would be abominable for any man who is not completely insensitive to think of taking away from them. The Portuguese possessions have right of seniority.

The great Vasco was sent on a third voyage to India, but this time in disgrace. He died there in 1524 at the early age of fifty-five.

He was another Columbus, a devout, silent and energetic man who had no need of anger to make his authority felt. To his daily *Ave Maria*, Comtesse tells us he added: 'Holy Mother, take the helm yourself and do not let *me* stray from my course.'

* * *

This strange route and its stages became a commonplace to the Portuguese, thanks to their experience of the prevailing winds, currents and monsoons. It was a route along which other savers of souls flagged—soldiers of Christ such as François Xavier from Navarre—and it was unusual enough to be described here.

They left in April, at dawn, from Lisbon, with a course set for Madeira, 150 leagues south-west. From there, they made due west for Brazil. Going about, tacking and making use of the same winds, they doubled the Cape of Good Hope. When they were late, they wintered in Mozambique and later sailed due east to Goa.

The return journey was made in December. The Cape was rounded again about March and they mounted the west coast by using the southern winds which on the outward journey had forced them to run towards Brazil. Then they put in at St. Helena and finally at Lisbon.

Another detail regarding the territorial distribution agreed to by the Popes, which has been so much discussed. Ferdinand, the Catholic King, reported Columbus' discoveries to the Borgia Pope. Alexander, a Spaniard by origin, granted to the King of Spain, by a Bull of the 4th May, 1593, all the lands situated west of a meridian 100 leagues west of the Azores. Portugal protested. The Bull was adjusted on the 7th June, 1594 and the famous line was definitely fixed at 370 leagues west of those islands.

It was actually far more complicated than this, for everything came under review again with the discoveries of Magellan. This Portuguese, sailing due west at the orders of Charles V, inevitably had to trespass on lands which had been granted to the Portuguese.

Magellan was lucky enough to round South America by beating a passage through the Straits which bear his name, although without actually touching the Horn. He sailed up the western seaboard as far as the isles which he christened the Philippines, in honour of the Infante, and died there, supporting an ally whom he had won for his prince. Del Cano, his lieutenant, with a flash of genius, continued to sail westwards until he came upon da Gama's Portuguese settlements. But there is still a dispute as to the number of days for, as Jules

Verne reminds us in his *Round the World in Eighty Days*, the dates differed. Del Cano was behind and the others ahead of time; the latter had sailed east, while he had been sailing west.

When he returned to Lisbon, after three years and fourteen days at sea, Del Cano was the only man who could sport on the blazon which the Emperor had granted him a terrestrial globe with these words: 'The first to have rounded it.'

64. The *Santa Maria*

CHAPTER XII

Spain

THE great and arrogant Spanish monarchy, which rose to
such supreme power, started in a very paltry fashion in
the Mediterranean. It is certain that in their initial efforts
the Kings of Aragon were very inferior admirals compared with
the Venetians or the Genoese, although one must admit that the
Spanish navy helped in the first real attempt to shake off the
Saracen yoke: the recapture of Almeria in 1147 was a significant
victory. Spain, however, should have realised that she could not
recover without a navy since part of her misfortune had been due
to maritime negligence.

The history of the Spanish navy progresses by leaps of a
hundred years. The victory of Almeria was due to Catalonia
which already possessed a Grand-Admiral in default of a grand
fleet. In 1247—and this is an important date—Boniface,
Admiral under Ferdinand III of Castile, retook Seville after a
few naval skirmishes in which his squadrons proved their
mettle. After this the navy of the Spanish kingdoms established
itself and supported the policy of expansion and the defence of
the Peninsula against the Infidels, the kings of France and the

JACQUES COEUR'S NEF

Fifteenth-century window. *Musée de Bourges*

PLATE VII

THE BA[
Detail. By Vi[

PLATE VIII

LEPANTO

ge's Palace, Venice

SPANISH EXPEDITION AGAINST THE ISLAND OF
TERCEIRA (1583)

Toledo Museum

PLATE IX

Genoese. Carving itself out a respectable place, it participated in 1341 in the victorious defence of Tarissa which decided once and for all the fate of Spain, throwing out the Moors when, in great waves, they resumed their conquest.

But it is with Ferdinand V that we see the beginning of her real grandeur with its maritime victories. This King is ineluctably bound up with his wife, Isabella the Catholic, the heroine of the siege of Granada. The Knights above all paid her homage because of the colour assumed by her chemise which she wore in fulfilment of a vow during the entire length of a four year siege.

Ferdinand, before giving support to the journeys of Columbus, from which he won his greatest glory, had been a redoubtable champion of Christendom in the Mediterranean basin. He foresaw the naval possibilities of his kingdom and realised that his fleets could balance those of the Ottoman Empires and become the western counterpart of the eastern arsenal. He intervened with some weight in this astonishing battle, this fray which convulsed the waves: from the year 800 to the year 1830, the Mediterranean was constantly at war. It was the thousand years' war. The grandeur of Ferdinand V suddenly heralded the majesty of Spain. In three reigns the monarchy of Castile passed from petty provincial kings to potentates, masters of Europe and of the known world. It may have been partly due to the injection of our best French blood as a result of the Burgundian alliance. Ferdinand gave to Philip the Fair—a blond Apollo—the hand of his poor daughter, Joan the Mad, whose weakness, however, would not suffice to check the fire and the force of the race she engendered.

Ferdinand V's grandson was Charles V, his great-grandson, Philip II. A mere mention of these names conjures up the ardent exaltation of Spain and the magnificence of her fleets. Ferdinand attacked Mussulman power beneath its very walls and pointed the way to be followed. He captured Oran.

But obviously he owed his supreme glory to the great naval figure of the fifteenth century, the tall, red-headed Christopher Columbus of Genoa.

Columbus is certainly one of the best-known men in history, but at the same time an aura of mystery still surrounds him. A great deal of ink has been spilled on his account. The facts about his birth, his tomb, his ships and his discovery are all uncertain. We do not know, we hesitate, and with each new fact that comes to light, we seem to have found the answer. Even psychologically his character is difficult to analyse. We still wonder if we are dealing with a scholar or a visionary, a logical prospector or a lucky adventurer. He appeared on the scene, made his discoveries and disappeared: we must be content with that.

His birth is in doubt. Undeniably he came from the territory of Genoa, but he may not actually have been born in the city itself. The theories that he was born at Calvi in Corsica have been officially refuted, but they still worry innocent and conscientious historians. Corsica belonged to the territory of Genoa.

The man himself is both simple and complex. On the one hand we have an honest sea captain who should have been content to bring his tropical cargoes safely back to port. And yet, on the other hand, this merchant seaman is both artist and philosopher. He exceeded his task; his imagination was so vivid that he might have been a novelist of the sea, but one who actually lived his novel. A large Genoese concern commissioned him to bring back sugar and colonial products, and we must admire the fact that in his spare time, he used to draw and to paint those fine rutters and maps of the world, illuminated in the tradition of the great medieval miniaturists. He was the forerunner of the great cartographers of the following century of whom France possessed such masters as Jacques Devaulx and Le Testu. But behind this desire to portray, something seemed to haunt him. From long reflection on these drawings and these plottings of the land, Columbus' thoughts went beyond the known. The hand, hardened by salt water and hempen ropes, which traced the maritime regions so delicately, obeyed some intuitive anxiety. Art added its intimate balance to the balance of the world. Those seas could not fail to contain to the west something comparable to the eastern continents. His hand lingered. . . .

* * *

The silent man sought for information, read the old documents and listened. We find him sailing the known world in all those winds which covered the charts of the period like a vast spider's web. Christopher Columbus sailed to and fro, up and down and along the cardinal lines. Jewelled Cap Verde;

the Ionian Isles of molten gold where the legends of the Phoenician Atlanteans lingered; the snowy gulfs of Iceland where the whalers spoke to him of the continent to the west which, 50 years before, a sea of ice had separated from men for ever . . . and where, in the old days, further to the south, the men of the north had colonised a land where the vine grew.

We follow him through his novitiate. In 1482 he married the daughter of the Governor of Madeira: he himself was the son of a weaver. In the following year he remained for a long time in the Azores, always staring westwards, always anxious about the *Mare Tenebroso*, the 'Shadowy Sea.'

Half Portuguese by marriage, he revealed his plans to John II, who basely tried to betray him and despatched his own ships. They returned defeated, with battered wings. Now everything abandoned the prophet. Felipa, his wife, was dead and he no longer went to sea. Taking his child Diego, he entered a monastery, where he lived for many long years as an oblate. He was finished and nothing seemed to count any more here below. But his ardour seeped through and in some miraculous way finally inspired the monks to dwell once more on earthly hopes. One of them procured him an audience with the heroic Queen Isabella, who agreed to engage him and promised three ships.

Feverish triumph! Already victory could be sensed in this indecision. His nautical experience was used to the full. Nothing was neglected and we are assured that he was one of the first to embark with a chronometer to determine longitude, which hitherto had been calculated only by dead reckoning. At last, one Friday, on the 3rd August, 1942—a Saint's Day—he sailed from Palos de Moguer with three ships.

He bore the title of Vice-Admiral and his ship was commanded by Juan de la Coza, the owner. Yes, the *Santa-Maria* had been hired by the Crown—and the two other vessels by the Pinzón brothers, seasoned filibusters, brutal sea rovers who had all their wits about them.

An appalling existence began. He sailed on into the unknown, an unknown which grew more and more oppressive, imposing and elusive. He found himself with diminishing stores and provisions, lost in a nameless solitude, in a sort of oceanic void beneath the implacable, windy bell of heaven. He floundered among fields of seaweed which fouled his bottoms. He had to bear with the pathetic fears of a rebellious crew who on all his voyages pestered their captain with cries of 'Put her about!' He persuaded them gently, for he possessed that gentleness to be found in the very strong and the very devout. One day, when the current brought the *Santa-Maria* within hailing distance of the *Pinta*, he called to Pinzón: 'Alonzo, they're grumbling in my ship. They all want to turn back.' And the stout sailor roared back: 'Strangle half a dozen of 'em and fling 'em overboard.'

He obtained a few hours' respite which he spent in prayer. On the 11th October one of the crew, with a trembling finger, pointed out to him in the water an object more significant than an island: a branch freshly broken from a tree, its scarlet berries still full of juice. Then the whole crew stood on deck in silence watching excitedly until, at two o'clock in the morning during the dark night of the 12th, the famous cry rang out: 'LAND.' It was Rodrigo of Triana who gave it, thus winning the promised bonus of 10,000 *maravedis*.

At dawn Columbus landed and planted a crucifix on the soil of the New World, on an island. This story is fraught with mystery—which island still remains doubtful. It is believed to have been Watling Island or perhaps the small Samana or Mariguana; one of the Bahamas which lie like an outpost guarding the West Indies. We still do not know for certain.

Only much later was it learned that the *Santa-Maria* perished miserably near French Cape, at Santo Domingo, dragging her anchors. Today the spot is out of the water and one of the anchors responsible has been discovered in the middle of a field.

Alonzo Pinzón abandoned Columbus who had to return on the little *Niña*, leaving behind 25 of his shipmates. He took two and a half months to return and nearly sank in a storm: he had already made preparations to consign to the waves a document giving an account of his exploits. I have always wondered what would have happened, had the discoverer drowned and it had been left to the bottle to announce this breath-taking discovery.

*　　*

Although he received a triumphant reception on his return, this voyage was only a reconnaissance. The following September Columbus set sail again with seventeen ships, an escort, almost a fleet, but they were ships full of adventurers, with whom his moral tribulations began. They explored the whole of the southern part of the West Indies and roughed it there for three years; but piety had given place to the bitterest concupiscence. Columbus was plagued by the most hideous greeds and sordid rivalries; his orders were flouted and his punishments stored up in rancorous minds. The Admiral returned from the third voyage in chains. In 1500 he was destitute.

His glory gradually crumbled away; it was worse than a death sentence. Then came the last voyage, from which he returned defeated and forgotten. He died, ruined and obscure, in Valladolid in 1506.

He wanted to be buried in the land he had discovered; no one dreamed of granting this wish and his poor ashes began their odyssey which was to last for 60 years. At first they reposed in the Convent of Santa-Maria, a reminder of that other famous name; then in the charnel house of the Observantines; then, seven years after his death, in the Carthusian Monastery of Santa Maria de la Cueva, after an almost royal ceremony in the Cathedral of Seville accorded him by the remorseful Ferdinand. Not until 1536 did they decide to fulfil his last wishes. He was transported to Santo Domingo, with the remains of his beloved son—an act of piety which made slight amends for previous ingratitude. In 1655 English aggression caused the tomb to be hidden. In 1673 an earthquake added its disorder to that of humans. After this we know little more: in 1795, however, with the cession of the island, it was decided to transport his remains back to Spanish soil. On excavation an enormous coffin of gilded lead was found. It was taken to Havana and interred with great pomp near the High Altar.

But this was not all. After the defeat of 1799 the Spaniards reclaimed the body of the man who had brought such prodigious wealth to their country. What purports to be the body of Christopher Columbus now reposes beneath a splendid mausoleum in Seville Cathedral.

In 1877, however, during repairs to the Cathedral of Santo Domingo, another coffin was discovered with the following inscription: 'P. AR. ATE', which might well signify *Primer Almirante*. The other coffin probably contained the bones of Diego. It is therefore possible that the last wishes of the Admiral were

complied with, and that his remains still lie in the conquered
land.

And now let us consider the ship that was instrumental in
achieving such discoveries, both Spanish and Portuguese. It
was a single vessel more or less adapted to the purpose: the
caravel (64). This famous name, with that of the galley, is used
by every antique dealer to designate an old ship—unless it has
black and white gunports, when it becomes a frigate. In any
case, do the scholars know very much more about this kingly
little ship of the fifteenth century? The specifications of Columbus' ships are still a matter of controversy. It has not yet been
decided whether they had a round or a square stern and there
is doubt about their aftercastles. It would be interesting but
rather disillusioning to continue this discussion. One always
becomes sceptical as soon as one tries to go deeply into history.

There are, however, certain indications as to this type of
vessel to be gleaned from drawings and descriptions. The
descriptions are invariably confused and contradictory; even if
one reads them in the original language they are, in effect,
'translations' since nautical terms form a special dialect which,
despite philology, often refuses to relinquish its keys. As for the
drawings, they belong for the most part to the sixteenth century
and are therefore of only relative value as regards the ships of
Columbus or of the Portuguese. Naturally they give certain
information, for in 30 years, and particularly at this period, a
nautical type would not have evolved to the point of becoming
unrecognisable. These admirable documents are in water
colour and gouache from the hands of those magnificent
designers of marine charts. Can one possibly suggest that these
pilots did not know what they were drawing? They were of
course artists, but they were primarily sailors.

The caravel they show us is, to begin with, a small ship, not
exceeding 200 tons burden; a swift, solidly built and seaworthy
ship, not over heavy and with a fair sheer to take the best
advantage of the wind when heeled at any angle. Normally
lateen rigged, since it was Mediterranean in origin, it was a
ship of the vanguard, a reconnaissance ship. In any case the
sixteenth century caravel is too well suited to this role not to
have been the result of a well-thought-out design. It left traces

which are found even today in the polacca and the xebec. It would need very little change to transform the *Niña* into a xebec. The caravel was the corvette of the nineteenth century. It was birdlike, with a sheer, able to extricate itself from a bad spot with the help of the oar, but, above all, a good sailer. In

65. Caravel, Sixteenth Century

the sixteenth century it carried a delightful highly intelligent rig and was manœuvrable to the last degree. Three lateen masts and a foremast, square rigged.... We know that the caravel spun like a ball and why should it not with so many ways of throwing it off balance? Its three lateen yards allowed it to sail close to the wind and its square foresail captured a stern wind as perfectly as possible—we all know the difficulty of running before the wind. The foremast, stepped very far forward, 'pulled' the long slender hull and kept it on course—a difficult matter with a following wind, which constantly causes broaching-to. Two huge lateens were employed, one forward and one aft, and between them the square lighthouse of the bow caught the gusts and turned like a weathercock. At a single glance one can imagine the speed. I myself have obtained astonishing results with models rigged in this fashion.

But to return to the fifteenth century and to Columbus: we

must admit rather more heaviness, larger sides to suit a long journey and for artillery defences, and we shall not be far wrong if we substitute square rig for lateen rig as was the custom when sailing in the Atlantic. It is futile, however, to try and make the type uniform when each port had its own way of building. This can be seen by the caravel of Palos (65). My correspondents have been kind enough to send me from various countries all the existing models of the *Santa Maria*. I have reproductions of the one in the Louvre, those in Spain, in Genoa, in Boston and in England. To be frank, they only resemble each other by the Latin cross on their lower sails. The *Niña* alone remains undebated and is represented as a large launch rigged with three lateen sails.

However, the discussion would become more bitter still if we trusted the words of Columbus, who always called the *Santa Maria*, the *Não* (the *Nef* or 'ship'), while he described the others as caravels. I think we can assume that the discoverer's vessel had a fairly solid superstructure, heavy enough to merit this name.

Except in the case of the *Niña*, they were square rigged. We only know about the sails of the *Santa Maria* from Columbus' own writings. He wrote in his log on Wednesday, 24th October, 1492: 'The weather has become calm and pleasant. I set *every* sail on the Ship: the mainsail with its two bonnets, the foresail, the spritsail, the mizzen and the topsail.'

I must draw the attention of men of goodwill to the bad faith of the naval historians for whom this remarkable precision does not suffice when they reconstruct the rig. Our good Auguste Jal insists upon attributing four masts to the *Santa Maria*, which he persists in making a caravel type of the sixteenth century: he assures us that 'every sail' means 'all the sail the weather allowed': an astonishing conclusion. Linguistically, 'every sail', placed after 'the weather has become calm and pleasant', obviously means that had there been other sails, Columbus would have hoisted them, as he had even gone so far as to run lace on his bonnets.

In support of his fourth mast, the auxiliary mizzen, whose sail is not mentioned, Jal replies quite subtly: 'They sailed with a stern wind and in this case the lateen of the auxiliary mizzen always remains furled'; but Vice-Admiral Pâris retorts: 'Columbus did not sail with a stern wind but with the wind on the beam, since he loosed his mainsail; otherwise, with a stern wind, the foresail would have flapped, lost the wind and been of no use at all. If he hoisted *all the sails* he was reaching and there was no auxiliary mizzen because Columbus would have mentioned it with the others.' This is the type of discussion that arises. My grandfather the Admiral, a great sailor and a fine seaman, said 'Pâris is right'.

But since even Columbus is not believed, I am afraid that my version will inspire little confidence. So if I may be allowed to sum up: the caravel was a reduced ship, smaller than the *nef*, smaller than the galleon, capable of great speed and of changing its sails according to necessity. There is nothing to prove that, in the manner of the pinks, which were almost contemporary, it did not carry its yards on deck ready to hoist when it had to sail close-hauled in a good wind. The *Santa-Maria*, on the other hand, was a *nef*, for here is the list of her cannon, which a small ship could never have carried: a battery of four cannon firing 20-lb. balls, six 12-pounder aspics, eight 6-pounder demi-culverins fifty times longer than their bore, several 14-pounder culverins, stowed, it is true, as ballast; springales in great number, swivel perriers and a hundred enormous one-pounder muskets.

And finally, a few words on Amerigo Vespucci, the famous, rather too famous Florentine, that seeker after glory who, in the service of the Spanish bankers, set sail on the western ocean in the wake of Columbus. It is maintained that he arrived on the western seaboard before the great Genoese. However, we cannot accuse him of having robbed or wanting to rob Christopher Columbus of his glory. His name was only somewhat contemptuously given to the New World. The geographer who based his map on the ideas brought back by Vespucci, called that little strip of territory claimed by the Florentine 'the Land of Amerigo.' Only much later was it noticed that this snippet, this enclave, formed a fairly large domain. Columbus, the discoverer, stood as patron to only a very small portion of the New World.

* * *

Charles V plied the Mediterranean to such a degree that it almost became a Spanish sea. He also dealt heavy blows to the pirates and captured Tunis. Brantôme portrays him standing impatiently on the deck of his galley or pacing nervously to and fro. But he suffered great defeats. In 1541 the whole Mediterranean echoed with the terrible set-back met with by the Emperor off Algiers although all the vicissitudes of this defeat have never really come to light, thanks to the reserve of the survivors who wanted to safeguard the honour of their Prince. Thousands of men perished in the muddy waves, ravaged by hideous diseases. A hundred and forty huge vessels sank and 15 galleys. Nearly the entire cavalry was wiped out by a storm and the waves threw up on the shores of Africa the corpses of the finest steeds in Europe.

Philip II was to accomplish with Lepanto a great arresting action in a collapsing, bewildered world. This was the supreme contribution made by Spain to civilisation, and it counted far more than the stream of precious metals she poured into Europe. This King must always be considered in the light of his victory at Lepanto: it explains and absolves him. It has not been sufficiently stressed that he found himself the main target of a pincer movement which was to prove fatal. The King of Spain was squeezed between the south and the north, between the Arab and the Anglo-Saxon drives. The Armada can be excused by Lepanto. This passionate but logical monarch thought that having won the latter, he could undertake the former in a symmetrical movement.

*　　　*　　　*

With Salamis and Actium, Lepanto remains one of the most important naval battles in history. The interests at stake went far beyond bitter national rivalries. It was no longer commerce or gold that was in fee; it was a question of *souls* and a civilisation. Lepanto, in which all the Catholic nations except official France took part against the pagans, assumed the value of a Crusade, a defensive Crusade against the Orient, against Islam.

The situation must be studied in all its gravity. The Crescent had found new paths and favourable prospects. The Mediterranean was becoming Moorish once more; the Christian retreat had taken on the proportions of a catastrophe. The already grave set-back at Algiers was followed by the capture of Cyprus in the most atrocious circumstances, arousing terror and discouragement. The Ottomans threatened Christendom from Andalusia to Hungary.

* * *

The fleet which triumphed at Lepanto was created and led by a man of genius, a bastard son of Charles V, Don John of Austria, to whom, with a broad mindedness one cannot but admire, Philip II delegated his authority on the sea.

Don John dazzled his contemporaries. Brantôme's portrait is one of the most sensitive and the most moving: it reveals the charm and the prestige of this handsome, thoughtful and resolute young man in all his gentle majesty. He was one of those individuals who are governed by the spirit and who place a private conviction and secret integrity above everything. He used to say: 'I should kill myself if I thought that anyone loved glory more than I do.' The Pope immediately singled him out and, delighted at the opposition from the Dukes of Anjou and Savoy, entrusted to the young twenty-six-year-old General the heterogeneous ships of this Holy Alliance.

But fortunately Don John was not only a man of goodwill. He was one of the innovators of his age and very much ahead of the warriors who were his colleagues. His victory was due far more to preparation than to leadership. A navy in any case demands detailed planning and can never be left to improvisation.

Don John was not afraid of original ideas. He supported the plans of the Venetian Bressano and the building of large galleys. Where, doubtless for greater speed and to avoid possible hitches, Venice would have only commissioned a few types, Don John caused fifteen to be built (61) at a moment when they were still on trial. It was these ships which obtained the decision.

One of these models can be seen today in the Armeria Réal of Madrid—at least it was preserved there until the Civil War. We can judge from it the radical, almost barbarous fashion in which the problem was solved if we compare it with the magnificent model in the Musée de la Marine of the galleass, built later by Venice. It is a model of the *Sphinx*, Don John's flagship in the action.

This vessel must have been 150 feet long with a 21-foot beam and gives the impression of a formidable crustacean, the ruggedness of certain parts contrasting with the power and the breadth of others: note also the roundness of its carapace. We are no longer faced with an instrument of speed such as the galley, but a powerful weapon of destruction where, in a period so devoted to decoration, luxury and elegance, everything has been subordinated to efficiency.

The most surprising feature is the bow. It has a real, absolutely circular turret (61*a*), completely different from anything previously built—an oak redoubt reinforced with wales, an artillery cauldron. Inside were installed the basilisks, with a calibre double that of the cannon carried by the galley; among others there was an 80-pounder bow gun like those used against Malta, augmented by four 30-pounders.

Forward of the turret the *Sphinx* carried an enormous ram, armed with a point which the best workers from Toledo fought for the honour of forging and welding; and, to add to the cruelty of the instrument, two oblique claws attached to the spherical bows, two gigantic catheads to ravage the enemy's upperworks.

Then there was a series of covered decks—complete decks or parapets—with slanting shutters to parry the arrows: the muzzles of culverins and *veuglaires* peep through the port lids above three tiers of oars emerging from ten oar ports which could be closed when under sail. Three lateen sails and, finally, a raised poop, heavy and squat, a tough crupper bristling with guns and crowned by a square fort, a blockhouse which, in the case of the *Sphinx*, was covered, despite everything, with brocade in honour of the occasion. . . . Three navigating lanterns, the centre one the height of two men. . . .

Certain galleasses carried a remarkable stern superstructure, a sort of protruding tail, very pronounced in shape, which must at the same time have protected the huge curved rudder from the shock of collision and allowed it to be replaced in case of loss.

The panels of the Captain's quarters represented the siege of Troy: they were painted by Sancho Coëllo, the sensitive portrait painter of the Royal family. On the head appeared one of the first figureheads, which would later be found on the bows of ships: a Sphinx sculptured by Bautista Vasquez, whom Georges Comtesse calls 'the Puget of Madrid', but of whom I know nothing.

*　　*　　*

The following is the constitution of some of the Christian detachments in this incredible affray, of which we are still reminded by the Angelus we ring three times a day (this at least is the popular legend, although it cannot be denied that Calixtus III, after the fall of Constantinople, had already recommended this prayer to the Catholic world). All honour to every lord; Venice put to sea with 105 or 106 of her largest, most powerful 32-bench galleys and two or three galleasses. Giovanni-Andrea Doria brought two galleys of which he was not only the Admiral but the owner—a wealthy age which allowed such generosity. The country sent 12 ships commanded by Antonio Colonna, that impassive mariner who replied laconically to Don John in the council of war: *Etiam si oportet me mori, non te negabo.* 'Even if I must die, I will not deny you.' This same Colonna paid brilliant homage to Don John's galleasses, which the rest of the fleet referred to as buckets or pitch barrels. Officially Genoa only produced three galleys, while the pretentious Duke of Savoy supplied a mere three small frigates of 15 benches! The Knights of St. Stephen (a new Order founded in Tuscany on the model of the Knights of Malta and which rendered great services) brought 12 galleys. The poop of one of these galleys was striped with a long black band in memory of a defeat. The Faith provided only three ships. Its fleet, under the Commander of Saint-Clement, had just suffered a serious setback at the hands of the renegade Lucciali as it left Messina.

A few lords turned up with their ships, as they might arrive today with their yachts. The one which caused a sensation belonged to a Venetian, Ambrogio Bragadino, whose father, in the teeth of convention, had been flayed alive after the capture of Famagusta. The skin of the heroic defender, stuffed with sawdust, had served as a standard for the Turkish Captain. In token of inexpiable mourning Bragadino's galley was painted black from masthead to rails.

185

Spain, in addition to her famous galleasses, provided 46 ships. France was not represented. The stigma of her collusion with Barbarossa remained, but many French gentlemen, among them Crillon, had come of their own free will.

Tall ships mingled with this crowd of long-oared ships, but they appear to have been used merely to transport material and for the disembarkation of troops. The very faithful engravings which are so easy to reconcile with the documents show no *nef* or carrack in the famous battle.

It is asserted that the *Sphinx* was preserved until the middle of the eighteenth century in Cartagena harbour.

* * *

The expedition of 1571 was one of the only combined operations which was carefully prepared both psychologically and materially, doubtless due to the influence of the youthful leader. Thus, while the Ottoman armies merely used Christian slaves to extort more from their suffering flesh, while they kept their 30,000 captives on the benches, Don John insisted for this occasion upon either free men or those condemned to short sentences, men who would be worthy of the battle. It seems, too, that the fleets were massed according to national affinities or rivalries.

The artillery was carefully chosen as regards calibre; the small arms studied and detailed for specific purposes. Europe at that time had a great lead in musketry. The arquebus had become a commonplace, and one must read Montluc to appreciate the support given to the fleet by these companies of musketeers against an enemy who, apart from his cannon, had nothing but spears or blades.

They went even further: at Messina, we are told, while waiting to set sail, Don John assembled everyone in a vast hall for a technical conference, indicating on a blackboard the position of each ship. He even foresaw six possible eventualities and gave his instructions regarding them with the signals to be used in daylight and at night.

* * *

This stresses the naval occasion: these carefully prepared evolutions could have taken place only under oars. They were considered in the light of a manœuvre by land battalions. A good general did not have to forget his art when boarding a ship and was able to command the various units like regiments. He could see at a glance the weak points or the advantages and fling in his troops accordingly. The wind was discounted. Everything was reduced to a question of formation, of artillery, decision and courage.

However, Lepanto was the last naval battle which still allowed this facility of manœuvre. It marked the decline of the galley, thanks to a conflict where mobility gave a full return; for the galleasses, by their firing power, weight and solidity, appear in the last analysis to have outclassed the others; and weight, solidity and firing power are the inherent qualities of tall ships. In future the victory would rest with vessels manœuvrable in themselves, not in formation, as one sees in the Armada and the battle of the Azores. In the old engravings of Lepanto, the galleasses look like panthers crushing cheetahs.

Galleys, too, allowed neither sustained effort nor the risks of bad weather. Combat was offered in autumn—despite the activity of Pope Paul V, who knew he was dying—and this was one of the causes which prevented the victory being followed up. The galley slaves were exhausted. The equinox was passed but they were far from confident at finding themselves on the waves after St. Michael's Day. Had Lepanto been won a fortnight earlier it would have resulted in the fall of Constantinople, from which all the pashas had begun to flee.

*　　*　　*

The fleet sought the Ottoman army and sailed on a south-easterly course after putting in at Corfu. It was on Saturday, 6th October, that the enemy was sighted in the Gulf of Lepanto and that the Christians took their last decision.

It was a battle of the Crusades. Don John attended Mass on his knees and received Communion the morning of that famous Sunday. Then, brandishing a crucifix in the manner of a Commander's baton, he passed behind the three groups of ships, raising the cross towards each vessel. One realises with awe what supreme power the young Commander wanted to invoke to give strength to his men. It was no question of reprisals or of some more or less vainglorious idea: it was the very essence of spiritual ardour that he was arousing.

The galley slaves were unchained and given their weapons. Their enthusiasm earned them this. The crews roared; there were only saints aboard.

Then Charles V's son returned to the *Sphinx* and temporal magnificence was restored to its rights and its prestige. He hoisted the famous banner of crimson or blue damask which men knew only from hearsay, the banner given by Paul V, with a Christ whose expression brought tears to the eyes. Below, supported by chains, the personal armorials of the late Emperor, a little of whose flesh was still alive and in command.... Don John hoisted his flag at the masthead to show that he was on board and appeared on his quarter-deck in his incomparable armour. He may have worn the famous dragon-headed helmet which has been attributed to him. In any case his cuirass, gleaming with gold, must have been ennobled by the cream habit of the Knights of Calatrava, with jagged, full-blown, scarlet *fleur de lys*, by the high boots of soft leather and the gilded spurs.

All the ships of Christendom were covered with iron. This naval army advanced in three widening rows. In the centre an arrow-head of six galleasses formed the spur of the whole fleet. The Ottoman army advanced in a crescent with its wings well deployed. It was eleven in the morning, with a light wind and fair weather.

* * *

The Turkish fleet was commanded by Petrov the Russian, Ali, the victor of Famagusta, and Uluch, the old corsair whom we have already met. A furious *mêlée* began. The galleasses spread immediate consternation. They broke through the enemy lines without suffering any damage, tearing and sinking. The surprise they caused was the beginning of the defeat, even before terror set in.

The left Christian wing was commanded by Venieri the Venetian; Don John was in the centre and Doria on his right to seaward, faced by the cautious Uluch who did not want to be on top of the shore.

Venieri already had the upper hand of his foe, but the fray in the centre did not weaken. Don John engaged Ali with furious shock tactics. While giving his orders the giant Turk, seeking a duel, launched a hail of arrows from a little steel bow which might have been forged for Hercules. Ali defended the Turkish flagship, the finest ship of the fleet. He was carrying, as a protective talisman, one of the most precious relics of Islam, the right canine of Mahomet contained in a single diamond.

Ali repelled three assaults by 400 Spanish musketeers. The fourth thrust him back to the cabin where he went on fighting, while a dark, smooth Venetian vessel which was seeking him out, drew alongside his stern. Suddenly, the avengers were vomited on to his deck, an eruption of fighting men in mourning. . . . It was Bragadino's galleass. The crew broke and fled. The men in black set upon this savage pasha, who flung them off and hurled them back. Finally they overwhelmed him and made him kneel on his own deck. He stabbed himself, but the son of the man who had been stuffed at Famagusta, a good family executioner and a worthy heir, rose up, axe in hand, and, crying his father's name in the Muslim's ears, decapitated him.

The Admiral's head was brandished on a pike and terror reigned among the Turks. But this did not satisfy Bragadino; he wanted an eye for an eye. He seized the head, lashed it to the feet of the corpse, beneath whose armpits he passed a rope, and hoisted the whole thing on to his main yard. Bragadino's great galley passed among the Ottoman ships proudly exhibiting its trophy of flesh, muslin, satin, blood and gold.

On the right wing, in the turmoil, Doria saw Uluch fleeing in an attempt to save his galleys. Giovanni-Andrea's galleys carried two companies of Spanish veterans taken from the Moncade *tercio* (regiment), one of them being the company of the valiant Diego of Urbina who fought on board the *Marquesa*. Among his men was a gentleman and titled soldier, though not yet an *alferez* (ensign), whose name would become even more famous than that of the Generalissimo.

The *Marquesa* drew alongside the flagship from Alexandria, killed 500 men and captured the Egyptian standard. Propping himself up, despite his fever and three wounds which had put one hand out of action—fortunately the left hand—the soldier went on firing his *escopeta*. His name was Miguel de Cervantes. In addition to his literary glories he liked to recall his wound received 'in the most brilliant occasion that past and present centuries have witnessed . . . like stars which should guide others through the heaven of honour. . . .'

The battle lasted five hours before the Turks, making use of their speed, were able to slip away with a favourable wind: five hours of marvels of strength, endurance and tenacity. We must remember this persistence if we want to appreciate fully this incredible expenditure of human effort.

The Pope was informed the same night, thanks to a magnificent system of relayed signals. All the Christian navies were filled with just pride and their strength had been doubled by the Ottoman prizes.

With Lepanto, however, the naval Middle Ages came to an end

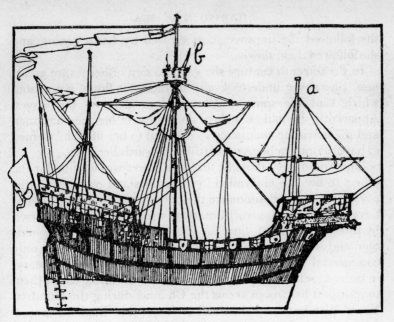

66. The *Mary Fortune*, A.D. 1500

CHAPTER XIII

England

WE arrive at last at that island nation which was later to play so important a part in maritime development and ultimately to rule the seas. She was there in the misty, spray-lashed north, sheltered by her black rocks and white cliffs. She vegetated, little known and still mediocre during those years when the Latin sun spread its glorious rays on the sparkling waves. Mysteriously she awaited her hour, which would arrive when the bell tolled for Spain. She was feared as a proud and obstinate Power, but her soldiers, those particularly hardy soldiers, were dreaded more than her sailors. Admittedly her navies appeared several times in that Mediterranean she would one day make her own as a natural dependency, but the time had not come when the nations and the maritime cities would look to her as an arbiter and a model. It was known that she had in her service brave, rash sailors, but, like the others, she followed the improvements created by Latin genius, and she followed them slowly.

In the fifteenth century she gave no sign of her future greatness. She never undertook any of those far-flung expeditions which kept the spirit of Christendom alive on the waves. Apparently she had enough to do to protect her merchantmen and the maritime commerce so essential to her life. She seemed to have adopted a bourgeois attitude towards her navy.

One would have thought that this Power was waiting for the others to become embroiled in difficulties and expense, to discover new seas and announce their conquests, so that she might have a choice of the world markets without weakening herself by prospecting. For a time she was content to exploit her heritage and her immediate possessions. Her squadrons were only commercial fleets which she armed for war when necessary, in order to settle her quarrels. She made admirable use of them to transport her troops across the Channel during the Hundred Years' War but one is inclined to forget that England shamefully lost this famous struggle, chased by a woman from the territory to which she laid claim; she had just exhausted herself in the Wars of the Roses—unique floral designation for a savage butchery—thus dissipating the authority she might have had in Europe. Without the accession to the throne of the wise Henry VII, England would never have known her final triumph.

Another stroke of luck came to her aid: the rivalry between Francis I and Charles V, with the web of alliances it engendered. The whole Latin world turned towards the large island and its choleric King. It was felt that the aid of Henry VIII would tip the scales. English prestige, which would perhaps become the most effective and most frequently employed weapon of the United Kingdom, was born. It is from this moment that the English nation took on in the minds of Europeans the bogey-man aspect she was never to lose. Furthermore, she very soon learned how to foster the fear she inspired. She seems suddenly to have understood the advantages she could wield and just as suddenly entrusted her future to the exploitation of the sea. She was driven to this by the Spanish threat, and her victory over the Armada confirmed her new power.

She invented nothing, and still invents very little. She merely improves and her workmen are the best in the world. They are slow and scrupulous and fully prepared to improvise but their improvisations are incomparable. The English trade mark is synonymous with expensiveness and excellence. The pride the nation takes in it is justified by the workmanship put into the softest fabrics and the most trenchant steels.

In 1500 an old English pilot showed Henry VII a map of the world which still survives. It was a sort of tacit reproach. On it smoked Iceland with its volcano; on nearby Newfoundland could be read: 'These islands are full of demons.' Greenland had for emblem a polar bear and the text: 'Here the ice reigns.' The great West Indies almost touched it and one could read: 'This is the Atlantis of Plato.' Then, below Florida ('much gold'), could be seen a channel opening on to a broad expanse of western ocean : 'This is the Strait through which we should go to Cathay.' Actually, it was joined to Xipangu (Japan) and a huge land on which were drawn chimpanzees and elephants, with the inscription: 'Kinsay, the town of a thousand towers (Pekin).'

All this, however, bore the seal of the Kings of Spain or Portugal and even the King of France. Columbus, Diaz and also Master Cabot. . . . What would Master Henry discover?

Henry VII grew enthusiastic. He was the true founder of English naval power. Instead of hiring or requisitioning the ships he needed at all costs to form a nucleus from which he could develop a professional navy, he sought information, studied documents and started to build four vessels whose names have become historic: the *Regent*, the *Sweepstake*, the *Sovereign* and the *Mary Fortune*, all representative of their period and forming the point of departure for the illustrious English fleet. Now one has only to follow attentively British construction to learn everything about the ship.

* * *

Henry's ships were carracks, a naval type which we have already met on our voyages. Like the majority of maritime inventions it came from Venice. The Carrack was essentially a large, tall ship; later, again essentially, a fighting ship which would completely abandon the use of oars. It was employed in trade certainly, but of course nothing in the naval world can be

absolute. But in its structure it was made for the warrior and
not for the merchant. It did not have to worry about load; its
capacity only existed for the purpose of artillery and its shape for
the purpose of domination. This determination would render

67. The *Henry-Grace-à-Dieu*, 1514

the carrack difficult to handle when the type was developed to
extremes. It was the modern battleship, the sailing fortress. Its
probable etymology is really rather curious. It derives from *cara
da rocca*, 'the face of a citadel.'

Let us consider the question of size, to begin with. There were
no carracks below 500 tons burden; they surpassed in power the
nefs, which, lightened and modified, eventually became galleons,

particularly in Spain. It frequently achieved 1,000 tons burden, and Portugal in the sixteenth century launched some which exceeded 2,000. It was a ship that won great prestige, less among the sailors than the taxpayers who returned amazed by what they had seen and ready to disgorge more money, conquered by the formidable aspect of these wooden walls.

In plan the carrack is distinguished by a double fortress fore and aft dominating the deck (67a, a). In the reign of Henry VIII this deck bore the weight of the big guns; their muzzles aligned between the shields on the bulwarks. There were no regular batteries: the two bastions—that of the stern being twice the length of the one forward—bristled with artillery along the sides, and even inboard, to enable them to cross and lower their fire if the enemy came between them. The *Mary Fortune* (66), for example, epitomized the efficient naval instrument of war, devoid of exaggeration or danger, for her castles did not tower to those giddy heights they reached later.

*　　*　　*

In Henry VIII's ship the masts are better proportioned. The obelisk mast has disappeared: it has become lighter and more balanced. The foremast (66a), on the contrary, has developed and acquired real power. The mizzen is still lateen-rigged. Only the mainmast carries a top (66b) and can sport a modest topsail which these English vessels, at the same time the height of audacity and of caution, only adopted very late. They were medium ships, unpretentious and probably excellent. The first ones did not exceed 4-500 tons burden. The stern was raised into a round poop on which was a rectangular, two-storeyed castle.

But the blustering personality of Henry VIII was to destroy all this wisdom. His desire for opulence and imperialism inspired British shipbuilding and in the guise of exaggeration brought about the greatest progress. It is not without reason that, despite all his cruelty and savagery, the English consider him one of their greatest kings and are devoted to him. The enormous fellow was one of them and very much more so than they would like to admit. Henry VIII saw in the navy an instrument of glory and he drove it vigorously to produce ships 'worthy of the monarch of the English nation'.

To replace the *Regent*, which a Breton hero had sunk, Henry VIII laid down the *Great Harry* or *Henry-Grace-à-Dieu*: although at one time these two were confused and later separated, they are now identified again as one and the same ship. With a remarkably revealing speed, the ship was built in a year. Her success attracted the attention of the whole of Europe, which

68. Bows of Holbein's Ship, 1552

realised at once the changes that had taken place and what they boded for the future.

The actual size of the vessel is not known: at least 180 feet in overall length; more than 1,000 tons burden and less than 1,500, and this must suffice. She was built entirely of oak and with her new solidity was the first British or European ship to carry two complete, superimposed battery decks (67d, d), with the gun-ports arranged in a chessboard pattern and not one below the other—a far happier disposition. Even if we do not know the exact dimensions, we know her cost to a penny—£8,708 5s. 3d. What magnificent accountancy! She carried 21 large bronze cannon and 231 small. The result: a pincushion.

Her castles (67a, a) were in three storeys, which gave her seven decks. The aftercastle hung well over the rudder and the forecastle finished in a point, prolonged by a kind of ram above the water. At the tip of this arrow appeared for the first time in Europe a sculptured emblem which would become the figure-head (68). The castles inboard fell sheer to the deck. So far she was merely a large-scale version of the *Mary Fortune* (66), but in her rig she suddenly became modern. This rig was quite exceptional for the period and some of its novelties would be abandoned. Four true masts. . . . The foremast (67*b*) was almost as high as the main and definitively found the proportion it would keep to the end, as did the mizzen, which was much lower. Previously the two mizzens had only carried square sails but the modern English, who must have considered the matter carefully, equipped the mizzen with three superimposed lateen

69. Ship of the Reign of Henry VIII

sails. This seemed very rash. It is impossible to see how they could be lowered. The after mizzen also carried two lateen sails. It was not very seamanlike but we are not entitled to laugh at it. The mainmasts now show two tops, a proud innovation which made possible the modern extensions of the mainsail— the topsail and the topgallant, 'the bold sail at the masthead.' It is true that the *Great Harry* was the only ship in the reign of Henry VIII to use these topgallants.

This famous ship, in which the English King sailed to the

Field of the Cloth of Gold, was sober in her decoration. Her impressiveness lay in a hull of black, oiled oak, contrasting with the light paint of the upperworks and castles, cut by the vivid colours of shields hung all along the rails and bearing the arms, or rather the emblems of England: the famous Tudor Rose, the Cross of St. George, the Fleur-de-Lis, in memory of the French

70. English Galleon used by the Conquerors of the Armada, 1588

conquest (Edward VII was the first, I believe, to renounce his title, King of France). . . . The main luxury of the ship was provided by her flags, whose profusion rather disconcerts the modern mind. Until the eighteenth century the beflagging of ships—this was found in the galleys throughout their life—surpassed imagination. One has to read about them to believe. The flags at the *Great Harry's* masthead reached 120 feet in length; 28 banners of silk, embroidered with gold and silver; 10 flags of St. George and 7 other heraldic banners. . . .

The huge vessel completely dominated the fleets of Henry VIII. Beside her the *Mary and John*, the *Catherine Pleasaunce*, made a poor effect: this was the 'capital' ship. However, the *Great Harry* wisely seldom put to sea. She was re-christened the *Edward* in 1552, when the young King came to the throne, but sailors will always tell you it is unlucky to change a name and she went up in flames the following year in Woolwich dockyard.

However, her career was successful and her object had been achieved. She had proved what the English shipyards were capable of doing, and that Spain could now no longer afford to ignore them. Robert Brigandine, the leading English shipbuilder, had impressed Europe. From then onwards until modern times

71. Bows of the *Golden Hind*

the British Isles set maritime fashion. Venice was a thing of the past.

* * *

Queen Elizabeth's navy (71, 72) was very different from the sensational vessels Henry VIII had inspired, but I must stress once more the value of these exaggerations. They are marvellous in stimulating progress. They allow all methods to be perfected and the unusual becomes the commonplace. From a bad, rash prototype excellent modified specimens are produced. The Queen's navy could never have been what it was without a *Great Harry* behind it. England now knew how to build big ships and she could lend an ear to the more prudent advice of two seamen, two merchants—one a slaver and the other a pirate—who created for her the leading navy of the world. Hawkins, the slave trafficker and Drake, the petty captain of commerce, gave seaworthiness and a goal to these ships from which, first and foremost, they demanded manœuvrability. However, it was Drake who set the fuse alight after some amazing adventures at sea. He must be considered the English Magellan, but before he was officially recognised, he had already distinguished himself in the most sensational manner. Molested in his modest traffic by the Spaniards, this skipper declared a private war on them. In 1573 he set out with a 70-ton vessel, the *Dragon*, to attack Spain. No more, no less. . . .

Drake sailed to the colonies over which Spain, never envisaging the possibility of competition, held undisputed sway. He crossed swords with her round Panama, where she had

72. The *Golden Hind*, Drake's Ship, 1575

founded some very prosperous trading stations. After a glorious campaign he returned to Plymouth, where he obtained recognition: the Queen gave him her personal protection. When he undertook his voyage round the world—the second man to do so—he already nursed warlike plans. He succeeded in winning California, Chile and Peru for the United Kingdom and conceived the idea of annexing the Indies.

Then he fitted out the *Golden Hind* (71, 72) and in his ship one can recognise the very latest improvements from both the north and the south. The carrack had lost its arrogance, except in Spain, who would pay for this dearly. It became the galleon: another ship to become famous although we do not quite know, particularly in its infancy, what it represented. When Spanish galleons are mentioned the imagination runs riot. It is a golden word. Moreover, it is intimately associated with those transports of precious metals which linked America to the Spanish ports, with those ingots and bars of gold which Spain unloaded in Lisbon, Cadiz and Barcelona, and which she was supposed to have sunk in the Bay of Vigo. The galleon glitters and flames and a shining silhouette looms against a dark background. But leaving this lyricism aside, it was an excellent ship, derived from the *galea* or *gaulus*, a sailing ship, but still aided for a long time by oars and on this account less lubberly and not so tall as the *nef*. A hybrid, a cross between the *nef* and the caravel, it was nimble, sufficiently well armed to defend itself and stable enough to weather a heavy storm. It was our frigate, replacing the carrack with its fairytale castles and outrageous audacity. There are certain luxury and prestige ships to which some routes are forbidden. Thus our poor *Atlantique*, with her victories of Samothrace in the saloons and her six-ton chandelier hanging from a glass dome, could not have been used on the New York route because her precious furnishings would have been knocked about in a gale.

The galleon (70) was perfected in England and one might even say that the type became specifically English.

When she tolerated the carrack, Great Britain submitted for the last time to Latin influence. By creating the more subtle galleon she became herself once more, practical, self-willed, with that balance between modernity and tradition she has always known how to preserve and in which perhaps lies her greatest strength.

The English galleon lay very low on the water compared with those cathedrals which had flaunted their pinnacles. It was built for solidity and one is inclined to find it stocky. Its development over a period of 30 years was not revolutionary, but intelligent and painstaking. Drake and Hawkins created a craft completely subjected to efficiency. It never exceeded 150 feet and was between 500 and 600 tons burden. In its perfection it was to become the leading type for 200 years and its variations would never alter its fundamental characteristics.

The hull was still dominated fore and aft by superstructures for combat, command and living quarters, but these were no longer castles; they were already quarterdecks and poop-decks. Some of Louis XIV's ships would be more heavily charged than Drake's galleons, as were certain ships of Charles II's reign. The quarterdeck was an upper deck extending from the mainmast to the sternframe. Another deck was laid aft over the last quarter; this was the poop-deck, beneath which were the pilot's quarters.

A novelty in the stern, later to become the richest ornament of the poop, was the gallery (70,73) which jutted out at the height of the main deck. In the Elizabethan galleon it was merely a narrow balcony, attached by upper arcades to the hull but still remaining uncovered.

The bows, too, carried a deck running back a fifth the length

73. Jacobite Stern

of the ship, which would be the forecastle, another novelty. This forecastle is cut off sheer, six feet from the stem, leaving a triangular protruding promenade, prolonged by a spur above, the water, rather like the galleasses of old. This would become the ship's head and would last as long as sail. It was bounded by ample bulwarks. This platform also served for handling the anchor and the head sails and as an advance post for musketry in battle. Its object was to give an open field of fire to the battery, which was always carried forward and could fire along the axis of the ship in a chase.

The rigging had become modern. The masts were balanced and carried three tiers of sails. The galleon often had four masts, including the *bonaventure*, lateen rigged. The bowsprit had become a powerful mast. This had already been found necessary in the *Great Harry* to support the increased height of the foremast by spreading its stays. A very important item—this became a point of honour with the English specialists—which one must never overlook unless one wishes to be regarded as a novice in shipbuilding, was the principle of no bobstay, that passive rope which was later to unite so naturally the stem and the bowsprit. For the British the bobstay only became legitimate at the end of the seventeenth century. Moreover they themselves were surprised that they had taken so long to arrive at this simple idea, although there is an explanation. Firstly, for a long time the bowsprit carried only the spritsail, which tended to make the vessel plunge while the jibs pulled it up again. Moreover, the support of the foremast was easy as long as it remained rudimentary. But there is another thing which the moderns always forget: the general elasticity of the rigging. Our ancestors, even down to our grandfathers, attached so great an importance to this that when in flight or giving chase, they eased their masts and slackened the shrouds. All the best sailors have noticed that too tight a rigging 'kills' the course, but no new design has taken this into account: only the Chinese and the Polynesians still profit by it.

However, thanks to a succession of links, after the sixteenth century all the masting of the sailing ship was supported by the bowsprit. The fore stays were secured directly to it; the main-mast stays, being made fast to the foremast, depended on it again, just as did those of the mizzen, being joined to the main. When a cannon ball cut off the bowsprit, the whole masting was imperilled. Thus, to gain the elasticity which they deemed indispensable to the whole structure of the rig, the early designers only used the bowsprit as a longitudinal spring. They attached it to the hull only by a cable, the gammon, which secured it at the masthole. This gave sufficient flexibility and the whole rig balanced on this long, free stalk. When they began to forget intuition and experience and to trust solely to the draw-ings, the bobstay appeared. And what a bobstay: the most rigid chain support that could possibly be devised!

At the extremity of the forecastle was placed a sculptured ornament, usually the figure of a dragon or a basilisk. Eventu-ally they carved a fantastic animal with the body of a snake.

The Tudor ships had a characteristic which disappeared under the Stuarts: the blocks of wood holding the shrouds fast were in the shape of a heart pierced with three holes. These 'dead-eyes' (71, 73) became circular with the more frequent use of the turning lathe (the lathe had a great vogue under the Valois and Louis XVI). On the big ships they were pierced with five holes and became oval in shape.

The ship was not steered with a free helm; it was too big. It could only be controlled by the aid of the 'whipstaff', a huge vertical lever which had to be manipulated with both hands. The helmsman's look-out post rose above the quarterdeck like a submarine's conning tower.

A final detail but a very important one: the stern was flat (69), cutting the decks at right angles. Its terminal point dragged in the wake. This was a retrogression which endured until the end of the seventeenth century, when the French ships were the first to change it to allow the wake to slip by more easily. It is probable that this simplification was due to the haste of the English to defend themselves against the imminent attacks of Spain. These sterns were the most delicate part of the whole design. They demanded great care and selected timber.

In the struggle against England, quick action was essential. The Mediterranean, purged of the Barbary pirates for the time being, ceased to be the main political field. Spain frowned at the north. She had acquired a material power difficult to imagine today unless one pictures a union between Great Britain and the United States. To this must be added the moral authority she wielded, which doubled her strength. Spain had everything, devotion, aristocracy and art. This is not the place to extol these virtues of a country I hold very dear, but I should like to give a few details of the Spanish wealth obtained by sea, for it compares with the British fortunes. We remember the second wave of Conquistadors—Cortez and Pizarro—who with magnificent rashness and abominable cruelty conquered Mexico and Peru for the might of Spain, taking everything with an ill-advised ease—ill-advised because it would dictate colonial policies from which, in 1949, we suffered an enormous reverse. In 1580 Spain possessed three-quarters of the gold in Europe, so much precious metal that its value dropped at one fell swoop. This Spanish finance was the beginning of the high cost of living in Europe. The import of precious metals in such abundance produced nothing less than an inflation which rapidly became as dangerous as that of our paper money today. Gold, fundamentally, is only a token and not a vital commodity although we make a fetish of it. Too much gold, as it has always done, gave enormous purchasing power, but it was expended on sterile and non-productive creations, on armaments or palaces; her people finished by dying of hunger under a golden cope, disgusted with slow and badly paid work, while England fortified herself with merchandise and raw materials.

But there was always the wherewithal to pay. After completing his southern crusade Philip treated himself to a fleet for his northern one. He wished to destroy British power on two counts; first because of its interference with Spanish colonial policy and secondly because England had become the champion of something far more dangerous than paganism: heresy.

The great naval interest of this conflict lies in observing medieval Spain at grips with progressive England.

*   *   *

Spain mobilised against England the ships and the tactics which had gained her a great Mediterranean victory, but England triumphed with her new ships and her original strategy. When we study the two battles, so close in time—1572 and 1588—they seem to be a century apart rather than 16 years. What would these outdated derelicts do against the English merchantmen? Were they fossils? We are back again with galleys, galleasses and hookers. Why not *nefs*, that word which disappeared with the sixteenth century and is now used in France only as an architectural term? What would be the result of the dashing tactics inspired by Medina-Sidonia like another Don John? This Alonzo de Guzman, seventh Duke of Medina-Sidonia, who has been nicknamed the Good and the Handsome and who was the equal in physique of the imperial bastard, was in fact another Don John. Opposing him was a great noble, Lord Howard of Effingham, with nothing of the courtier about him; an English athlete with a ruddy face who, going on board, would lift a block with one hand and immediately win the hearts of his crew; a splendid yachtsman, perhaps the founder of the Royal Yacht Squadron; in any case, with a stomach as unperturbed at sea as in his park, whereas the handsome Medina soiled his ruffle at the slightest roll of the ship.

Philip II, when he commissioned his Armada, was thinking in terms of the last war instead of the next one. He planned a kind of epic and almost feudal struggle in which each clan and each province was to furnish a detachment. The whole of Spain joined in and played its part. Nearly every Catholic nation sent a detachment or a squadron.

Barcelona, Tarragon, Valencia, Alicante and Cartagena together sent 40 ships of 600 tons; Almeria, Malaga, Cadiz and Lagos, 20 galleons of the same tonnage. Seville, the richest and most generous, produced 25; Guipuzcoa and Biscay, 35; the allies, 30 caravels or demi-galleons of 400 tons. Medina flew his flag in the *San Martin* of 1,000 tons burden and 49 cannon, but the *Regazone*, the flagship of the Levant, exceeded 1,200 tons. The heavier and more bedizened Spanish galleon had begun to be covered with sculptures and gilt, flaunting the wealth Spain considered seemly for any attribute of her kingdom.

In addition, 40 hookers, double-purpose ships for battle and cargo like our flutes of the seventeenth century; 50 vessels from the Asturias and Galicia; 310 medium ships; more than 20 Spanish galleys; 20 Neapolitans; 55,000 fighting men and 1,200 horses; 1,500 naval guns; 200 disembarkment cogs with 1,400 mules; three thousand gentleman 'adventurers'; 180 priests; secret ships loaded with women and a poet, Lope de Vega. This whole world, assured of victory, sang with him:

> . . . *Spain arise*
> *to the raucous vibrant sound of the war trump.*

But a pack of English bulldogs dispersed the procession.

*　　　*　　　*

The Queen had collected under the command of Howard a first-class team well capable of taking the initiative. Philip himself had also thought of reinforcing Medina's incompetence by a selection of stout sailors, but Spain did not produce men of the same calibre as the English. Under Howard were seasoned mariners; Drake, who had rounded the world and pillaged

Lisbon; Raleigh, the sailor poet in love with his sovereign, who had discovered Virginia and named it after the Virgin Queen; Frobisher, the polar bear from the Arctic; and above all, Hawkins, the ex-slaver, the great freebooter who knew how to build a ship as well as to command it.

They built ships swiftly in the Themistoclean manner and their very speed served them by making the new fleet homogeneous. It was a small fleet—only 200 vessels and 16,000 sailors—which engaged in this new Salamis, but a fleet of the highest quality.

Appalling days; Spain's naval Calvary. After two soul-destroying months spent at Ferrol, when everyone had begun to waver, the Armada finally entered the Channel. The first contact took place on the 30th July; a short but costly dogfight in which the English terriers drew blood from the Spanish greyhounds. On Tuesday, 2nd August, a new engagement in which, without being given time to take up its positions, the Armada was subjected to a mad charge of marauders, so that Medina grew nervous and ran for Calais to wait for the Duke of Parma. This was retreat. Everyone felt it and was jubilant. The same evening Howard could write to the Queen: 'We are plucking them.'

The Armada re-formed in good order off Calais but during the night the English sent in their fire ships and the *San Martin* blazed. Drake went into the attack under full press of sail and the wind took a hand. All the cables were cut; panic reigned in the storm and under the resolute attack of the English galleons. A rout ensued such as the world had never seen, and which has remained legendary, but of which the truth surpassed the myth. They dispersed in all directions. The *San Salvador* ran aground on the rocks of Asnelles; the natives would corrupt the Spanish name and call them the rocks of Calvados. A galley from Guipuzcoa was lost far up on the Norwegian coast. The Spanish Admiral did not even try to return through the Channel, which, with the wind in their favour, the English were barring. Still assailed by the storm and the British sailors—everyone attacked, even the mongrels—he tried to make his escape past the Orkneys and Shetlands down the west coast of Ireland. These bright, sunny ships reached the 62nd parallel. The weather was exceptionally bad that summer. Reaching the coast—where the very natural fury of the English makes us tremble—the Spaniards were slaughtered everywhere, on the mud banks, on the rocks, on the beaches. Even drowning men were battered to death.

For months the seas were strewn with these unfortunate hulls, completely unrigged, laden with martyrs. Abandoned to the waves, with only a jury sail, these condemned men did not know what to expect. In the eighteenth century it was maintained that only one ship and 30 supply boats returned to Spain.

England did not lose a single ship and announced 200 dead. Never has there been such a defeat. The sea belonged to the north and Britannia ruled the waves.

74. *Boier*

CHAPTER XIV

Holland

ANOTHER Venetian State had been founded in the north and it, too, lived by its navy alone. It was perhaps even more original and characteristic than Venice. Among all peoples and nations this land of the United Provinces appears as the most deserving and the most sympathetic, the most resolutely and peaceably national, for its most intimate conquests were not made with gunpowder and blood, but, as De Ruyter said with his customary energy, 'with the sweat of our brows.' Holland was built on the sea itself and has expanded by hard work, by a thousand-year effort of piles and polders, dykes and dams; an ever-precarious labour, always sustained and immediately resumed when the anger of the waves destroyed this work of ants. Even today, by means of reclamation work and new dykes, Holland expands by six acres a day.

Shipping here is doubly important, on salt water and on fresh. Impossible to concentrate on warships; they have to think of barges, for inland circulation is even more intense than navigation on the high seas. Holland is a leaky ship living by its pumps and only remaining afloat by baling; she has as many canals as roads and there is a constant traffic on the straight gleaming waterways. In each big Dutch port there is a corner

75. *Boier*

for barges. It would be an interesting study to follow the transformation of the barge into the ship—a transformation which in any case was almost imperceptible. The vessels which cross

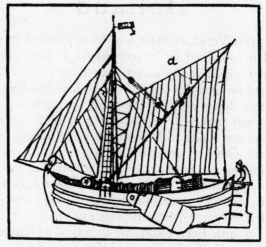

76. *Hektjalk* with Spritsail

the seven seas to bring from all parts of the world every type of merchandise, finally glide between carpets of flowers, chessboards of tulips, hyacinths and windmills.

Although a nation without forests, Holland was the country which produced the greatest number of ships. Without iron or mines, she warehouses every metal and without vineyards, every

77. Rudder of a *Boier*

conceivable wine. As an old book says: 'Apparently the groceries grow on the spot, the oils collect, the salt crystallises, the silks and the drugs for medicine and dyeing are products of her

78. Rudder of a *Tjotter*

own growing.' Today, in addition to this, she has acquired most of the diamonds in the world. These are the results of maritime power.

Things were not always so bright and the first efforts seem rather pathetic. The Dutch had to struggle against great disadvantages before devoting themselves entirely to the sea. They only began to reap their harvest in the sixteenth century. They were by nature gentle and patient, sons of a difficult soil demanding untold sacrifice, but they grew energetic and violent when they found themselves bullied by all the nations whom their productive activity offended. Their first victories were won over the Hanseatic towns which had grown jealous of their

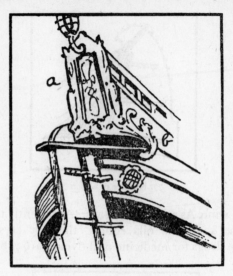

79. Stern of a *Flute*

maritime commerce. But from the sixteenth century onwards, they were tacitly recognised as the most able navigators in the north, as well as the best and most prolific shipbuilders. In 1512, they provided Charles V with 100 vessels.

80. Rudder of a *Tjotter*, with carved and painted head

However, Protestantism had already alienated them from the Spanish monarchy, under whose protection and flag the Dutch squadrons had been able to establish and to perfect themselves.

It is the admirable story of the 'Sea Beggars', more sailors than soldiers, whose bravery and skill, after innumerable naval combats, ultimately founded their country in 1579, when, by the

81. Seventeenth-century Gallery

Treaty of Utrecht, seven provinces united as a Republic. The defeat of the Armada allowed them to establish themselves in freedom and power, so much so that it was they who in turn attacked Spain in June 1596.

Then began their long voyages. In 1597 they returned, loaded with produce, from the Indies. They had reconnoitred Madagascar and established themselves in Java in the East Indies. From there came the fabulous wealth of the United Provinces, which, without any stable territory and with no agricultural wealth, could wage long and costly wars and unremittingly commission fleets. They defended their rights against the most powerful maritime nations until the eighteenth century. Their War of Independence, moreover, only really ended with the Treaty of Münster in 1648 and had lasted 80 years. Münster was the sign of the admitted decadence of Spain.

In 1650 it was still maintained that Holland, finally established in her own sovereignty, possessed more ships than the whole of Europe put together. Each year 1,500 large merchant-men sailed from Amsterdam; 3,000 fishing boats fished herring; 40 ocean-going ships ensured the traffic with Archangel and

82. Stern of a Pinnace

Northern Asia; Turkey chartered 35 of her privateers and there were 150 at Batavia. Her gold reserve was one of the greatest in the world: Amsterdam warehoused 3,000 tons of gold.

The specifically Dutch ship forms were reserved for small craft, the big and medium ships conforming to the requirements of ocean travel. They were very broad (75), with splayed lines and practically no draught, and seemed to glide over the water. They all carried the leeboard, that characteristic aileron or fin which can be seen on all Dutch prints of small boats. It replaced the keel in the struggle against drift caused by their round, flat shapes. It was only used close to the wind. There was one on each side, that to leeward being immersed. The construction was as solid as possible. Big beams were in favour and always appeared to the Dutch, who had no trees, the epitome of naval beauty. They tried not to conceal them more than necessary beneath the paint so that their intrinsic value might be seen.

But there was also something special in Dutch ships, 'the

83. Bows of a Pinnace

Dutch twist,' a tendency to accentuated curves, angles and powerful sides. The fact that they were forced to sail over shallows partly explains these enlargements and bulges, for the boat could not have a big draught; the need to withstand heavy seas is another reason for these sturdy dimensions. Both these factors joined in determining the curves which made Dutch ships recognisable everywhere—the ship of *Mijnheer*. But there was also a certain Chinese influence. This has been little noticed but I find it undeniable after my study of junks. This influence can even be felt in the rig of small ships, many of which hoist a spritsail (76*a*), that compromise between the sail of the north and the lateen sail: a large, completely square, piece of canvas of which the front is attached to the mast and which is kept taut by a long pole stretching from the foot of the mast to the top corner and the outer edge of the sail. It is not quite the sail of the Chinese coasting lugger, but it recalls its shape.

Dutch shipbuilding surprises on first sight, but then begins to please, as do the Dutch themselves, by strength, quality and sincerity. One feels grateful to the shipwright for having had such a feeling for the powerful and nothing really seems preferable to this vigour in their boats. Heaviness becomes an element of beauty. The small Dutch craft last for ever and can stand up to anything. There is an infinite number of types, both clinker and carvel built, laden with superstructures or low in the water. They all bear very difficult names, from the *boier* (75), to the *hoeker*, the *buss* and the *kaag*. It is always best to point at them even if you know how to spell their names. Notice

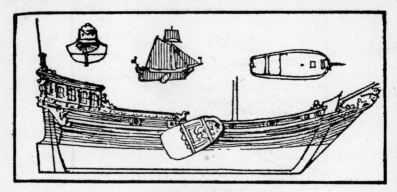

84. *Statenjacht* 1678

the fine design of the rudders, their sweep and their carved figurehead (80, 82, 83, 84).

I have no space here to give a detailed study of the different models, which vary with each port, but a single *boier* hull is enough to give some idea of the local construction of small craft; just as the stern of a *flute* (79) enables us to know the big ones. It is enough to bewilder the enthusiasts of the so-called subtle line.

When you see these big insects floundering about you cannot imagine that they could ever be nimble and you have to make a trip in one to appreciate the way it sails, hugs the wind and resists the sea. I recall an outing in a herring boat which will always remain firmly impressed on my memory.

*   *   *

The big Dutch ships have upperworks like *flutes* or pinnaces. The former presented a very large, almost circular stern (79), surmounted by a small carved escutcheon, as insignificant as a broadbean on a gourd. Below it, piercing the rotundity of the stern, yawned a huge oval hole (*b*) for the tiller, which was used also for stowing the great pine logs from the north which Holland imported for her masts, or the oaks from Poitou for the gigantic piles on which most of her towns are built.

216

The pinnace (82, 83), too, was of large tonnage and chiefly used for war—the term employed here has a very different meaning from the one current in the south, where it is a kind of fast sloop. It differed from the *flute* in its numerous gun ports and particularly in its stern with a gallery and a raised and grandiose escutcheon. Each of the great maritime nations, Holland, England, France and Spain had its own particular stern forms.

In the seventeenth century the Dutch poop had only a gallery without a balcony (81), but forming a pronounced

85. *Kopjacht*

double curve (*slingerlijst*) (82a), very simple and handsome, joined to little round-houses on each side. These houses jutted out with decorated windows to port and starboard. They took on more and more importance and lasted until the end of sail. Here were installed the baths and the officers' heads. The English stern had almost as many balconies as decks, together with round-houses, or demi-quarter galleries as the British called them. It was therefore more burdened than the Dutch stern and was square, rather clumsy and confused in shape. The open galleries of the lower storeys, however, provided fine deep cover. The Dutch form came from Spain, where the after-castles climbed proudly to form a very tall stern which preserved, more than in any other navy, the pious attribute, 'the stairway to God'. As for France, I can modestly state that she produced the most beautiful sterns, taking into account both dignity and naval requirements, with richly carved woodwork; a decorative subtlety which never clashed with the trim lines of the vessel.

Holland gave Europe the pleasure ship, reserved for persons of high estate. The English brought it to the height of navigability and subtlety, but British yachting really started with two little ships called the *Mary* and the *Bezan,* presented to King Charles II by the Dutch East India Company. Samuel Pepys sailed in the latter ship on the Thames. The English name for a pleasure ship in fact comes from the Dutch *jacht.* Moreover, English yachts retained for a long time the main features of Dutch construction, more than ever inspired by the junk. The Science Museum exhibits two very interesting models, one of the Dutch gift, the other England's adaptation of this, possibly the *Katherine,* designed at Woolwich in 1674 by Phineas Pett. The British yacht retained the upperworks of the original but tapered the vitals in an astonishing fashion, so as to make greater headway when under press of sail. This vessel, of course, no longer carried leeboards, for its deep keel and rising floor timbers sufficed. The English were prepared to sacrifice comfort to speed. The essential requirements of the Dutch *jacht* were stability at all speeds and a shallow draught to enable it to pass everywhere and to beach on any shore.

Amsterdam has admirable models of these small pleasure craft. They possess a discreet and powerful beauty which seems the apotheosis of the highest tradition, for most of them date from the eighteenth century and they hardly vary from the lines of their predecessors. The Dutch *jacht* was always full-bellied and normally clinker built because this gave the most solid and stable form of hull. It had a central cabin, particularly in the older vessels, for the motion is less noticeable in bad weather in the centre of the ship. A small skylight lit the cabin. Later, with progress in building, and when the owners grew more seasoned, the roof was carried aft to the stern in imitation of the English; but the most beautiful of them retained the central cabin.

Another interesting point. From the seventeenth century onwards, there appeared on the small ships, and in particular on the yachts, the jib, that important sail which the warships only adopted 150 years later!

* * *

With Tromp and De Ruyter, the Dutch navy reached the peak of its naval glory. French battles with the ships of the United Provinces were long and painful but were always marked with a reciprocal esteem exceeding the usual courtesy of the period: bullets were exchanged more often than smiles, but this mutual admiration made the battle worth while. Louis XIV presented his portrait, set in diamonds, to De Ruyter and the old

86. De Ruyter's Ship, 1666

sailor had himself painted wearing the collar of St. Michael on his cuirass. The most famous French seamen were pleased to pay him homage as the leading sailor of his age.

The ships in which this great admiral hoisted his flag were among the most important and the most heavily laden on the seas (86). They became so powerful and heavy that they could no longer enter port and the Dutch had to build a harbour to serve Amsterdam. When the ships of the fleet had to put in an appearance there they could only approach by the use of certain machines which typify Dutch tenacity: the camels (87). Two hollowed out pontoons shaped to fit a ship's bottom were immersed under the vessel to be transported and made fast beneath its vitals. The pontoons were then emptied by a pump

—there were about 50 on each—and thus, as though on a pedestal, the *Seven Provinces* or the *City of Haarlem*, loaded with booty, bedizened with flags and weighed down by the cannon

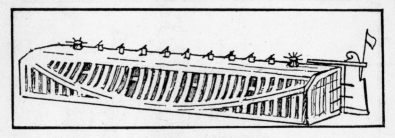

87. Camel for Raising Ships

balls embedded in her timbers, arrived in triumph at the banks of the Amstel.

In Holland all the scholars took an interest in ships and Dutch shipbuilding gave foremen and engineers to other navies anxious to perfect themselves. Peter the Great worked for several days in a shipyard in Zaandam until, in spite of his incognito, the hold really became too full of inquisitive spectators. We owe to the Dutchman Huyghens the spiral spring which, replacing the pendulum, made possible the naval chronometer and at the same time an approximate estimation of longitude.

Finally, Holland possessed the best marine artists of the north. Breughel left us some magnificent pictures and even if today they are considered a little too accurate and dry, it must be acknowledged that in maritime matters precision is the most admirable of faults. No seaman, even the would-be seaman, can help doffing his cap to the dynasty of the Van de Veldes, the first of whom, Adriaan, was the most sensitive, or being grateful to Backhuysen, rather smoky and severe, but the first to portray a fleet as though he were painting a brotherhood, with a detailed portrait of each brother. The Dutch ships were dark in colour. A certain Puritanism accounted for this and since the first marine painters belonged to the Netherlands, it was thought for a long time that all the old ships had been reduced to a cold sobriety, to sombre oak, a few plain mouldings or raised wales. On the evidence of Backhuysen, the French

LARGE ENGLISH CARRACK

By Boutewerk after Holbein. *Musée de la Marine, Paris*

PLATE X

BATTLE BETWEEN THE DU
By Van de

PLATE XI

ENGLISH FLEETS IN 1666

m Museum

VESSEL

Drawing by Pierre Puget. *Louvre*

PLATE XII

museum models were re-painted and we only realised much later that the curators had betrayed the gleaming hulls of the French squadrons with their whites and royal blues, giving them the colour of leather and spices to be found in the Dutch ships.

88. Small Galley, 1550

CHAPTER XV

France

THERE have always been great and glorious French sailors, but not always a French navy. If one wishes to make a broad generalisation, then it only appeared under Francis I. In actual fact this delay was quite logical. For many centuries France had no fixed naval frontiers. Normandy, recaptured in 1204, was immediately invaded and occupied by the English. Brittany was independent; Guyenne remained British and Provence was an appanage. From time to time the King of France managed to break through to the sea but alliances, dowries and also wars rapidly closed the coast to him. Moreover, he hired the greater part of his ships from maritime nations and only manned them with French crews. Furthermore, when artillery appeared, the heavy burden of a regular fleet did not seem so essential since it was easy to convert a merchantman into a man-of-war by installing a few cannon.

I must add, alas, that we French were never sea-minded despite the exploits of our captains and our corsairs. It was always said, 'The French gardener won't leave his lettuces.'

Our navigators and admirals, however, won a most flattering renown, Jean de Béthencourt, lord of Grainville-la-Teinturière, being one of the first to win fame by his quests and naval explorations. The ancient blood of the men of the north flowed

222

in his veins and setting sail from Dieppe in 1402 he colonised
the Canaries, which had already been discovered. He assumed
the title of King so that the great north-western province had
two monarchs; the King of the Canaries and the King of
Yvetot. Béthencourt was only an organiser, but his activities
were of great service to the age of discovery because of the safety

89. Jacques Coeur's *Nef*, 1450

he managed to give to long voyages. He really created a 'line'
between these remote islands and his Norman fatherland and
was thus able to demonstrate the advantages of colonisation
even at this uncertain period. He shipped 80 families from
Normandy and his stewardship would have been brilliant had
not the war destroyed it. In 1418 Béthencourt, fearing that the
Canaries would fall into the hands of the English, ceded them
to the King of Spain. French was spoken there for a long time.
Legend has it that Béthencourt originally intended to sail to
Florida and America, the New World—which the pilots of
Dieppe and Fécamp talked of long before Christopher

Columbus—under the aegis of the Templars who probably obtained the greater part of their disturbing wealth from there.

Thirty years later France claims the energetic Jacques Coeur, whose character and activities have always remained somewhat mysterious. His qualities as a financier, diplomat and merchant are known, but they were all born from a practical knowledge

90. L'Ecluse, 1340

of the sea. He became one of the last great ship-owner navigators (89). He brought precision and efficiency to maritime expansion, which was therefore far less precarious than might have been expected. Jacques Coeur kept up a fleet of merchantmen which was the source of his vast fortune. He was very much loved. When he was shamefully and quite unjustly accused and flung into gaol, his sailors rescued him. He died in action in 1456 leading a squadron against the Turks. Had Louis XI had a man like Jacques Coeur he would have done wonders on the sea, for this great experimental King sensed the possibilities in this field; but he possessed only three galleasses, two galleys and a few small cogs. However, his common-sense inspired him to lay the foundations of a Company on the lines of that which would later make the fortune of the Western countries.

* * *

As warriors, our admirals made history. Eustace the Monk, a

91. *Nef*, 1500

former Benedictine who turned corsair in the thirteenth century, for a long time contested the supremacy of England. He very nearly established the son of Philip Augustus on the English Throne. Philip the Fair blockaded England. At l'Ecluse (90), under Philip VI, we suffered a great naval defeat which opened France to the English, although it was a glorious battle. 'Buchet de l'Ecluse,' the treasurer Béhuchet, before being treacherously hanged as a pirate by the English, had himself wounded the King of England when the *Saint-Georges* attacked the *Thomas*. Queret, our admiral, was executed. Under Charles V

225

we pride ourselves on a great mariner: Jean de Vienne, his gold whistle round his neck, made London quake by burning everything as far up the river as Gravesend. A few Bretons, four brothers from Ploësquellec and four from Coëtivy, brought the Hundred Years' War to a glorious close; as, later, Jean de Porcon and Prégent de Bidoux, under Louis XIII, brought fame

92. *La Grande-Nau-Françoise*, born and died at Le Havre 1532–1533

to French skill and courage. Prégent de Bidoux was the only Frenchman to fight with Villiers de l'Isle-Adam during the famous siege of Rhodes. A great Breton, Hervé de Portzmoguer, called 'Primauguet', in August 1512 blew himself up in the famous *Cordelière*, at the same time destroying the *Regent*, the English ship which was the forerunner of the *Great Harry*.

*   *   *

The foundation of Le Havre, of 'Franciscopolis', by Francis I, is characteristic of the new French trends. In the future France

226

would have a Royal Navy for which she now laid down harbours and shipyards. The régime of hire was officially over, at least in theory. The country began to take an interest in great ships, though, as was always to be the case, only spasmodically. Francis I gave the order to build at Le Havre a man-of-war to eclipse the already almost legendary *Great Harry*. Tradition assures us that the gentleman-king suggested to his astonished engineers a ship twice as large as the *Great Harry*. In the prince's mind this probably meant that the carrack should be double the length of those which were the pride of the English navy: a giant ship for a giant king (Francis I was six foot six). But this would have meant an impossible tonnage, since volumes correspond to the cube of their dimensions. The engineers got round this by only bothering about the tonnage, so that the *Grande-Françoise* (92) reached 2,000 tons burden without exceeding the length of the model by more than a third. The king was very gently hoodwinked.

The speed of the construction goes to prove the skill of the French and their resources at this period. The keel was laid down in 1532 and she was finished in a year. She was built in Percanville Creek which is now the yacht basin at Le Havre.

She was the largest vessel afloat. We know few details but they indicate an exceptional strength, together with a quest for beauty which heralded the future lavishness of the fittings. The *Françoise* was a four-masted carrack. Her mainmast was twenty-five feet in girth, which meant a trunk nearly eight feet in diameter: it carried four tops and must have measured some 210 feet in height. She was the s.s. *Normandie* of the period. The shape is known: a fore and aftercastle with an open deck between. But, as in the case of the *Normandie*, luxury and comfort were carried to excess. She had been built as though she were to remain ashore. An impressive forge allowed all mechanical repairs to be carried out aboard; there was a baker's oven so that the crew could have fresh bread each day and better still, to avoid shipping flour, which easily deteriorates at sea, a windmill was erected in the bow. Between the castles, the engineers had provided a tennis court such as one finds on modern trans-Atlantic liners and to prevent the balls from falling into the sea and to protect it from the rain, a huge awning was stretched right over the waist.

There was a private chapel, entirely in gilt, where members of the King's religious house officiated and distributed consecrated bread to the faithful on Sundays. Order was ensured by Italian guards who directed the stream of visitors, for the ship aroused universal curiosity. It was never empty. People flocked in from all parts, not only from the neighbourhood, but from

93. Newfoundlander, Seventeenth Century

Paris and the distant provinces. They came in groups, in festive bands. They arranged meetings there. There were excursions by coach or by water. The ship gleamed with sumptuous decorations: a phoenix on the stern, and at the bow a statue of St. Francis, larger than life size. The salamander surrounded by flames, with the proud device: *Nutrisco et extinguo* (I feed on it and put it out), was greatly in evidence. The King appointed as Commander, Villiers de l'Isle-Adam, a nephew of the great Philippe.

She was probably built in a dry-dock to avoid launching, for accounts mention that to take her out the equinoctial tide (22nd or 23rd September, 1533) was chosen. All she managed to do, however, was to get half way across the harbour. The following day, as she was being towed seawards, she drifted into the estuary and fouled the famous Francis I tower—that dowager of Le Havre, with its diamond-shaped embossments, which was for so long a landmark in the grand harbour. Some sailors leaped onto the platform of the tower which was on a level with the upper gun-ports: this detail reveals the height of the carrack and its moonlike sheer. They had not yet reached the open sea. The *Grande-Nau-Françoise* came to a standstill at the end of the little dam protecting the north-west entrance. Everything was attempted to drag her off. An enormous girdle of barrels and hogsheads was attached under her sides; boats and sloops were unable to rescue or refloat her despite the advantageous conditions of Le Havre which had been chosen because the high tide lasts for two hours as a result of contrary currents.

They did not manage to get her across the bar and since they could not leave the passage blocked, she was brought back ignominiously to her berth. But on the 14th November, in a terrible north-easterly gale, the carrack, insufficiently shored or top-heavy from her enormous superstructures, capsized. She could not be raised again and, like the s.s. *Paris* a few years ago, she remained there for a long time on her side. At last she was broken up. The St. François quarter was built from her timbers.

Le Havre appears to be fatal to our huge ships. The big carrack, the 100-gun *Philippe*, was built there; she was destroyed by fire in 1545 during a naval review by Francis I of the troops destined to invade England. The fire started during a banquet given by the King to the officers and their ladies. The galleys saved the treasure and fled before the menace of the loaded guns which, in the conflagration, hurled their cannon balls at the fleet. The *Philippe* sank in the midst of 25 galleys and the 150 tall ships which formed the French invasion fleet under the orders of Claude d'Annebault. A sad omen which subsequently came true: the squadron never managed to engage the British home fleet. But these vessels and this concentration were a proof of our new strength.

*   *   *

From the early part of the sixteenth century, we have to record exploits by the French in the field of discovery. Already our Norman and Breton sailors boasted with justification that they had been the first to land in Brazil. Honfleur became one of the busiest centres of discovery. In 1503 the *Espoir*, a little ship from Honfleur, under the command of Gonneville, discovered the Southern Indies, but the Portuguese possessed the rights to them by Papal approval. The Bretons were well acquainted with Newfoundland and had fished there since 1450. The fishing was done from the deck and the men sheltered in wicker niches along the bulwarks (93a, a).

In the same century our ships played a great role as pioneers, admittedly under Italian captains, at the expense of the big Lyons business houses which fitted out their merchantmen at Le Havre. Next appeared the Seigneur de Varengeville, whose manor still exists today, Jean Ango, Viscount of Dieppe. Like Drake, he declared his private war and, in reply to Portuguese atrocities on his sailors, blockaded Lisbon with 30 ships equipped at his own expense. Ango was an astonishing character. Princely, humanistic and Christian, he seemed determined to get the very best out of life. And finally Jacques Cartier, the stubborn, dreamy, but rather too imaginative sailor from St. Malo, who went in search of precious metals in the 'New Isles' and penetrated the St. Lawrence. There, thinking he had found a gold and diamond mine above ground, he loaded his ships with talc, mica and copper and returned immediately to France, spied upon by every pirate on the sea. He had discovered new France but neither nuggets nor gems, and his mistake was so jeered at that his glassware was soon known as 'Canadian diamonds'. Moreover, his prestige and that of colonial discovery were tarnished for half a century—a delay by which others knew how to profit. Our expedition to Brazil, to uphold Catherine de Medici's claim, also came to grief with the defeat of Philip Strozzi the Magnificent, the Queen's cousin, whom the Marquis of Santa Cruz conquered off the Azores and flung into the water like a common scoundrel.

*　　*　　*

The ship became more intelligent and generalised. Lateen sails were completely abandoned by the big ships, except in the stern, and for long expeditions even the small vessels no longer carried them. Magellan used square rig. Vessels were modelled

on the English galleon and usually carried three masts, the
foremast and mainmast being almost equal in height, and the
very much smaller mizzen merely tall enough to carry a triangular sail. The topsails were now quite rigid—the Normans

94. The Siege of La Rochelle. Tall Ships, after Callot

called them *jeannettes* in memory of the Portuguese Joanete who
had been the first to rig them, still mobile and flapping, by
lengthening the tall mainmast. The mast which carried them—
the topmast—was fixed on all northern ships. It was a quarter
the height of the mainmast. The mass use of cannon had necessitated the use of topsails in battle, the sails thus remaining
completely out of range of fire. In the Breton battle of Pertuis

against the citizens of La Rochelle, in 1625, all the ships furled their lower sails. The galleys struck all sail and sent down their masts. The bowsprit was lengthened but was still used only to carry the spritsail and, above all, to give support to the masts. But it was not so easy to get rid of the Spanish fashions and their mania for castles. No one had the courage to copy British sobriety to the full. The French ships still had large citadels. One can even say that at the end of the sixteenth century a new fashion arose for high sterns (94).

Henry II continued the paternal work but Richelieu, more than Francis I, was the main founder of the French navy. He was driven to this originally in order to fight against Spain, then against England and the Protestants; and, finally, against the citizens of La Rochelle who, in their fortress town, possessed experience and a high degree of naval audacity. In 1626 the great Cardinal took control of the different jurisdictions which had previously been distributed along the coasts among several admirals who were invariably jealous of each other and played the most monstrous tricks from which only the country suffered. He appointed himself Grand-Master, chief and superintendent of shipping.

He grouped around himself a board of directors composed of six old sailors, including his uncle, Amador de la Porte (I believe his monument is in the Louvre), Commander of Malta. We find once more the profound influence of the famous naval order to which the new ships would be entrusted.

The Cardinal divided the French forces into two groups: the western in the North Sea and the eastern in the Mediterranean. He carried out a far reaching enquiry into French resources, found employment for the coastal populations, put various commercial companies on their feet, and decreed that any French gentleman might engage in maritime trade without it being considered derogatory. In this way he created new subsidies and opened an inexhaustible bank for the great families, many of whose fortunes came from the sea. However, he forbade any workman or French sailor, naval shipwright or fisherman to serve anyone but the King of France, thus inaugurating that policy of recruitment which later, under Colbert, would start the real system of naval enrolment. In 1595 Henry IV had only half a dozen vessels and Marseilles possessed a couple of dilapidated galleys. In 1642 Brézé, the Cardinal's nephew, was in command off Barcelona of 40 tall ships and 22 galleys, all French-built and French-manned.

*   *   *

Richelieu had approached the naval problem with ruthless efficiency. As a first step he turned his attention to the harbours and shipyards—Le Havre in the north, Brest in the west (the

95. The Siege of La Rochelle

latter port being put into commission again); Brouage in the south-west and Toulon in the south. Marseilles, already an ancient port, kept its galleys, but Toulon sheltered large sailing ships which were now in their heyday. First class shipwrights were lacking or were extremely difficult to find. Most of them were simple artisans who transmitted their secrets from father to son—secrets of routes as well as how to draw, to build and to use the materials. Unable to call upon England or Spain, who were both enemies, the Cardinal sent for Dutch builders and immediately produced prototypes, while the siege of La Rochelle, for which he had chartered ships from Dunkirk to Bayonne, allowed him an overall review of French ships.

The siege of La Rochelle (94, 95, 96) increased even more Richelieu's determination to build a powerful navy. This attack, so resolutely and so cruelly led, has often quite unjustifiably pained the admirers of the great Cardinal. They overlook the harm done by the Protestant corsairs, even on their own, before they had called for aid from the British fleet. The Rochelois were enemies of their own country and viewed in the light of their times their insolence was intolerable.

Already, under Henry IV, France had tried to take the town
—a nest of insurgents sheltering beneath the cloak of religion—
but her sailors had been undaunted. One must judge by the
following details. In 1617 four of her captains blockaded
Bordeaux; in 1621 the corsairs of La Rochelle attacked any
King's ship that sailed along the coast of Aunis. In 1625

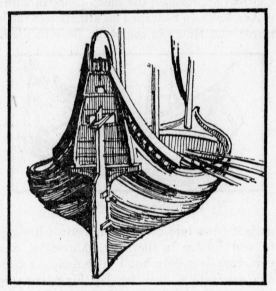

96. La Rochelle, 1627, Half-Galley

Benjamin de Rohan-Soubise entered the Blavet where ships
were being built for the King and carried off six of the largest.
On the way he seized the isles of Ré and Oléron. It can be seen,
then, that the Cardinal was justified in his reprisals and that he
was compelled to take naval action against privateer attacks.
On the 1st November, 1627, All Saints' Day, when La Rochelle
surrendered, after a siege of a year, Richelieu presented the King
with a naval programme which would ensure France a navy
that could hold its own against any country.

*   *   *

The siege brought to light an artist who remains one of our
best marine draughtsmen. Jacques Callot, whose royal draw-

ings record the efforts of both sides, portrayed the movements of fleets; the camps, the redoubts and the fortifications. He drew in great detail the ships of the period, both English and French, which were now indistinguishable except for their flags.

The high-charged ship was *de rigueur* (98). This was due to the tumble-home which became obligatory with the increase in fire

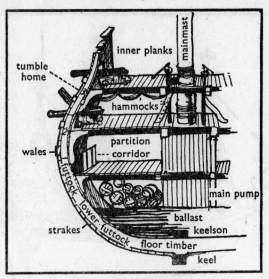

97. Cross Section showing the Mainmast

power. Tumble-home is the waisting of the upperworks to bring the weight of the batteries nearer to the centre of gravity. It already existed to some extent in the *nef*, but it was accentuated and after the seventeenth century assumed great importance. Thenceforward, there was no other type of construction. The result was a sheering of the sterns, an increase in their height, for the natural shape, starting from the tumble-home, tended to compress and to taper them almost to a point. In the ships of the first half of the seventeenth century, it was impossible for three men to stand side by side on the extreme end of a man-of-war's poop. However, it made a very favourable post of command and also a military strongpoint. On the other hand, the tall stern made the ship keener and more determined to hug the wind; in case of complete dismasting the vessel's stern brought her to the wind and she did not fall across the seas.

Tumble-home (97) made boarding more difficult, for even when the ships came alongside each other their upper decks were more than ten feet apart. Another effect was increased seaworthiness even when the ship was hove-to, the curved side diminishing the shock of the waves. This design was discussed until the middle of the nineteenth century when it became

98. The *Couronne*, 1638, according to the most modern reconstruction

obsolete, although it still had many partisans who were neither old-fashioned nor blockheads. Certain grave vices of many fine ships were attributed to their 'straight walls' (for example, the instability under sail of the famous *Valmy*).

*　　*　　*

Two French men-of-war raised the reputation of the French shipyards sky-high—a new reputation they were never to lose: the *Royal* and particularly the *Couronne* (98), the work of the master shipwright Morieu, of Dieppe. The *Couronne* was built at

236

La Roche-Bernard at the mouth of the Vilaine and has to be mentioned in any history of sail; she was specifically French and set the fashion for all the other navies. This was the first sign of that creative faculty which would put France at the head of material progress, though in theory only, for she combines inertia with disorder to such an extent that she has never known how to profit by her discoveries.

The *Couronne* exceeded 2,000 tons burden, but her size was nothing compared with the logicality of her planning both in-board and outboard, her efficiency and manœuvrability. When she arrived to join the fleet in the Bay of Biscay, she stupefied the old whalers who did not believe it possible that a ship of this build, so heavily armed, could still hold the wind. She put about like a caique and carried a weight of guns that had never been seen before. She sported a mainmast of 216 feet and offered 12,000 square yards of canvas to the wind. She was a 72-gun ship.

The *Couronne* had been royally planned, on a grand scale. Richelieu, in an epic manner, had ordered that the great cabin should be larger than the principal apartment of the King in his Louvre, and this served as the point of departure. The ward-room was 30 feet long and 18 feet wide. Onto the sides were built those galleries we saw on the English galleon, so that the room could easily hold 100 persons. Barbicans jutted out along the stern, relieving the heaviness of the poop. Nothing was spared as regards magnificence. The white silk flag em-broidered with the arms of France, countless *fleurs de lys* and coats of arms, was presented by the Queen, who spent 14,000 crowns from her privy purse. Only the Duchesse de Rohan complained. She considered this 'edifice' mediocre, although it had cost her husband a whole forest.

A remarkable characteristic of the *Couronne* was her long head, of English origin, but which had been lowered still fur-ther to allow the gunners to fire at water level and ahead, in order to repel galleys which would never risk her broadsides. The head ended in a figurehead portraying an allegorical Hercules killing the Hydra. The St. Francis of the *Grande-Nau* had been an anomaly but these figureheads were now in current use. In France they applied rather ingenuously to the name of the ship. In Spain a lion was carried, which the English used as a support for the Royal coat of arms or the portrait of the King in a medallion. In Venice a bust of a woman was usual.

The *Couronne* was born in 1638. She was the result of a kind of joust between France and England who had just launched at Woolwich the *Sovereign of the Seas*. Phineas Pett, the shipwright

99. The *Grand Saint-Louis*, Flagship, 1646

who created her with the aid of his son Peter, did not manage to equal the power or the quality of the *Couronne*. The Petts produced a ship of 1,637 tons burden and it was a pleasant conceit on the part of the designers that the capacity and the year of launching (1637) should coincide.

She carried more guns than the *Couronne* and was the first of the northern ships to be a complete three-decker, whereas the Frenchman had only two. It is true that they were obliged to scrap one, and that the English vessel sailed with reduced sails aloft, being distantly related to the Spanish ships. The figure-head represented King Edward trampling no less than seven Kings beneath his charger's hooves. Not a single foot of the superstructure escaped the decorators, so that the Dutch called her the *Golden Devil*. But she was very heavy.

She cost £40,000, of which £10,000 was for decoration. The *Couronne* cost half a million French *livres*, just two-thirds of this price.

* * *

The big ships of this period have some peculiarities which allow them to be dated to within 20 years. Firstly the deck, which was covered with a perforated roof, reminiscent of the carracks. This was sometimes a sort of wooden trellis with large meshes—very apparent on the *Grand St. Louis* (99), the flagship of France (1646), and on the *Sovereign*—over which the sailors

100. Man-of-War, 1650

passed fore and aft. There was no actual barbette battery. The rigging itself was specialised. The stays resembled very thick ducks' feet which made the masting look over loaded, but at the same time elegant since the eye is attracted by the multiple ropes all running from the same central point. This feature was designed to distribute strain over several points. It disappeared in 1660. Finally, after 1640, the spritsail flaunted at the extremity of an oblique spar (100*a*), a small, well-secured spar which carried a sail important for manœuvring, a little vertical mast stuck into a small top. At the same time, to compensate for this eccentric sail, the mizzen also carried a topsail above the lateen yard. In 1628, on Callot's plates, this rig did not exist (the modern English put a spritsail on their Jacobite vessels), but in December 1643 all Brézé's men-of-war were equipped with it.

*   *   *

Colbert put into practice the ideas of Richelieu and his efforts on behalf of the navy place him in the ranks of our greatest ministers. The obstinate fight he put up until his death (he was killed on the battlefield) was justified by its results, In 1661, when he began, he was faced with a score of dilapidated, rotting hulks, almost without crews, lying in silted-up docks. When Colbert died France had 270 ships and nearly 60,000 sailors. However, the minister did not live to see the crowning achievement of his great efforts since he had been dead nine years when Tourville won the famous battle of Beachy Head over the Anglo-Dutch fleet, thus upsetting the naval balance of the day. This was the work of a man, or rather two men, for his son Seignelay, too, was worthy of great admiration and of the gratitude of all sailors. Colbert remained the punctilious minister and politician; Seignelay wanted to see for himself and take command and in his keenness, which was sometimes exaggerated, often choleric and excessive, he is one of the most sympathetic figures of the seventeenth century. Madame de Sévigné compared him with 'a young and gay Bacchus who will conquer the Indies'. She called him 'Splendour'.

Colbert had to start from scratch both with ships and recruitment. For the ships he summoned shipwrights from everywhere and had vessels built in the big foreign shipyards, which were only too eager to carry out his orders. Holland was his largest supplier both in ships and men. She had a tradition of high quality. Richelieu had also called upon many master ship-wrights from the United Provinces, certain of whom brought a whole team of workers with them. In our ports could be seen families who continued to speak their own language and to observe their own customs. But, in addition, there were excellent native recruits such as the Hubacs, the Coulombs, the Chapelles,

101. Warship of Louis XIV, 1680

the Honorats and the Rodolphes, who, joining their skill and taste to the technique of the newcomers, managed to create a French type of ship (101). Jan de Wert, for example, from Holland, and Blasio Pangello from Naples, found worthy associates and emulators who already possessed a certain doctrine of their own.

Next came the ports, the arsenals, the factories, forests to be managed and exploited. The effect of creating an active navy is to encourage the whole country, its industry and even its commercial policy. This period, however, was very fortunate in not having to negotiate for oil; they had only to sow fields of hemp to obtain motive power for the fleet. But, on the other hand, what trouble was caused when, instead of merely signing a contract, they had to interfere with the customs and routine of an industrial and peasant economy in a society where every man, beneath the appearances of legal absolutism, remained so implacably master in his own house! The struggle for tar shows what difficulties the Minister weathered.

Modern Toulon really dates from Colbert, who ordered Vauban to build a port capable of receiving a hundred large ships. Rochefort was a new creation. Lorient was designed to ensure the traffic of the Companies—which were also organised and subsidised—for the flag of trade inevitably follows the flag of war. When Colbert assumed his naval apostolate he could search in all our harbours and only round up 200 sea-going merchantmen, compared with the 10,000 possessed by Holland and 4,000 by England.

As regards crews, he inaugurated a system of rating by which all the fishermen and sailors were classified, enrolled and bound in the King's service. Every five years they had to serve one year in a warship. Between their periods of service they were indemnified by half-pay and enjoyed special privileges. This was only a partial success for since their pay was often in arrears, the sailors were quick to sign on in merchantmen. Recruitment before Colbert, of course, had been through the press gang. The 'press' usually closed a port and picked up all the sailors to be found ashore. Force was used and it is understandable that there were many desertions. Finally, as regards officers, the minister created the *Gardes Marines*, young men of good family who were taught ashore and in ships with a view to appointment to the naval staff.

* * *

But Colbert had to compete more with contempt than with general inertia. At the close of his Ministry the navy and the naval officer had risen to first rank in national esteem, but before him the sailor in France was considered as a kind of robber and perhaps the most dangerous type of robber. The navy merely served to get rid of 'bad hats'. This attitude persisted well into the nineteenth century: when a boy caused his family too much trouble, he was threatened with the sea or embarked as a midshipman. The navy was the scarecrow and the ship was the bogyman. However, at the sight of Colbert's brilliant, well-organised fleets, the integrity of his quartermasters and the courtesy of his officers, everything changed. He knew how to foster an *esprit de corps*. With Tourville's aid, the French warship became the most resplendent and best of its age; the officers formed an *élite*, a nursery from which sprang our naval type. The French naval officer is still a man of quality, respected not only by his own countrymen but by the most jealous of the other nations.

This result was not easy to achieve, particularly as the King remained to a large extent indifferent, if not actually hostile, to the navy. Only once did he visit a ship of the line—the Chevalier de Lhéry's *Entreprenant* at Dunkirk—and when he received Louvois' proposals for better conditions for the men, he considered the Minister's demands exorbitant. Part of the splendour displayed in the ships of the line was due to this antipathy. It was hoped that the prince would take pleasure in them and consider his fleets as branches of his palaces. In vain: after La Hogue, considering the navy a failure, Louis XIV gradually lost interest in his squadrons.

*   *   *

The naval scene had changed. The Mediterranean was no longer the centre of the maritime world; the Atlantic, and with it the tall ship and the square sail, was supreme. The Mediterranean even today has managed to preserve individual shapes and rigging, but only in her coasting vessels and fishing fleet. In the seventeenth century the last remaining lateen-rigged vessel was the galley and this was condemned for all practical purposes after that memorable date 10th July, 1664, when, near the Isle of Elba, the *Le Bon* stood up to 37 Spanish galleys. The galley, under the *Roi Soleil*, achieved unparalleled perfection and luxury but its day was over.

France set the tone and led the fashion in European ships. Unhampered by traditions or conventions, she incorporated the improvements evolved by other navies, merely adding her own particular genius and her inventive faculties. The French ship was a mixture of Dutch and English. The ideal aimed at was Dutch solidity and English lightness. Spanish influence was ignored except as regards luxury, that luxury which would take 200 years to die and which defended itself as hotly as did the dazzling uniforms. Men were prouder to fight

102. The *Réale*, 1680

in a vessel that combined art and science than in a tar-bucket. The beauty of a ship is a moral stimulus. Courage is composed of the most delicate elements.

* * *

The French ship was remarkable for its moderation and its trimness: no trace of the Dutchman's hippopotamus beam or of brutal English stiffness. It had a sea-going line. It floated instead of cleaving the water (101). The stern was still raised and

244

the bows lowered but this was achieved with the balance of a
water bird; the ship of Louis XIV seems to have been designed
more for stability than for speed. Its trim could be seen at first

103. The *Soleil-Royal*
Burnt at Cherbourg on May 31, 1692, after Barfleur

glance. One felt that it could carry sail and resist the wind
without needing too much ballast. It was a great consumer
of knots, a quality which is expressed by a French proverb:
Grand rouleur, grand marcheur.

Two French vessels epitomise the great period of shipbuilding
under Louis XIV; for the tall ship, the *Soleil Royal* (103) and
for the low vessel, the *Réale* (102). It is a pleasure to reproduce
these beautiful craft.

There were four *Soleil Royal*s in the French fleet, but here I
shall mention only two, the one, the most sumptuous, laid down
in 1669 and broken up in '89 and the other, the most beautiful,
Tourville's ship, which was burnt at Cherbourg after Barfleur. Duquesne, from a love of contradiction, perhaps grossly
underrated the former by keeping her as a prison ship at the

104. Quarter-galleries of a Three-Decker, 1725

entrance to Brest harbour. Colbert had ordered her to be re-
gilded and painted sky blue like a reliquary to inspire his
sovereign with a taste for ships. The second *Soleil Royal* was
merely painted grey, but her carving was much more important
and beautiful, as was also her design. Tourville, who loved
her, tried to provide her with all the naval qualities. She was a
three-decker, with, in addition, a quarterdeck and poop. She
had been given ports for 110 guns but never carried more than
104. One can see with what care her sea trials must have been
carried out since it was decided to decrease the artillery on this
unit which was to become a prototype of the powerful French
warship. The lower battery consisted of thirty 48-pounders, the
largest calibre used at the time. Her second battery had thirty-
two 18-pounders. At the outset two 48-pounders and four
18-pounders were removed to lighten her, but this still did not
satisfy the engineers, for her 48 battery was exchanged for 36's.

These guns were in *fonte verde*, a green bronze with the patina
preserved, bronze composed of old bells, red Swedish copper,
yellow copper and pure tin. The soft iron cannon, cast at
Ruelle in the factory created by Colbert, was considered less

honourable. A vice-admiral carried only bronze and insisted upon it as soon as he took command of his ship. These admirable pieces of artillery, chased and embossed and gleaming on red carriages with dolphins for handles, bore the device of a full sun and the words *Ultima ratio regum*, 'the last argument of kings.' But the artillery had definitely abandoned its picturesque names;

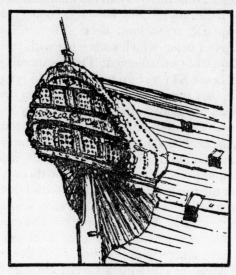

105. Stern, 1600

no more culverins which suited so well the long pieces of the galleys, the bow-chasers on movable carriages; no more *passe-volants*, basilisks or falconets, merely numbers corresponding to the weight of the cannon balls. Of all this ancient nomenclature, there only remained the perrier, a small piece mounted on a pivot and lashed to the bulwarks or the tops. This had no calibre because it was stuffed with anything that came to hand, even stones.

Ornament on ships was restricted to two main points, the bows and the stern (105). In the case of the flagships these were joined by a band, a painted and carved stripe. The head was shortened and turned into a beak. The *Sovereign* (it was still afloat and Seignelay had visited and studied it) seemed ridiculous with this long, useless protuberance. The French ships, followed by all the others, had already replaced the forecastle with a forecastle deck that showed no obvious elevation, at least from outboard. Above the cutwater rose the beakhead, like a Bourbon nose, and French sailors ever since have called it their 'nasal appendage'. It formed a curved spur which carried the figurehead, an important piece of sculpture. In the case of the first *Soleil Royal* it was a seahorse ridden by Glory, sporting butterfly wings. From there to join the bulkhead ran three open curves, large handrails forming bulwarks connected by vertical stanchions—quarter stanchions. These were joined to the bulkhead by a carved beam which connected with the supports of the bow, also richly ornamented. The outstanding feature of these rails in Louis XIV's reign was their rigid symmetry. Seen from the side, they presented a curve which later on, when they rose to the level of the forecastle, would also run down as far as the lower deck. This allowed the use of bow guns on the beakhead frame, the beakhead bulkhead ending the bows.

The ornamental band was on a level with the main deck and pierced with gun ports, of which there were three types: simple bull's-eyes on the quarterdecks, windows with bowed lintels on the upper deck, while in the British ships they were framed with round fillets or wreaths. The two upper rows were without port lids because they were set too high to need them, but those of the lower decks were square with port lids. Later the red lining of the lids was edged in gilt with a carved gilt *fleur-de-lys* in the centre. Curved ledges reinforced the whole, gilded or black wales more boldly sheered than the decks, so that the ports eventually cut them towards the stern. This gradually decreased in the eighteenth century, when the vessel tended to become flatter.

We arrive at the magnificently complicated poop with a quarter-gallery and three storeys with windows. A large bracket secured it to the hull and its first storey began at the second deck. These storeys corresponded with the balconies which gave so rich an appearance to the stern, with their glittering windows and the vigour of their carved marine deities, giants and famous men. Three balconies on the second *Soleil Royal* served as great cabin, wardroom, and the private quarters of the Captain. Above, to replace the Holy image on the Spanish and the earlier French ships, was an Apollo driving his quadriga, very cunningly placed since the bas-relief was seen head-on.

But one should examine this profusion of sculpture on the

drawings and not on the models, for the model-builders in their struggle with reduced size altered the proportions and exaggerated this decoration. The effect is overpowering. Actually it was infinitesimal compared with the grandeur of the hull. All this extra wood did not weigh half as much as a medium anchor and to the eye was completely harmonious and by no means ostentatious. The sculpture was so detailed that it resembles a bronze bas-relief forming half pillars rather than round supports, so great was the respect for proportion. The taffrail was adorned with three gigantic lanterns of crystal and gilded copper. The Admiral carried a fourth at the masthead.

* * *

The masting of the Louis XVI ship was immature compared with the hull. The rigging remained heavy and rather clumsy. The components of the masts, which were in three pieces, were not sufficiently inter-related. One feels that the ship could be very quickly dismasted. The blocks were heavy, like huge black coconuts, and overloaded the rigging. The tops remained in the tradition of the old navy, circular and in the form of shallow baskets. To prevent the topsail getting foul below, the topmast was joined to the stay by a typical device which was soon to disappear, the crowfoot (106) and its brails. That profusion of stays so common during the first part of the century, has almost disappeared. It survives only for the lift of the mizzen yard, the mizzen brails and the backstays of the spritsail topmast. Finally —and this is very remarkable—the yard braces, the ropes which contact the angle of the yards, lead to the stays and not to the rigging so that one sees them hanging down rather untidily between the masts. The aim of this arrangement was to ensure the suppleness of the whole. The mast was painted in black and white rings, the yards were black.

A new ship appeared, the bomb ketch (106), designed by Petit-Renaud and tried out by Tourville. The frigate had as yet no official status.

The Musée de la Marine possesses, in addition to the bas-reliefs of the woodwork, the most beautiful model in existence of the galley *Réale*. It must delight the heart of any boy and shows to what state of perfection this 5,000-year-old warship type had been brought. The galley had become a complete and definite type. Nothing more could be done to it, whereas the round ship continued to develop for another 200 years. It is the ship of the commander of the galleys. The flagship came later, like the *Sultane* and the *Capitano* of the Barbary pirates. In the seventeenth and even in the eighteenth centuries the galley was

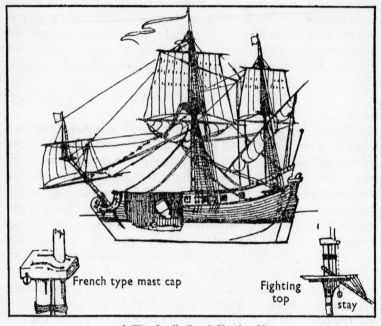

French type mast cap

Fighting top

stay

106. The *Cruelle*, Bomb Ketch, 1680

the prerogative of officers of noble birth. The general in command of galleys was much more than a vice-admiral. Under Louis XIV, the obese and witty Duc de Vivonne, Madame de Montespan's brother, showed himself to be worthy of the tradition. Toulon owed its elegance to being near Marseilles where the galleys rode at anchor. It became the fashionable port, the snob port. It has remained so. In the navy of olden days, to describe the naval qualities of Brest and the advantages of Toulon, they used to say: 'At Brest one *sails*, but at Toulon one *climbs*.' A little of the luxury which had been introduced into the round ships in the Colbert spirit must have been intended to compete with the galleys and attract the gentry.

But the craze for galleys also originated from the fact that they needed far less nautical knowledge. A nodding acquaintance and a little temerity were enough. The officer was only concerned with the battle: a good cavalry colonel would have made an excellent captain for the *Perle* or the *Arrogante*. Some old shell-back from Marseilles took charge of the crew and the wind was of little account. They fought with sails furled and topmasts struck. No knowledge of hydrography or navigation was needed. The galley hardly ever lost sight of the coast and courses were set by guesswork.

The *Réale* was 150 feet long and the others between 126 and 135. French construction had acquired such a reputation that the Knights of Malta demanded French galleys. Nothing was left to chance or to the fantasy of an engineer. Each piece of wood employed bore a name, a standard pattern and even a weight. The exact number of nails needed in construction was known. Although Venice had produced some measure of standardisation in her arsenal, Colbert achieved it entirely. It was brought to such a pitch that when the Marseilles arsenal was ordered to assemble a galley in 24 hours, the navy estimated 14 and actually carried out the work in 7!

*   *   *

The main differences from its forerunner, the sixteenth century galley, were greater solidity and increased lightness resulting from the sheer (107), with the admirable up-tilted line which is one of the prerequisites of superior navigability and at the same time a precaution against the craft breaking its back; the fore and after parts have a tendency to hog, receiving less support from the water because of their slenderness, and the sheer, by accentuating a contrary arc, managed to preserve a balance. Thus, protected against flexion, the timbers can be reduced to save weight. The great master of this new line was Chabert of Toulon and Marseilles. He devised a series of patterns of such variety that one has to see them assembled to understand their cut and to grasp their continuity.

This vessel achieved a maximum of speed and seaworthiness for its tonnage, and although it was despised by certain great seamen of the seventeenth century, this was only because with it their nautical skill was set at nought by dandies lacking naval instruction. Tourville realised that five galleys could catch a sailing ship without exposing themselves to anything but a salvo from the stern gun ports, which did not amount to very much.

Even in a rather heavy sea they still kept up the pursuit and in spite of their slender lines managed to carry sail, thanks not

107. Galley, 1680

only to their movable ballast, which they placed to windward, but also to their oars. The oars were taken in to leeward but the more venturesome sailors even risked rowing on this side to act as counterweight. In a stiff breeze and a moderate sea it was futile to chase them even under sail for their lateen sails could be sheeted in in a manner forbidden to square sails.

The seventeenth century galley introduced an important development with the rembate, an upper deck which covered and protected the battery and gave to the musketeers and the boarding troops a place where they could wait. A musketeer stood between each oar but the majority of the attackers formed up on the rembate.

The battery was standardised: no more calibres left to the whim of the captain. It remained rudimentary, however: a bow gun, the central 36-pounder, two 9-pounder bastards and two 4-pounder medium guns—all of them on fixed carriages as in the Middle Ages, to be aimed in unison with the ship itself by the helmsman, on the principle of the modern fighter plane. The four helmsmen in a galley were all qualified gunners. The attack took place after five salvoes from the specialist gunners, two, at the most, from the ordinary seamen. Then they went in to board. But, lying so low in the water, one can understand the disadvantage they suffered when they had to attack high ships. Finally they built inclined planes for the oars, but to use a 33- to 36-foot oar is no child's play (the oars reached just over 41 feet in the case of the *Réale*).

The galley was essentially a hull, a spindle, bearing a long square platform, and the *talar* where the men rowed; in the bows forward of the rembate, the little triangular space terminating in the ram, a long decorative arrow; further aft the *espale*, an open space following the benches just forward of the deck cabin, the staff quarters; between the benches, a long narrow catwalk along which the galley sergeant ran with his cat-o'-nine-tails. The deck cabin, instead of being a heavy sentry box, had become an arbour. On vertical walls half the height of a man were mounted arches, trellis-work covered in waxed cloth against the rain and against the sun by a lofty rectangular awning. The cabin allowed all manner of luxury in the way of sculpture and hangings.

The galley had only one deck; each compartment, each hold, had its own hatch. The quarters were rudimentary. They were funk-holes, stuck away in the stern and the dandies found them very uncomfortable. Actually no one lay down, they slept on the benches—the galley slaves on their thwarts, the officers on the benches of the cabin and the musketeers on the open deck.

The *Réale* carried only two masts, two 'trees' which could be lowered onto the deck, although this was hardly ever done. For convenience and to prevent fouling the mainmast, the foremast was stepped slightly to port. Enormous yards twice as long as the masts allowed the big mainsail and foresail—the largest sails then carried—to be hoisted and take advantage of the Mediterranean wind (there were no reefs; the sails were changed to suit the weather).

The galleys became raiders. The crews could not remain

aboard for long. They only went to sea from St. Urban's to St. Michael's Day, from the 18th May to the 29th September. It was rare to spend a night aboard: when this occurred the officers spent it gambling, drinking and smoking in the cabin. They smoked and perfumed themselves outrageously because of the stench of these fine warships. The galley was, as a matter of fact, far less evil-smelling than has been maintained; but it is certain that the smell of 300 men sweating in the sun, mingled with the odour of food rich with garlic, must have been horrible. It was a warm and infectious stench of which the officers got the benefit in their quarters when the crew rowed against the wind. True they relied as much as possible on the wind and used oars only for leaving port and in battle. The galley slaves were reserved for increases of speed.

*   *   *

I should like to say a few words about these slaves, although they have been dealt with many times before, and I want only to record my personal views in this book.

The principle of the galley slave is undoubtedly what repels us most in the old days—days which are not so very far distant, for in the nineteenth century the Italian States still equipped galleys. We find in it traces of the most ancient form of slavery, not the more or less good-natured compulsion enforced upon the negroes, but an absolute contempt for life and for humanity such as Rameses or Darius entertained; the oarsman was the human beast of burden. This represented a complete denial of one's duty towards one's neighbour, that Christian precept which was to revolutionise the world and which will one day, perhaps, render it uninhabitable by the confusion it will cause.

As soon as a man arrived on the galley benches he no longer had a soul, a spirit or a heart: only a back and a pair of arms. He became an automatic cog in a machine which must not be allowed to lose its power. He was beaten to death, unchained and then flung overboard as a broken tool. It needed a Saint, a St. Vincent de Paul, to bring a little humanity into the lives of these human automatons, but this was harmful to the rhythm of the oars and the captains looked upon him as an agitator.

There were three sources of recruitment: prisoners of naval warfare taken as reprisal for the customs of the Barbary corsairs; men condemned in common law, and volunteers, known as *bonnes-voglies*, or 'bow-oars'. The latter kept their moustaches and even if their heads were shaved for the sake of hygiene, they were chained only during combat. The Mohammedan prisoners—the Turks were the best and it is from their calm vigour that we have the old expression, 'as strong as a Turk'—kept a long lock of hair on the top of their shaved skulls, a distinction of which they were very jealous and which was stipulated in the treaties with the Porte. They were chained to criminals who had neither beard nor hair and whose heads were smoothed with sandpaper. Subconsciously, this indignity was resented for a very long time. A man who was entirely plucked immediately felt that his self-respect had been wounded: convict skull! The red convict bonnet also came from the galleys. The slaves wore it on parade.

The revocation of the Edict of Nantes enormously increased the horror of the oar. Men of honour, who preferred martyrdom to apostasy, were herded with thieves and murderers. One has only to read the poignant document written by Jean Marteilhe, Protestant and galley slave. It is possible that this infamous treatment of men of quality was the cause of disaffection in the galleys and the end of their prestige which took place in the eighteenth century and which ruined them.

*   *   *

The wars of Louis XIV were waged in support of the Grand Monarch's continental policy: the trade wars belong to the eighteenth century. In France they brought to light first-class seamen of two types, the regulars and the corsairs; two groups who have always trodden on each other's toes but who were established in their prerogatives and in their special functions during the eighteenth century.

The King's two greatest admirals were Duquesne and Tourville. They impressed Europe by their valour and skill: no British admiral of the period achieved the same repute, nor can one quote a Spaniard to compare with them. A part of their learning, however, came from a Dutchman whom they had defeated, De Ruyter, the son of a cordwainer from Flushing, a town which was the counterpart of St. Malo or Dunkirk for naval warfare and Dutch privateering. Thanks to these three sailors, naval combat under sail and the art of navigation left the realm of empiricism. Naval science developed side by side with naval art and brought it, along with its uncertainties, even more liberty and imagination.

De Ruyter remains the patron saint of seamen. He was the epitome of the Dutch character, a mixture of joviality and will-power, gentleness and the most terrifying aggressiveness, intuitive science and stark reasoning. In every good Dutchman there is a mixture of the dreamy philosopher and the mad dog. He is slow, patient and thoughtful, but as soon as he loses his patience, is ready for action and sure of what he wants, he is a dangerous man to thwart.

Duquesne was brilliant, with all the intemperance and awkwardness of a genius. He stuffed his superior's instructions into his pocket (nevertheless Colbert continued to write to him with constant admonitions), and harried the quarter-masters and the stewards. He was a Protestant and was amused at having acquired the title of Marquis in spite of the persecution. He was magnificent and ignoble, with the face of a drunken cod-fisher. He knew only one master, '*Monsieur le Duc de Ruyter.*'

Tourville differed completely from these two seadogs. He remained the smart promoted officer who knew his job. He codified the precepts which De Ruyter and Duquesne had learned from naval practice and humanised the profession. His reserve, courage, skill and enthusiasm created the French naval officer type.

I shall not refer to his role at La Hogue. In any case he came out of this defeat with a marshal's baton. The tragedy is that this man who made the French navy the finest in the world, had to watch its decline and even foresaw it. The defeat at La Hogue cost only 15 ships, a loss which could very quickly have been made good, but its echoes made the King and his ministers decide to give up all large-scale battles with ships of the line. Tourville had reason to deplore the passion of sailors for privateering.

* * *

For a long time French ship-owners made great fortunes at the expense of the enemy by attacking their merchant fleets. They operated on a grand scale on the three seas, and were given all the support they demanded by Vauban. It was a rush for spoils which became extremely popular. Normans, Bretons, Basques, men of Dunkirk, all participated eagerly. The names of Jean Bart, Doublet, Duguay-Trouin and Coursic—the latter, whose real name was a rather difficult Basque one (Joannis de Suhigaraychippi), sailed among the icebergs to board the whalers—are remembered still. Undeniable material profit, a marvellous school for battle, but nevertheless a strategical retrogression. Privateering could only succeed with the aid of boarding tactics and this was a return to the most barbarous methods of the navies of antiquity. And yet privateering benefited the yards by forcing them to build fast ships; from this necessity emerged the great improvements in sail of the eighteenth century.

But, taken all in all, privateering favoured one of the greatest mistakes of all maritime ages, the taste for small units, together with a belief in pinpricking and a faith in the blockade; a blockade is never successful, because the sea is too large.

*   *   *

The great marine artist of the period was Pierre Puget, the famous sculptor whose pictures are preferable to his somewhat flamboyant high reliefs. With Carpaccio and Willem van de Velde, he ranks as the most accurate of the naval draughtsmen and his lyricism, which never flags, surpasses that of all the others because he has created poetry with the most solid realism. His imitators tried their best, but their vessels never managed to convince like those of the artist from Marseilles. Pierre Puget brought to his drawings the powerful conviction of the sculptor, the three-dimensional spirit and the realism which the painter ignores. One can examine all his ships, and with little trouble his most fiery images become blueprints. This integrity is one of the highest qualities of an artist and there is no reason why we should under-estimate it in the past even if today it has been replaced by *verve*. This applies particularly to the ship which, like the horse, is a very bad subject for fantasy.

Puget's designs are of special interest because, for him, they represented eagerly nursed plans which were on the point of realisation. He was a great craftsman. He burned to cut in elm or lime the decorative masses he expressed in charcoal.

He played a great part in the maritime splendour of the period and the warship of the Grand Monarch owes much to him. He was a dark, violent, integrated man. He quarrelled with and flouted the authority of the administrators as Michelangelo flouted his patron Julius II. One day, refusing to tolerate their criticism, he fled to Italy. The Marquis d'Imfreville ran after him, caught him and brought him back. But Puget imposed his conditions. In future he would answer only to the King or the Admiral direct and no changes were to be made in his plans. The King and Colbert agreed.

The somewhat heavy decoration he applied to the ship is always majestic in the extreme, but it is not without melancholy. This creator of caryatids seems to be bearing himself the burden he placed on their beautiful shoulders and to be thinking incessantly of the one which Fate imposes upon mankind.

*   *   *

At the end of this reign, the navy had lost half its effective ships and the men-of-war lay idle in the fine harbours which had been built for them. The grandiose constructions of Colbert no longer served except to disguise the emptiness of the arsenals, to give employment to the ship-breakers and the warehousemen. It was a terrible moment for real sailors, of which, however, few echoes are found, for privateering had flung dust in the eyes of the young just as it had given an alibi to the cares of the statesmen. Velez-Malaga, in 1704, was the last great naval action for 60 years: one cannot count the capture of Port Mahon because its importance has been overrated. It was only a lucky raid.

England led the field and she played the game well, powerfully and secretly. She was in the course of founding her immense and fruitful colonial Empire at the expense of France and Spain. It has perhaps been stressed too much that Cardinal Dubois was in her pay and connived at the ruin of the navy; that Fleury had no naval policy; that Louis XV was a defeatist, but this fashion for rehabilitation leaves me cold. I am prepared to admit that the great mass of the French people still remained indifferent to long-distance expeditions and that few people regretted the 'dotage' or the abandonment of warships until the end of the Seven Years' War. Without provoking a general up-roar, as it should have done, and in fact without disturbing any-

108. 74-Gun Ship, 1780

one, the loathsome Berryer, the police lieutenant who became Minister for the Navy, could propose that everything remain-ing in the harbours should be put up to auction.

Trade with the colonies, although more prosperous than ever (commerce with the West Indies rose from 25 to 240 millions), was monopolised by the Companies and insufficiently distri-buted throughout the nation. It still appeared to be in the nature of privilege and almost of abuse. The public turned its back upon the navy.

Thus the two great wars supported by Louis XV completely

ruined France, despite the magnificent exploits, the *tours de force* of Dupleix or La Bourdonnais with no navy to support them. The Treaty of Paris on the 10th February, 1763, is one of the most melancholy dates in the whole of French history.

* * *

But France lived on and we shall see another of those renaissances which arouse such hope in times of chaos. This resurrection was due to Choiseul, that ugly, witty, lively little

109. Stern of the *Océan*, 1786

man, the incarnation of the best French qualities and the most pardonable of our faults—one is always inclined to excuse French faults: even if they are dangerous for the Fatherland let them remain agreeable for individuals!

The failures of the Seven Years' War had modified the outlook of the most sceptical, except perhaps Louis XV, whose cruel, oppressive pessimism was prophetic. Choiseul had the genius to interest the whole nation in the navy. He had the courage and audacity to sink his pride and open a general subscription. And the whole of France contributed, even the Church, which disgorged a million pounds. The provinces acquitted themselves magnificently. Artois presented the magnificent *Artésien*, a first-class ship of the line. Burgundy gave a three-decker, the towns produced money and one can fairly say that nobody failed to produce his mite. It was perhaps inspired by self-interest, but, on the surface, it appeared to be a great movement of sudden passion and love.

The decree of 1765, one of the pillars of our navy, made everything ship-shape and under a new administration there was a return to important works, ports, arsenals and hulls. And incredible as it may seem, notwithstanding our defeats and our neglect, the inspiration which bore the imprint of the *Grand*

110. Stern of the *Valmy*, 1847

Siècle had been so powerful that the stirring towards perfection had not been halted. Our officers and engineers, deprived of everything, reduced to so small a ration that even the terrified administrators dared to refer to the fact in their reports—these men who no longer received their pay, who went to sea in order to live, who brought back any trash in order to survive, continued to explore, to learn and to teach. Their vocation was deeply anchored in their hearts. It was Frenchmen who brought about progress in naval science. Bernouilli, Bouguer, Bourde de la Villehuet, composed treatises which laid down procedure and introduced new improvements. The Marine Academy, founded at Brest in 1752 while all the French hulls were rotting, encouraged the whole corps of officers to follow an intensive course of study. After Euler, the old master shipwrights became engineers, ships were built from blueprints and nothing was left to individual fantasy. Strangely enough this resulted in admirable vessels, probably because, in addition to the newly codified science of hydrodynamics, the hereditary naval sense of these designers came into play. We were soon to see the English stealing the ships of P. Sané to copy them strake by strake. Could we have had a better reference?

Choiseul, in his elegance and his apparent futility, was a great worker and knew how to take care of everything. The famous decree laid down many points which still hold good today: the navy respects them without remembering the man who inaugurated these practices.

In this decree there is mention for the first time of the supreme duty of the captain, and we can read:

'In case of shipwreck, whatever may be its cause, the Commander must encourage the men of his crew, superintend their disembarkment and be the last to leave his ship.'

The French navy has remained magnificently faithful to this regulation.

Despite so many great qualities, Choiseul succumbed to too great a love of intrigue and his tendency to favour those whom Louis XV knew to be evil. Madame du Barry, whom he had certainly plagued unmercifully, was given the task of dismissing him. But this was a more serious affair. He was not even angry with the favourite and as he left, thinking he saw her in the distance, he blew her a kiss from the tips of his fingers. I have mentioned this because it is the very essence of France, which should never be despised: she has always been epicurean. After evoking Colbert and his jaundiced insecurity, it is curious to see his successor disappear with this last gallant gesture.

It is not necessary to frown and to clench one's fists in order to accomplish a good job and Monsieur du Boynes, the serious-minded man who succeeded the brilliant Duke, very nearly compromised the work that was under way. With the new reign, it was high time for the appearance of Sartines and later Castries who, with the support of Louis XVI, completed the reconstruction of the navy.

Poor Louis XVI was one of the only French princes who was

really devoted to the navy. He may have been hesitant and timid, but when it was a question of the fleet and of the sea he showed no shortcomings. Louis XIV, as we know today, loved to take refuge in one of his smallest apartments to study the maps and tales of travel while stirring as little as possible, but his grandson was quite different and he did not allow his taste

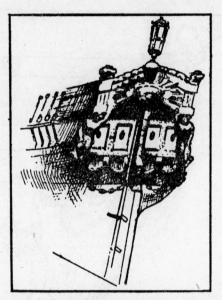

111. Stern of Frigate, the *Aurore*, 1767

for geography to remain sterile. He has been called 'the restorer of the navy' and had circumstances been the least bit favourable, under his rule France would have won a position which Louis XIV had been unable to give her.

*   *   *

The ship of the line has become the modern ship. What had once happened in the case of the galley now happened here. The type became entirely static. Until the end of sail, they would continue to build the Louis XVI ship. The conquests of Louis XV were exceeded and the Chevalier de Borda, that great engineer who gave his name to the naval schools—what events, what hopes and triumphs in those two evocative syllables—carried out constant surveys and hydrographic work. That he gave his name to the school of naval instruction may perhaps have shocked a few old sailors, astonished to see themselves under the aegis of a scientist rather than the flag of a great admiral. I once heard a few excitable admirals dis-

112. Quarter-Gallery of the *Venus*, 1760

cussing him. When the noisiest had finished his din, his antagonist, Admiral Galibert, replied: 'There was no need to teach us courage, merely mathematics.'

The ship at the end of the eighteenth century (108) became flattened and lost the shape I personally admire—that sort of amplitude which allowed it to settle gently on the water—but it acquired another beauty from its strong, nervous lines, far removed from the austerity that set in fifty years later. The heavy majestic hull has fined down and become a thoroughbred

without succumbing to that emaciation which is so fatal to
buoyancy. It is no longer the ship to run before the wind but
one to beat against it, crouching to cleave the wind and hold
its course, to rout the waves which the breeze throws up over
its bows. No more deck houses, no more castles; the fine stern
edifice is restrained. The balconies are narrow, with that

113. Great Bilander, 1825

stirrup-like form (110) which is so pleasing to the eye in its
simple vigour. No more mythology, no more Olympic figures,
only a couple of Atlantes or sirens (111), which support the
quarter-gallery, and the figurehead on the bows. Even this
figure often disappears, to be replaced by the Royal Arms.
Colour has gone the way of ornament. It has grown more sombre,
with less blue—that brilliant blue which still gleamed on the
upperworks even under Louis XV. Scarlet, however, covers the
inboard works and the port lids are vermilion. But natural polished wood, and black and white, play an important part. For
some years the bottom was white, but later became a glittering
bright pink, for copper sheathing had arrived. This was one of
the few inventions borrowed from England and admittedly it was

very effective. Sailing polished the sheathing and it gleamed at the slightest list. After too long a rest in port it turned green, like excavated bronze, but after ten leagues at sea the bottom recovered all its brilliance.

This sheathing also increased speed by a third and allowed much longer cruises without the need to return for careening, particularly in warm seas. Careening: one finds the word on every page of the old sea books. Seaweed, cockles, and barnacles seem from some jealous predilection to flock to the vitals; the ship immediately wears a beard which slows down the speed in an unbelievable fashion. Furthermore, a wooden ship was attacked by all manner of destructive worms. In the old days they clouted the ships, that is to say, they drove in close-set leather nails with large heads to collect the rust, but this was not very effective and it is easy to see that a rough surface in the water did not encourage a smooth passage. The parasitic plants lived on undisturbed. Moreover, nothing was found to preserve the bottoms. Under Louis XV the clouting was covered with a triple layer of white lead in the hope that the barnacles would get colic from eating the mineral. Nowadays bottoms are vainly covered with murderous cyanide paint, one thimbleful of which would suffice to poison a sea lion; but the molluscs thrive on it. The man who discovers a paint they will not attack will become the richest man in the world.

After many experiments, they used copper sheets (in particular yellow copper or tombac because it was cheaper) and this quadrupled the length of the cruise. There were miscalculations, of course, one of which was quite remarkable. In certain places the sheathing was immediately eroded near the iron parts, even without contact with them, due to the action of the chloride in the sea water.

The Louis XVI ship was one of the most solid and carefully built. The timbers were almost touching and gave it a completely new power of resistance. Each timber was a cannon-ball distance from the next, reckoning eight inches for a 30-pounder. This principle was continued in the extremely stout inner planking. We have left far behind the ten-year ships of our first national efforts.

One of Sané's first masterpieces has remained famous for its extraordinary longevity. This was the 110-gun ship *Etats de*

Bourgogne, built in 1760, and in praise of her construction I propose to give her astonishing history. She was in service in the American War of Independence after her poop had been cut down. She fought on the 13th *Prairial* (June 1st) after a second

114. Brigantine

refit, a spanker replacing the mizzen and on her stern the ugly name: *Montagne*. Villaret-Joyeuse brought her back to Brest with 500 cannon balls in her hull. A third refit raised her waist and en-

115. Polacca, Seventeenth Century

closed her head. After a fourth refit she sailed under the name of *Océan*: she led the squadron and was obliged to reef her sails to keep her place as flagship. She was known in the navy for 90 years and was only put out of commission in 1850 for 'humanitarian reasons' as an old skipper told me.

The ship still maintained its waist. This was a sort of central well, a square depression, formed by the forecastle and quarterdeck and the gangways, between the foremast and the main-mast, the floor being the main deck. The longboat was placed there with all the small boats in it. The gangways were light, rectangular walks communicating between the quarterdeck and forecastle. The waist also housed the spare spars, which were piled up on each side of the longboat. The vessel's hull pre-

116. Toulon Gondola

served its tumble-home, for Sané opposed the vertical side for a long time. The cutwater was higher than in Louis XIV's time and the bowsprit was raised but still gave the beak-head a

117. Pink, Eighteenth Century

certain air. The rails took on a far more complicated pattern than under the *Roi Soleil* and finished off the upper parts of the bows in an admirable fashion.

But above all it is the masting (108) which distinguishes the ships of the period for the landsman. The spritsail topmast has given place to a jibboom prolonging the bowsprit, and the famous little vertical mast no longer tops the end of the great spar, which is now held rigid, too rigid, by the bobstays. The fore staysail appeared with the *Triton* in 1725 and now there are three of them which tend to lift the nose of the ship. The royals still crown the mainmast, royals (108c) still set flying while the topgallants are fixed. Aft, the mizzen gives place to the spanker and at the end of the century the old yard was cut at the mast-head and changed into a gaff. Nevertheless, the flag was not

118. Small Bilander, Seventeenth Century

always flown as it would be in the nineteenth century. It was sometimes hoisted on a staff at the stern. No more huge lanterns rising above the poop: now there were only signal lights with lowered lanterns.

119. Hoy, Seventeenth Century, Brest. Ancestor of the Lugger

The braces to the yards now lead to the shrouds and the spaces they occupied on the way down to the deck are now filled by staysails. The staysail is a novelty dating from Louis XV—a large jib set between the masts which gave great assistance when sailing close-hauled. The top is now absolutely flat. The tiller is worked by a vertical wheel; the artillery, of iron now instead of bronze, has changed neither in form nor in calibre.

*   *   *

The latest and most efficient type was the 74 (108) designed by Sané, strong enough to carry plenty of artillery, trim enough

120. Levantine Sailing Boat, 1825

to outsail the simple cargo vessels, stable enough to hold a course and handy enough to turn swiftly. I have piled on these 'enoughs' to show that with all these needs, sometimes paradoxical, the man-of-war was only a compromise and that it could only be conceived by a man who was both engineer and sailor. These 74's bore the brunt of the colonial wars. They represent the type we have called the 'battle cruiser'. Unfortunately, although France created it, England reaped the greater harvest.

Frigates also bowed to the needs of distant battles and long sea mileages. They grew in size and became more powerful than the fourth and fifth rates. The frigate ultimately carried 50 or 60 guns; she became the most popular ship, even among sailors. I shall quote the *Aurore* (111) which was one of the most perfect creations of the time. Or again, the tasteful decoration, the style of the quarter-galleries of the *Venus* (112), a slightly older but very famous ship.

The corvette took its place in the establishments. It was a reconnaissance ship used for exploration or as a scout. It was called a 'despatch vessel' because it carried despatches, but possibly this etymology is too facile to be true.

The longboat was no longer the auxiliary used by all the squadrons of Louis XIV, that sort of tall galley with two or three masts which carried oars to enable it to perform liaison duties in spite of the wind. It disappeared when the oar finally became discredited. As regards exceptional manœuvres, the *Surveillante* is often quoted for overhauling the *Quebec* by the use of two galley oars through her stern gun ports.

121. Brigantine, Seventeenth Century

Nothing of the galleys remained on the registers except those four or six enormous oars which were piled up with the spare spars and the barrels of fresh water, the galley casks. In 1748 they were condemned even in the Mediterranean. All their glory had been but a reprieve and Marseilles slowly saw the precious timbers broken up and the admirable vessels warp and buckle. Only the Pope, from love of tradition, used them rather lavishly and with big fat infidels chosen for their vigour and agility, some of whom, to the delight of His Holiness, were converted with great solemnity on feast days.

*   *   *

But this represents only the main classification of the fleets, for ancillary to these official fighting units there existed a host of small ships, all of them different, charming and useful. Each port had not only its own type, but its special types. As many ships as there are birds: sparrows and chaffinches flying round eagles and vultures. We are well informed as to the infinite variety of these boats. The eighteenth century constantly drew and painted ships and yet we must resign ourselves to the fact that we know relatively little of their numbers and their peculiarities. The best informed and most studious scholar will suddenly be pulled up in the middle of a naval document by a name which means nothing at all to him. The ships, however, were divided into two main categories, the Levantines and the western Mediterraneans. The former carried a lateen sail and were addicted to the use of oars; the latter were square-rigged and used the oar more modestly. France was the only great nation to mingle these different marine types, of which the intrinsic qualities were claimed and extolled by each important port. Toulon was proud of her polaccas (115), pinks (117), *coralines* and gondolas (116), launches, feluccas, *speronares* (two skiffs which carried spritsails) and *sacolèves* (120), but everyone was in agreement as to the merits of the king-xebec when brigantines (121) came to be discussed. The Mediterranean type retained lateen sails (114) whereas the northern type (121) had two raked masts with a fore and aft sail.

Brest claimed stout luggers (119), ketches, *picoteux* and *picots*, which put to sea in weather that a Muslim would not have entertained, and adopted the northern types, the cats, the galliots, the smacks and the hoys which, with the bilanders (113), braved the sand banks, currents and tides of the northern seas. But I have not named them all; in Brittany alone people used to say there were 'as many ships as coifs'.

One day, in a mood of depression, Louis XV declared: 'We shall soon have nothing except Monsieur Vernet's navy'. This was little enough for the defence of his shores and colonies but it was far from nothing. Joseph Vernet, a genial painter, prepared the way for the happy increase in enthusiasm for the navy, the great movement which would bring Choiseul to light. Everyone was delighted with the delicacy of his marine canvases and their poetry. Today, our decadent painting has made them unfashionable; our pictorial *morbidezza* has made us anaemic. Vernet was seduced by the sea and ships, as though he had suddenly discovered the ultimate goal for his talents. With a loving hand he portrayed the wonders of the sea, the mists and the waves, the ships that sailed them and the great crowds in the ports. Perhaps the most pleasant feature of his broad canvases is the brilliant crowds, the animation of his gentlemen, oyster girls and sailors. A figure in a red coat always figures as the centre-piece; to one side, some dandy quizzes a pair of lovers, a little further off a few young tritons splash each other in the warm waters. His favourite hour is the great moment when the sun tinges and colours more than it illuminates. The mountains are mauve, the waves vermilion and all the faces of his women, in that rich, dying light, speak of the poignancy of farewells.

Young Joseph not only excelled in his peace-time subjects. We can follow him into more tragic moments, though today these are somewhat disappointing. His vessels are swallowed by metallic-looking whales and tidal waves. One no longer feels sorry for the pretty, half-naked girls lamenting on the tortured shore, those sirens flung up by the sea. But one must admit that Joseph Vernet played a great part in popularising the shipwreck, a subject which was terribly abused by the literature of the eighteenth century.

*   *   *

There were hero explorers too, the strangest of whom was the famous Bougainville. Having started his career at the Bar only to become a fighting man—he was Chevert's aide-de-camp—then switching to diplomacy as an envoy, one would hardly have thought he would ever have become a great mariner. However, at the end of the Seven Years' War, obviously having found his real vocation, Colonel Bougainville transferred to the navy with the rank of Commander. Despite sarcastic crews and outraged shipmates, he was the first Frenchman to take his ship, well-named the *Boudeuse*, round the world in three years without any major mishap and with an insatiable urge towards discovery which he eventually transmitted to his countrymen.

It was in execution of a plan suggested by Louis XVI himself that La Pérouse, with his second-in-command, Chevalier de Langle, my great-great-grandfather, left for his round-the-world voyage. We know all about La Pérouse but my ancestor is little known. He had hoped to be in command of the expedition and was not very pleased to be a subordinate. He was an obstinate, melancholy Breton, a great sailor whose naval intuition was of great assistance in unknown seas, in the vast Pacific that had not yet been scientifically explored. The information brought back by Cook was not yet common knowledge. He was killed at Maouna on the 11th December, 1787, in the Navigators' Archipelago, unwilling to use his fire-arms at a moment when they would have proved most effective, for the King had ordered him to spare 'the good savages'. A few months after his death, the *Boussole* and the *Astrolabe* were lost on the rocks of Vanikoro. They had explored all the west coast of North America, the Hawaiian Islands, California, the east coast of China and all the larger islands of Polynesia. The names given to them by La Pérouse were changed by courtesy of the Americans and the English. Of the unfortunate La Pérouse no memorial remains except a Strait between Sakhalin and Japan, and of my grandfather nothing but a street in Brest as wide as a launch and a few plates from a service he ordered at Canton, with his crest and the crest of his beloved wife, Georgette de Kérouartz. Oh, I forgot; four sailor grandsons, two of whom became Admirals...

*   *   *

The tactics of the seventeenth century were due to De Ruyter and, under his influence, to Duquesne and Tourville. They made use of both wind and artillery and were essentially naval in conception instead of being on military lines as at Lepanto. The galleys and galleasses under Don John fought like well drawn up battalions. In the seventeenth century the fleets fired at each other in line of battle, that is in parallel lines or on opposite tacks, the ships crossing or accompanying each other firing as they went. Most of the time the vessels used the same rhumb and the same tack, proceeding on their course and firing their guns swiftly and with precision. They were fortresses, or rather a line of fortresses, playing follow-my-leader —a marching curtain. There was no longer a battlefield; it was perpetually fluid. The vessels followed each other at two ships' lengths, and all the crews' efforts were engaged in keeping the line intact. When one of them was too badly damaged, it fell out and went to the rear while another closed up to take its place. Thus one could see a long frieze of ships sometimes two or three miles in length, with the flagships in prominence. They resembled small models glued to a strip of endless canvas, travelling like automatons across a mechanical landscape, with a great deal of noise and smoke. Behind the line came the despatch vessels and the transports.

There was the advantage or disadvantage of the wind. They fought either to windward or to leeward of the enemy. If the wind was strong and they were weaker in artillery, it was to their advantage to fight to leeward, for the enemy, when heeled, was obliged to close his lower gun ports and lose the use of his big cannon. However, by remaining to windward, one retained manœuvrability, and this was of such benefit that to take 'advantage of the wind' always meant being to windward of the division being attacked. In fact, as they fought at the closest possible quarters, the one who was to leeward had to keep an absolutely straight course. If he sheered off or bore away, he found the void and drew away from the enemy—from an enemy 200 yards away whom he could not possibly approach. That was sail. But the one which was to windward was in a position to bear down at any moment on the enemy line, since he had only to bear away. He was free to board at his leisure, to cut the enemy line or to carry out an encirclement. Good gunners could find some advantage in fighting to leeward: good sailors only fought to windward.

But eventually this battle order, the only logical one with broadside batteries and the exigencies of sail, was transformed into a sort of naval review more spectacular than combative. It became a noisy, well-disciplined ballet. Instead of blowing each other up, they exchanged cannon balls—like some elegant game of battledore played by our grandmothers. But a Frenchman arrived to change all this, the Bailli de Suffren (his name is still pronounced *Suffrin* in the navy).

He was a huge, misshapen man, sweating, dirty, vicious, aggressive and about as refined as a brothel door. However, he was incomparably brave, a hero who flouted death and was afraid of no one. Endowed with a lucid intelligence, he knew how to express himself; obstinate, also, to a degree which was hard to reconcile with his untidy, sloppy appearance and his maddening gaiety. He was a Provençal, a native of that province which has always disputed the best sailors with Brittany and Normandy, who always retained, if only by his accent, that trace of vulgarity which the northerner could never tolerate. People used to say: 'An admiral has no right to make jokes.' In this respect, too, he upset everybody's calculations.

At first he was badly served and given little support by his officers who hated him until they began to admire him. Eventually they made a cult of him which he truly deserved. The seamen adored him immediately. Suffren was sick of following on the heels of Estaing and Grasse, of playing his part in the exchange of fireworks. It was all very well for the English to be envious of French skill and for John Clerk in 1782 to write: 'Our enemies the French have acquired a perfect technique in the use of their big squadrons. . . .' 'I don't give a damn for your evolutions', roared Suffren when he left for the Indies with his 74-gun ship the *Héros*, a ship he would lead in a dance quite different from these pantomime parades. His five battles were five semi-victories in which the English fleet was more disconcerted than battered. Let us add, as a point in favour of the English, that the British Admiral Hughes, almost as great a genius in some ways as his adversary, expressed his respect and his admiration for Suffren.

To crush the enemy at all costs, really to *crush* him; not to be content to pour a few doses of lead in his flanks, but to sink him and not to be satisfied with breaking a little of his timber and shooting his bonnets away. Never to relinquish what you attack and to sacrifice everything to the needs of the moment. Tactics: slip between two fires and only take the absolutely essential precautions. . . . Disjoint the enemy. Concentrate all your strength on a single point, pulverise it and then press on to another. Two ships sunk are worth more than ten damaged vessels.

Without the French Revolution the navy would have continued on the path Suffren had blazed in triumph, but it was Nelson who profited by his lessons.

*   *   *

Officially, Suffren died in 1788 from an attack of gout; unofficially, Brest tradition maintains that he was killed in a duel by one of his former officers, the Captain of the *Sévère*, Monsieur de Cillart. On the 6th July, 1782, before Negapatam, Monsieur de Cillart was accused of having struck his colours during the action. Ensign Dieu hoisted the flag again and replaced his commander. The *Sévère* escaped. The fleet, and Suffren first of all, circulated the jest: 'Cillart surrendered his ship but Dieu saved him'. Cillart was relieved of his command.

Six years later the Bailli de Suffren was accosted by an elderly, modestly dressed man. It was Cillart, who insisted on discussing his case and since Suffren hesitated, or grew angry, the other provoked and mortally wounded him. I have heard this story several times and once from a man of great integrity, a distant descendant of the Cillart family.

Had Suffren lived, the Revolution would have taken a very different course in the navy. This fantastic man knew how to appeal to the hearts and the heads of his sailors. There was something imperious and determined about him which would have made him play one of those roles that the great members of the Convention reserved to themselves. Suffren would have been the Mirabeau of the navy.

* * *

The Revolution entirely ruined thirty years of effort, and Napoleon, its upholder, was not the only one to bring disaster to the fleet. The navy, however, held out much better than the other services and the officers left only under duress. Rion and Castellet, when attacked at Toulon, only just managed to escape. MM. de Flotte and de Rochemore, after a mild form of torture, were strung up on the lamp posts and their wretched corpses swung there for a long time in the street. The workers from the arsenals—those magnificent craftsmen—became, as so often happens, blood-thirsty furies. At Brest, where Marigny, the Major-General, was nearly massacred, an executioner was appointed who actually dined at the staff table! When Jean Bon-Saint-André came to make a report on the harbour, out of the 640 captains and lieutenants on the roll, 19 were in prison, 28 asked to be relieved of their commands and 361 were absent without leave. They had emigrated, at the end of their strength and unable to control the fractious crews who, after having so long worn wide bell-bottoms, had now become *sans-culottes*.

The ships remained, but there were no men worthy of the command. This was so patent that the famous Republican

in Europe and the crossing of the Channel would have been easy but for the delay of the Spanish ships, cooling the ardour of the crews and ruining their health. Besides, the allied ships were valueless and the French squadron, after waiting at sea for them, deteriorating, for nearly two months, had to reduce sail in order not to leave them too far behind. Setting sail from Brest in June, d'Orvilliers only arrived in mid-August at the scene of execution, too late and having no more men to fire his guns. The *Ville de Paris*, says M. Tramond, had sixty-one dead and 500 sick out of a complement of 1,100 men. The plan was abandoned, but let us look at the end of the story. France could have assembled sixty-four ships of the line and 4,774 guns, against thirty-eight English with 2,968 guns!

Napoleon, with the Boulogne fleet, wanted to succeed by weight of numbers, by repeating the exploit of William the Conqueror, who had only taken one night to cross the Channel. A night free from interference, one single night was required, and for this it was necessary to gain at all costs temporary mastery of the Channel and to hold it for a few days: England had no continental army.

* * *

The Boulogne army was entrusted to gun sloops, gunboats, barges and prams. The former were brigs, small ships I have not yet mentioned, which began to enjoy a great reputation, particularly among nautical enthusiasts.

One finds the brig in all the books of the period which try to inspire a love of seafaring, and this tendency to extol it became even stronger during the last days of the sailing ship. Jules Verne really misused the brig. It did not exceed 75 feet and was rigged with two masts carrying the four usual sails one above the other. The mainmast, however, had no main course: this was replaced by a spanker. The brig was a development of the northern filibuster's brigantine but it did not possess the qualities of its ancestor. It was a bastard version of the three-master.

These gun brigs numbered 320 and, like everything else in the fleet, they were too well made. They were long-lived and the young officers who commanded them, who rotted in them in the

African estuaries, had very unpleasant memories of them. I have
often heard my grandfather curse them. Their primitive armament comprised four guns: two 24's, two 36's and occasionally a large mortar in the stern.

The gunboats were armed with one 24-pounder and carried
a field gun stoutly lashed in the stern ready to be disembarked
together with its carriage. A derrick on the foremast helped
with the landing of the horses. They were lugger-rigged,
another very remarkable invention of this century. The lugger
or *chasse-marée* carried a bowsprit and jib and three masts, the
fore and mizzen being stepped in the extreme bow and stern
respectively. The mainmast was lug-rigged with a square or
lugsail. It sailed close to the wind and was one of the most
active corsair ships in the Channel. It derived from the *baggala*
(141). There were 153 of them, 60 feet long with a 15 foot beam.

The barges, the general name for the flotilla ships, were
remarkably trim despite the flat bottoms they had been given
to allow them to beach undamaged. There were a great many
different kinds, ranging between 45 and 60 feet. They carried 30
oars with two men to an oar. Soldiers and sailors were harnessed
to the 'deadwood' and a spirit of competition inspired them.
They thought the great day had arrived and their hearts were
all in the regatta.

As for the prams, they constituted the artillery reinforcement.
They were heavy, powerful craft, 95 feet long, carrying a
formidable armament of twenty 36-pounders and a 12-pounder
mortar. Anchored near the shore, they were to have covered
the landing.

The outstanding feature of all these innovations, including
beaching facilities, was the essential part accorded to the oar,
for the last time in the naval world. In fact, the best
possible thing they could have hoped for would have been a
dead calm to immobilise the English fleet. The training of the
assault troops would have allowed them to row across the
Channel. However, there were many difficult problems to solve.
How could they all be embarked? How could these flotillas be
assembled without the enemy, with his active espionage
system, being informed? The four great centres were Boulogne,
where the flotilla formed a thicket of masts near the break-
waters, Wimereux, Etaples and Ambleteuse. William of Nor-

mandy, whose feat was never forgotten, had massed in a single day on the sands of the Somme, but he had only 50,000 fighting men. Now Napoleon was preparing to launch against Albion 2,350 small craft, 16,000 selected sailors, 150,000 crack soldiers, 9,000 horses, 3,000 large-calibre guns and 500 field guns, together with supplies and ammunition for a fortnight.

The disposition was covered by both a fixed and mobile defence, strangely reminiscent of the defence works undertaken by Germany on the same coast. Numerous forts and redoubts had been built, some of which were even submerged, the battery being covered at high water while at low water it had an increased range thanks to the flat beaches. The mobile defence at the least alarm could rush up guns mounted on wheels with huge rims to prevent them getting stuck in the mud. This functioned so well and so accurately that all English attempts to put the fleet out of action failed miserably.

The northern shores had never known such activity, such gaiety, such wealth and abundance. The officials of the Empire took a hand and the prices did not rise. The camp at Boulogne witnessed many splendid days. There, for only the second time since its inception, a distribution of the Légion d'Honneur took place on the 15th August, 1804, on the spot where Caesar had concentrated his troops before the conquest of Britain. The Emperor sat on the throne of Dagobert and on their shields and helmets his troops bore the crosses of Du Guesclin and Bayard!

The story of Admiral Keith's raid in October is still told on these beaches. The British Admiral brought strange fire ships of a new design; classic fire ships, but also long floats measuring 20 feet by 3, hardly out of the water, with rows of powder kegs which were exploded by means of sensitive antennae. Some of them had clockwork delay-action fuses. The French lost only twenty-one men, but the fireworks were visible at Arras, twenty-five leagues away.

It is very interesting to note the feelings aroused in the sailors by the preparations for this attempt. At the outset they thought it would be easy and they entertained every hope of success. The good relations between the troops and the sailors looked promising. The few practice sorties and battles went off well: the Channel became one more river for the Imperial armies to cross. Napoleon dared to forecast that six hours were sufficient. Then the Emperor resigned himself to doubling this figure and once his critical eye had assessed the position it soon became twenty-four hours and then a week. Next the protection of an important naval force was deemed necessary: after luring the enemy away from the Pas de Calais, it would return to Boulogne and give the flotilla the support of its wooden walls.

*   *   *

On the 20th August, 1805, after a skirmish with the British fleet, Villeneuve's squadron, instead of sailing north, entered the port of Cadiz. The Admiral considered it indispensable to carry out repairs and he was probably right, for he had only old material and weary, untrained men. But he remained there until the 19th October.

Everything was not yet lost, however, and a somewhat later arrival of the grand fleet could even have favoured the operation, for serious studies, already started under the old régime (Comte de Broglie-Ruffec) and continued by Napoleon, showed that the best moment for a raid on England was precisely that autumn period. The admiral, however, only decided to put to sea after furious orders from the Emperor. Napoleon could not bear Villeneuve and the Admiral could not 'take' the thunderous and insulting rages the Emperor reserved for him. But one curious fact remains—Napoleon continued to entrust the command of his fleet to this 'coward, this wretch who is capable of anything to save his own skin'. It is not what one could have called an encouraging atmosphere, and Villeneuve, well aware of the practical difficulties, with ships tired out by an absurd diversion the Emperor had ordered—a cruise to the West Indies—had every justification for sending in his resignation.

He was tracked down by Nelson who attacked him at daybreak on the 21st October. Throughout the night the battle had been expected and the French sailors showed an enthusiasm which gave rise to great hopes, although their valour was unfortunately greater than their training.

The battle was absolutely clear-cut and involved two great movements at right angles; the sailing of the Hispano-French fleet northwards; the thrust of the English fleet eastwards with intent to cut the enemy's lines. The French ships were in ragged formation and a disorder which did not allow the Admiral to profit by his superior numbers. In the centre, Villeneuve in the *Bucentaure*, closely followed in the *Redoutable* by the famous Commander Lucas who was one of the heroes of the battle. In the van, the ships of Admiral Dumanoir, badly led, and a few Spaniards. Bringing up the rear, the great Magon de Clos Dore on board the *Algeziral* and Gravina, a Spanish Admiral of equal repute. Nelson's original effort was directed against the rear, which is always the weak point of any naval formation. The leaders have to go about to rescue it and such a manœuvre in the presence of the enemy is always a delicate matter.

The English advanced in two columns without having achieved a very orderly formation. They had difficulties in any case because they were going before the wind. The northerly and most important column was led by Nelson in the 100-gun ship *Victory* and the other by Collingwood in the *Royal Sovereign*. The English ships were less numerous but more homogeneous and they had the advantage of a good preparation and a detailed training. The gunners of the *Victory* were supposed to be able to fire a broadside a minute. This demanded a disconcerting accuracy of movement: clean the gun, reload with cannon ball and primer, refill the touch-hole from the powder horn, bring it back to the gun port, aim and fire. A 36-pounder weighed 7,190 pounds. Nelson's division made contact with the French line about midday on a level with the flagship. It was seen that the English were not bothering about the van. The two columns prepared for a brutal and spirited action. The twenty-seven English ships closed in on thirteen French or Spanish, thus achieving a crushing superiority.

The allies fought with ardour and courage, the *Redoutable* and the *Algeziral* winning great glory. The Spaniards also did well and one cannot reproach them. The *Redoutable*, seeing that Nelson was about to slip under the stern of the *Bucentaure* and come round on the other side of the flagship, flung herself into the breach and received the *Victory* on the opposite tack. The musketry fire was intense. Nelson was hit by a bullet fired from the mizzen-top of the *Redoutable*, some say by a Breton and some by Robert Guillemard, a man from Toulon. The Admiral fell on the quarter-deck at the spot which can still be seen in the

Victory at Portsmouth, marked by a copper plaque. The bullet pierced his chest from above and broke his spine.

But the *Redoutable* was attacked to starboard by the 100-gun *Temeraire*, then raked by a 74. She did not strike her flag; it was shot away by an English volley which broke her mizzen mast. Only 123 men out of 645 remained unwounded.

Nearly the whole rear suffered the same fate as the *Redoutable*. Magon de Clos Dore put up the stoutest resistance. He sent below for a splendid suit of armour which some Philippine merchants had presented to him: he promised it to the first sailor who set foot aboard his adversary, the *Tonnant*, which he already dominated. But the *Bellerophon* came to the rescue, the 'Billy Ruffian', which later acquired an additional fame, followed by the *Royal Sovereign*. Magon divided his crew; but then came a fourth and a fifth Britisher. Magon, after being wounded four times and repelling three English boarding attacks, was killed by grape-shot in the chest.

During this time Admiral Dumanoir did nothing and the van looked on. The honour of the second squadron was saved by Infernet of the *Intrépide* and by Don Valdès of the *Neptuno* who, taking advantage of their inaction, put about and bore down upon the enemy. They fought with a vigour that aroused the admiration of the English. Villeneuve was captured and Collingwood received him on board with a distinction and courtesy which proved that the unfortunate Admiral had not been undeserving of honour. But when he was released and learned of the accusations levelled against him, in what detestation and contempt he was held in Imperial circles, he cut his throat. This happened at Rennes and, by a curious coincidence, at the Hôtel de la Patrie. Only eleven vessels got back to Spain and the Boulogne flotilla had proved a failure. For the French the word Trafalgar still expresses an irreparable disaster.

And yet the Emperor took a great deal of trouble. Under the administration of the odious Decrès—no one was more hated in the Imperial administration and his death by assassination was imputed to private enemies—the navy did not go to ruin. The French fleet was far from equalling the English fleet, either in quality or in numbers, but at the end of the Empire, still under the aegis of Forfait and Sané, who did not die until 1831 at the age of 91 (he could still draw magnificent plans with a steady hand), it represented a real power though there was a lack of high-ranking officers. There had been no time! The conscious-ness of this inferiority was so acute that decision in battle was no longer sought; as under Louis XIV after La Hogue, privateer-ing was the order of the day.

The end of the Imperial régime found all the new ports such as Antwerp or Flushing full of fine ships which hardly ever put to sea. In 1814 France possessed 103 warships and fifty frigates, double the number she had in 1801.

The warship, however, was popular. The sailor was a success. A strange anomaly: at a period when everything concerning war was strictly controlled by the burning and jealous will of the dictator, the uniform was left to the taste of the individual, except for the *Garde Marine* who were garbed and plumed like Hussars. The officers' uniforms displayed enormous individual-ity. They all looked like squires, with light buckskin breeches and hessians. Certain of them wore the cocked hat, a gigantic cart-wheel hat. Some of them even wore it in battle. The sea-man, however, provided the classic silhouette: very short trousers showing light-coloured socks, small blue jacket with a red waistcoat and a waxed cloth top hat with a cockade on the left. The dandies wore light bell-bottoms and a more ample jacket, a Danton collar and a broad-brimmed beaver hat with one side turned up. The hat was smooth on one side while the other was carefully brushed against the grain. The pigtail was still to be seen in 1815, as well as side whiskers and gold rings in the ears.

*　　　*　　　*

This was the garb of the corsair when he came ashore with his prize money to drink among the land-lubbers. However, one would not have recognised Surcouf by his dress. This hero, who abandoned privateering at the moment when the others began to know what it was all about, very quickly became a simple citizen of St. Malo. Obese, in a blue coat and light waistcoat, he looked like an honest lawyer and the umbrella he affected and hoisted in a squall added no warrior touch to his very civilian attire. Nevertheless he had been another King of the

Corsairs, whose exploits had far outshone those of the old pirates, with their Letters of Marque. His most extraordinary feat of arms was the capture of the *Kent*, an East India Company ship carrying a complement of nearly 500 sailors, with a detachment of soldiers and armed with thirty-eight upper guns. He boarded her with the *Confiance*, a little frigate with eighteen

122. Lugger, Nineteenth Century, 1825

12-pounders and a crew of 150. The fight lasted for three hours on the deck of the *Kent*. England set a price on the head of Surcouf, this being the first time that a reward of a million had been offered for the skin of a man.

123. Large Brig-of-War, 1825

But English commerce could afford to despise the corsairs however valiant they were. In 1810 Albion possessed nearly 24,000 ships against France's 350.

*   *   *

The privateering war brought happy developments and improvements to small craft. In addition to the brig (123) and

287

the *chasse-marée* or lugger (122), we see the hesitant appearance of the schooner (124), which was an excellent little vessel. A trim sea-worthy craft, it could sail fast on a wind thanks to its fore and aft sails. The schooner had two masts, each carrying a spanker, the after sail being the larger. Then, above these huge hempen trapezoids, were two topsails which ensured the best

124. War Schooner, 1825

use of a stern wind and made it manoeuvrable. Several staysails rounded off this high-quality ship. It was far superior to the brig and I shall mention it again in my chapter on the American clippers. The schooner remained for a long time the typical Channel craft for deep sea fishing. Everyone knows the New-foundlanders and the Icelanders, but these carry a single group of square sails forward.

Then came the cutter (125), developed from the British vessel of that name, with a 45 foot hull and a 60 foot mast, ignoring all the accepted proportions between canvas area and midship beam; an enormous mainsail, a topsail and below a very large square sail used only for going before the wind, and two jibs.

The cutter is the ancestor of the racing yacht and allowed a scientific study of the effects of wind on sail, for it was not expensive and for a long time it was used for experiment.

The cutters of 1814 registered the greatest speeds in com-parison with tonnage. The advantage they possessed over the schooner was the ease with which they could tack or gybe by a simple movement of the helm and a little hauling on the sheets. They could really turn on a plate and in this way could often escape from ships ten times their tonnage, merely by the speed of their tacking. They could never be caught in narrow road-steads.

*   *   *

And yet Napoleon was defeated. He did not love the sea and that was his misfortune. Had he as a child in Corsica felt him-

125. Cutter, 1815

self too insular and remote from the great continental theatres of war, or had he some presentiment that the sea would eventually prove to be his undoing? Did he foresee Porto Ferrajo, St. Helena and their barren marine vistas? To me this is mere literature. He suffered in actual fact from lack of naval discipline, like a Roman at the time of Carthage.

In this field, his logic, his orders and precisions, his superb braggadocio and his exaggerations, ruined him. This adventurer was no gambler, although with the navy one has always to take into account uncertainty and the caprice of Providence. One has to bow to natural forces and to slow tradition. One cannot make an admiral like a cavalry officer, nor a squadron like an army. Submission is the first essential.

And yet the sea was kind to him in the beginning. Of course he remembered Aboukir, but he remembered also how the sea had favoured him. Had Nelson overtaken Brueys, with his scurvy crews and his sluggish transports, what would have happened to the man of the Pyramids? As it was only his tender emotions had to suffer; the sea delivered to the English all the love letters written to Josephine, but faithfully brought him the anonymous missives informing him of his conjugal misfortunes. It is true that on his return he enjoyed a cuckold's luck and the fog descended to hide him from the British warships and their red spy-glasses. He entrusted himself to the *Muiron*, a good little Venetian frigate, docile but ageing, with forty-four pop-guns. A broadside from an English 74 would have blown her to pieces. In his gratitude he had a model made of her which is still in the Musée de la Marine. It once stood on his desk at Malmaison. The Emperor often looked at the *Muiron* and dreamed.

Out of spite, he invented the continental blockade, arousing a universal loathing for the name of France. He conceived a hatred for the sea. He enclosed it everywhere and would have whipped it like Xerxes; in private he spat upon it. He turned his back on his naval inventors because his rancour had made him obtuse. Fulton offered him an underwater device which would have blown up the English men-of-war like puff-balls: he did not even look at it. He was so enamoured of regularity that at one moment he tried to restore the oar to the navy. The Boulogne flotilla, in which everyone rowed, resulted from this. The gunboats, the *Gamelles à la Mouskin* as the old sea dogs called them, suited him. He even had half-galleys, a word which had not been used since Louis XIV. At least with them one was not at the mercy of the wind.

In spite of this, when the Marquis de Jouffroy appeared with his *pyroscaphe*, the steamship he had just invented and which, flouting the caprices of the Nereids, would make fleets as obedient as land armies, he replied with his usual grace: 'Let him go hang; it has no future!'

However, unlike Louis XIV, who was carefully kept away from the sea because it was feared he would soil his shirts, Napoleon was never seasick. I have questioned old sailors whose fathers had carried the Emperor: Caesar was never seen leaning over the handrail, feeding the fishes. 'Admittedly he always had fine weather, a calm sea and a gentle breeze,' said my ancestor the Admiral, and he added something which has been forgotten: 'He was a child of the ports: he must have paddled his own canoe as a boy in Ajaccio.'

People do not often mention his final voyage, the journey to St. Helena. It was swallowed up in the final storm, although in itself it was particularly tragic. As soon as the conquered man climbed up the ladder of the *Bellerophon*, pity abandoned him, and yet. . . . The *Bellerophon* took him to England before despatching him to the basalt island. They wanted to show the English this bogyman, this phantom who had given them so many sleepless nights. We forget that, but he must have remembered it.

On the 15th July, at dawn, the brig *l'Epervier* lowered its boat to take the Emperor over to the *Bellerophon*. On the 16th Napoleon appeared before Admiral Hotham in the *Superb*, and that evening, when he returned aboard, the *Bellerophon* set her course for England, where she arrived a week later at Torbay on the south coast and dropped anchor. An enormous crowd had gathered; obviously the slow return journey had been exploited to the full. She was sent on to Plymouth where she arrived on the 26th July. Curiosity was so great that the men on board grew scared. Their fear exceeded the satisfaction of showing 'Boney' in chains. They went so far as to give the order to fire on any ship which came too near her mooring cables. At this juncture, however, nobility took the upper hand. Neither a cry of hatred nor a sarcastic word was uttered; a silent crowd that merely stared. . . .

And what had happened to the ruffled eagle, who had been caged for eleven days and brought there? Well, he had wanted to kill himself and Las Cases had to keep an eye on the medicine chest. He remained seven days in the roadstead. When he learned the details of his deportation order, his courage returned. He was allowed only three companions. Las Cases then suggested that the two of them could write his memoirs there. Yes, the hope of a literary justification was enough to make the Emperor hold on to life.

Leaving Plymouth on the 4th August, Napoleon was taken north-east, as though to exhibit him to the whole of the English coast. He finally embarked on the *Northumberland* on the 7th. Now he was put in cells and officially stripped of his belongings: for the first time for many years he was addressed as General.

The *Northumberland* made her way down the Channel. She evidently had to tack for she arrived off Cherbourg which the Emperor gazed at longingly until the Roule fort disappeared below the horizon. Then, on the 11th, they changed course and sailed due south. It was a peaceful journey broken only by a few warm summer showers. The General came out at midday and walked up and down the quarter-deck.

Off Spain, it rained heavily. He refused to go below and his valet brought him up a coat—his grey riding coat! At this the *Northumberland* suddenly came to life. Men and officers appeared from all the hatches. In the rain, the deck filled with watching sailors; when the Emperor turned and made towards them they pretended to be working, but once the prisoner turned about and walked aft, heads followed him and eyes grew wider. The eternal silhouette was there in all its majesty: the little black 'square-rigged' hat, as the sailors called it, and the unique, famous, insolent, grey campaigning overcoat were outlined against the great white clouds. This was NAPOLEON.

*   *   *

With the Restoration, the navy went through a few very difficult years. Foreign nations had helped themselves and what remained in the way of ships was considered a costly frivolity. The sailors were put on half pay. This caused great resentment and much ink was spilt. This step was taken because of the diminution of the fleet and the ostracism of the new government. From the naval point of view hope returned only in 1820 when a new maritime programme began to be discussed. After a few beatings about the bush, difficulties and miscalculations, the fine fleet was born from which Louis-Philippe would benefit. Now appeared the magpie ship, the vessel reduced to the flattest and most sober lines, its only adornment the contrast of black and white painted ports and wales lacquered pitch black. Was it beautiful, hard, banal and brutal? Impossible to say, because it was sacred. For the men of my generation the magpie ship represents so much, so many dreams and memories that we cannot pronounce a fair judgment. The mere appearance at Brest of the *Borda* and the *Melpomène*, with their chequered sides, their draught boards, among the structures of iron, takes one back immediately to the great epochs. It is pointless to discuss it.

The memory still thrills me after fifty years. At the end of the Empire black was no novelty: it was the English taste. The French sailors often called the paint on their hulls *le black*; but the gunports were painted in very pale straw yellow or light orange. Now this black and white paint covered everything and it made such an admirable contrast that there was no need for further decoration. Only slender caryatids remained beneath the stern balconies and a bust or some rather mediocre figure-head at the bow. This was in harmony with the simpler tastes of the Empire. The great artistic damage caused by the Revolution and the decay of apprenticeship would hamper our creations for a long time. Beauty died with the craftsmen of Louis XVI. No one was capable of appreciating one of those thick, solid yet far from weighty mouldings. No one could carve gay garlands in wood. They had turned out too many sphinxes, too many emaci-ated Victories, metallic laurel wreaths, gryphons, eagles and lopped-off heads. Everything was flat, scurvy and 'utility'. So perhaps it was better to stick to that striking ship barded with stiff, square black and white gunports set in a dead straight line from bow to stern.

For the shape had changed, had lost all its sheer and compli-cations; elegance lay in the absolutely straight line. And it was understandable: another concept had been substituted for the genial rotundity of old times and there was beauty in this light-ness and economy which gave an appearance of suppleness and virility. Obviously this painting, hit upon by an old pensioned mariner, was a barbarous solution, but it was very nautical—or at least it became so. It was vigorous and warlike and it was to be the last grand livery of the sailing ship.

Intrinsically the ship did not make much progress. Sané was too old when he presided at the age of eighty over the famous commission to draw up the new programme. He let himself be over-ruled by the majority who wanted to turn the ship into a mere fortress, a block-house subjected to the laws of the sea and the wind. With a shrug of the shoulders he authorised ships with straight walls, suppressing the tumble-home so as to offer more space for the upper guns, at the cost of making the vessel heavier and lessening stability. He authorised the complete

u 293

closing of the bows, thus increasing the weight in a part of the ship already over-laden with the heavy raked foremast. Moreover, he was seduced by the English fashion which was paramount in our fine conquered navy. The old man considered these innovations to be experiments which it was impossible to deny. My head has buzzed with all these stories.

But his vigilance made itself felt in the actual construction of the ship. He tried to instil respect for the ancient craftsmen's laws which Imperial bluntness had swept aside. The Restoration ship re-discovered the old qualities of solidity and long life. It was time, for one cannot say to what extent the use of insufficiently seasoned wood would have harmed the constructions. Certain ships were deformed to the point of presenting two or three different curves, so much did the bows list to starboard and the stern to port. A ship built about 1799 was christened in 1814 the *Serpent*, because of its curves. Let me add that the progress achieved in woodwork allowed the ships to be ended with a round poop; the timbers were grafted on to the stern post and continued all round the stern. This gave much more resistance to cannon balls but certainly reduced the amenities of the officers' quarters.

In my opinion this period is rather pathetic and moving in its ingenuous pedantry. All the officers were intensely proud of their fine ships and wanted to try and rationalise everything. There were of course discoveries and improvements which brought some kind of glory to their inventors, but in our scientific days they would arouse a smile of pity. One saw officers turn pale at the new way of taking in reefs, grow enthusiastic about steel standing-rigging, and carry out endless trials. The Béchameil compressor was considered a major invention at a time when chains replaced cables, and a machine for distilling sea water ranked as a miracle. Iron tanks took the place of the butts and stinking barrels of olden days and the ballast, divided into lead blocks, allowed judicious modifications and an easy distribution of fixed weights. All this was of value, including the metal tanks which gave a chalybeate but healthy drinking water, and our only cause for mirth is the seriousness of these good folk. Apparently, feeling themselves carried away by a huge scientific current, they tried to show that the use of gigantic masts was not incompatible with progress and the whole navy boasted of them, giving them a rather exaggerated reputation.

*   *   *

But they were great sailors. With ships certainly less able than those of the Empire, they could nevertheless carry out the most

126. The *Sphinx*, 1829

remarkable evolutions. The whole French navy associated itself triumphantly with the manœuvres carried out by Commander, later Vice-Admiral Lalande, who created the most lively nautical school. To have been in his squadron remained until the end of sail the highest qualification a sailor could claim. Furthermore, a great stimulus resulted from the arrival of Baron Portal, the Bordeaux shipbuilder who, it was said, waged commerce like war, and war like commerce. The Board of Admiralty was influenced by him and he was instrumental in arousing one of those bursts of enthusiasm for the navy that occur spasmodically in France. Literature found a new field to exploit and countless volumes were written on ships and the men who sailed in them.

Navarino, in 1827, had been a revelation to the public and to other nations. On account of the confidence and hope it aroused the battle must be considered to be one of France's successes, but it would be wise to play down the glory derived from it. It

295

was an easy butchery and even if the Egyptian squadron was numerically superior to the allied fleets, its lack of experience and training reduced it to a mere cipher. In fact the real triumph of the Restoration was the Algiers campaign. The navy was mobilised and under the orders of Admiral Duperré did everything that could be expected of it. Its regularity, co-ordination

127. The *Gomer*, 1840

and ship-shapeness inspired respect even in England. I have in my possession the log-book of a young lieutenant, illustrated with drawings showing the magnificent appearance of these squadrons, all of which carried out their missions without a mistake or the slightest hesitation.

Now appeared on the scene the 'colliers', the steamers. For any mariner of those days they represented an impious enemy and everyone tried to avoid serving in them. Sweating and blowing among a forest of masts could now be seen seven smoky funnels, seven corvettes, mechanically propelled, at last, by steam. The paddle wheels (127) in huge light paddle-boxes bulged from the sides of the graceful shapes they propelled, shapes which had derived from the waterlines of galleys, with a centre beam an eighth of the length. Sometimes covered with netting so that the smuts could not fly and burn, pierce or soil the sails, a tall metal chimney stood amidships. They counted on those sails, for the engine, although simple and rudimentary, often broke down. No one believed in these vessels and as warships they were extremely vulnerable and unsuited to stand hard knocks. The first projectile in the paddle-boxes, which made a sitting target, and the paddles were wrecked.

However, it was the *Sphinx* (126) under full steam—this certainly did not strain the manometers—which arrived at Toulon to announce the successful landings in Africa.

128. The *Corse*, 1842

Algiers and the Lalande squadron were the last great achievements of sail. Two exploits were to relegate them to the past: the success of the *Corse* (128) from Augustin Normand's yards, which for the first time, with its screw and perfect lines, showed what could be achieved with steam; and the invention of the Paixhans howitzer, which finally put an end to wooden construction and then, with the appearance of iron, favoured the steamship, since the 'colliers' were always being set on fire.

*   *   *

The screw cannot be attributed to a single inventor. It was discussed long before the nineteenth century. Ericson, Smith and Savage were only adaptors and it seems likely that Augustin Normand, who reduced the long screw propeller to one with distinct blades, was the real inventor of this form of propulsion, the advantages of which were followed up by Dupuy de Lôme. The *Corse* was a kind of brilliantly won wager. Normand, in 1841, had contracted to build a ship to do at least eight knots but if he failed, it was to be at his own expense. This admirable little ship, a real masterpiece of design, shape and elegance, reached ten knots on her trials and thirteen knots under sail. Perfect sea-worthiness and speed were maintained in all weathers. It was the first screw steamship in the French fleet and at the same time the most brilliant success that had been achieved since the vogue for steam.

129. The *Napoléon*, 1850. Round poop

The Paixhans howitzer fired a hollow projectile stuffed with explosive material and fitted with a delay-action fuse. It burst inside the ship only after piercing it, in this way causing very severe damage. We know that the old ships were more or less indifferent to round cannon balls. A stout vessel would return to port after a battle cheerfully carrying five tons of lead in her ribs. A single one of the Paixhans shells would have sufficed to set her on fire. The red-hot cannon ball had been tried out with the same object in view, but its action had been quite different since there was no explosion

So, if they were obliged to build in iron, the major objections against stokeholds disappeared. Ships had now only to wait for the development of metallurgy to become armour-plated and finally entirely built of metal.

Prince de Joinville, who was one of the great sponsors of new inventions, contributed a great deal to the perfection of the squadrons. Despite his retirement in 1848 he remained active.

130. The *Valmy*, 1847

It was he who patronised Dupuy de Lôme and, incidentally, the whole of the modern navy.

With this young engineer there is no longer any need to leave France to find all the maritime improvements. Since then France has excelled in the art of prototypes without, unfortunately, thanks to governmental vicissitudes, being able to profit by its discoveries. After the success of the *Corse*, a triumph for private enterprise, the arsenals produced the famous *Vingt-quatre Février* (129), later named the *President* and later still the *Napoléon*—names changed according to the political climate. She was an astonishing vessel with two decks, 210 feet long, and a mast 156 feet high. Like her predecessor, she was designed for a screw with a 900 horse-power engine, ensuring a speed of eleven knots. It was a stroke of genius and the ship came up to all expectations. However, she was still rudimentary for I have heard, without actually being able to verify this, that her main reduction gearing was of wood with cogs of *lignum vitae* serving as teeth.

Her success was all the more sensational since the last three-decker built at Brest, in which it was expected that the latest refinements of sail would triumph, resulted in a set-back which was bravely but vainly concealed: the 120 gun *Valmy* (130), the largest warship with sails, did not like putting about and when she listed, all the stocky Bretons on board made the sign of the

131. The *Gloire*, 1859

cross. She was wall-sided and weighed down by her ostentatious artillery. The whole navy breathed a sigh of relief when at last, in 1864, renamed *Borda*, she was transferred to the naval school to replace the *Commerce de Paris*. With the *Valmy* severity of line and sobriety of silhouette had been achieved, but the sea and the wind had been forgotten.

* * *

At last, after several versions of the *Napoléon* type, Dupuy de Lôme built the famous armour-plated frigate, the *Gloire* (131), the most sensational advance since the adoption of artillery in warships; this was really progress since the new tendency was to imitate a fortress. For some years France possessed an unbeatable vessel, against which every other unit would have been powerless. This was the beginning of the navy as it exists today. The admiralties of the world were scared and hastened to build similar types, rushing at breakneck speed into this impasse of armour-plating from which they have never emerged. The *Gloire* was still shapeless, but gradually, after almost pathetic variations, efforts and experiments, a reasonable aspect was achieved. The naval citadel took shape.

A study of the ships during those years of anxiety is very

132. The *Amérique*, 1872

intriguing. One cannot watch without a great sense of pity the death throes of sail, its humiliation and submission to the engine before its complete disappearance. The agony was prolonged until the end of the nineteenth century when, in the navy and the merchant navy, the fine transport ships in which Pierre Loti set his *Matelot* still served officially on long voyages to the east. An amiable compromise had been reached between the two means of propulsion. This holds a great charm for naval enthusiasts and the antiquarian with a sense of artistry, for nothing is so interesting as a transition. A ship of those days is something comparable with the ornithorhynchus, the marsupial, the toed slow-worm and the frilled lizard. These sails and masts sprouting from armour-plating at last acquired an intelligent balance. The 'beacons' of wood and canvas were shortened, lightened and separated: they no longer dominated. Sails became discreet but remained decorative, a concession to the past, to the wind, to memories and as a last resource in case of damage or a breakdown of the engine. The officers of the old brigade still took a pride in handling them. I produce here a drawing of the steam packet *Amérique* (132). One must admit that the general aspect is extremely pleasant and satisfying to the eye and to the mind. One realises that thus rigged—even if for this purpose alone—the ship would roll less and be more comfortable. I have also reproduced a picture of the *Colbert* (133) and one cannot deny that this popular vessel, whose virtues I so often heard praised during my youth, also presents

133. The *Colbert*, 1875

an agreeable and discreet ensemble. The iron hull, the machinery and sails blend with an elegant conviction; the lightness of the masting stresses the power of the craft while the general effect remains majestic and almost *grand siècle*. Note the progress made since the *Gloire*.

I shall always remember my emotion, my admiration and bewilderment when, as a small child paddling about on the beach at Conquet, I saw the iron *Victorieuse* with her ram, and with all her sails hoisted against the setting sun. She was making her way up the Four roadstead. Massive but clear-cut with her armour-plating and armament, and yet, at the same time, diaphanous, ethereal, legendary....

*   *   *

This brings to a close our excursion among the shipping of the world except for a short chapter on the last great sailing ships and a visit to the exotic races where we find ourselves almost back in the Middle Ages, but also in the presence of that questing, that intuition, that experimental humility which is of such great interest. European shipping has become a scientific concept, which the honest man of general culture cannot follow; the humanities do not suffice; one has to be a specialist. Mathematics have taken the place of sense, good nautical common-sense, of that mysterious harmony, of that clash between the elementary forces and pioneering values, and of the adaptability of man trying to blaze a trail.

But this new marine is no less stirring and no less magnificent; so beautiful perhaps that it is dangerous to approach it if one wishes to preserve one's esteem and affection for the modest prowess of by-gone days.

134. Clipper, *The Electric*, New York

CHAPTER XVI

The Clippers

UNCLE Sam! A brusque, disturbing person, but always picturesque; tall, strong, skinny, dressed in a French coat with huge coat-tails fluttering in the wind as he strides along, arousing both irony and admiration; a tall top hat with the Stars and Stripes for tally; a goatee beard and implacable lip covering even teeth. At his belt, in a holster but ever ready, a six-barrelled Colt and later a Smith and Wesson, the latest type of this murderous weapon before the Browning.

For Uncle Sam nothing exists in any field, not even in the marine, before the founding of the United States. The ships he was to build were immediately superlative in everything except durability, but durability is not an American virtue. It is looked upon more as a vice, since it stands in the way of change. A kind of ruthless logic guides and animates Uncle Sam. Rudimentary conceptions pursued to the end determine his successes, obstinacy being the most effective agent. Experiment and contempt for risks make him go very far at a very great speed. When disregard for established theory reaches this pitch it is a great strength rather than a weakness. Uncle Sam was to produce the fastest sailing ships in the world.

Fenimore Cooper was right to boast of his country's frigates, to boast that they had shown a clean pair of heels to the English corvettes loaded with canvas like white clouds. English ship-building was completely outclassed by the ships of the rebellious colony. The little American ships made game of blockades and cruisers while John Bull followed, dreamy and melancholy, in the wakes of the sons of Uncle Sam. The first surprise came

135. Topsail Schooner

with the topsail schooners (135) which I referred to when I spoke of the schooners. In the sailing ships it was the usual practice to relate speed to the length of the ship: a sort of constant had been found, though it held good only for ships of similar shape but of different tonnage. The Americans really created—for that is the term—a ship designed only for speed. When I mentioned Sané, I spoke of the compromise he had achieved between the various and often conflicting needs of the warship. He would not have designed his hulls or rigged his famous ships as he did had he desired to deny one of these needs. The Americans, for example, wishing to sacrifice everything to speed, left out of consideration the possibilities of armament, load and resistance. They went so far as to build ships which could sail only close-hauled. The construction of these small craft, which did not exceed 90 to 100 feet, was of an exceptional delicacy, a delicacy such as had never before been dared. They had a draught a third or perhaps a half more than was cus-tomary and an incredibly light rigging with very close-winded cotton sails which really carried them, lifted them up, with the help of supple masts very heavily raked aft. They

achieved results which have probably never since been equalled.
Unfortunately, we have very few written documents concerning
the speeds of these small vessels. Despite their diminutive size
they were supposed to attain 17 to 18 knots. I have heard it said
that the *Résolue*, sailing at 12 knots, was passed in 29 seconds by
one of these schooners from the West Indies, which meant that

136. The *Velox*

it must have been doing nearly 16. Officers and men stood
dumbfounded at the rail.

Only the *Velox*, a true schooner without a square topsail,
built by Augustin Normand, can be compared with them (136).

* * *

The Americans brought the same improvements to the big
ship and from this emerged the Clipper (134), a term that
was also used to denote a winning race horse. The point of
departure of this transformation was the end of the privileges of
the East India Company in the tea trade. One then saw ships
lining up to bring back the new harvest as fast as possible. The
great master in speed building was John Griffiths, who changed
his hulls into long, tapering fishes with no more of those comfortable tumbling-home sides on which the ships used to roll.
Here everything was trenchant. There were no upperworks: the
Yankees sailed with their feet in the water so as to have no dead
surfaces to offer resistance to the wind. At the same time they
gave great length to the ship, often by the use of iron ribs. In the

great period, however, the sides were always wooden, for wood, sheathed with copper, gives the best gliding motion and also a certain elasticity which was probably the real secret of the Clipper: possibly a forgotten secret.

The appearance of these craft is a delight to the enthusiast. One can *sense* the speed, as though these strong yet fugitive lines had been moulded by the rapid embrace of the water. The bows are well protected but all the rest is flat and condensed. One can imagine the use of unconventional materials chosen for their lightness as well as their strength. Soon, the three-master was replaced by the four-master. One of the most famous of these was the *Great Republic*, of 4,500 registered tons, built to weather storms in which, while others hove-to, she continued on her way with an almost full press of sail. She was a Boston bottom, 285 feet long, and for a long time was one of the largest ships in the sailing fleet.

The California gold rush also gave rise to a struggle for speed among American ships and instigated new and sensational improvements. Among the 'cracks' one must quote the *Flying Cloud* from the yards of Donald McKay of Boston, which, with the *James Baines* from the same yards, achieved speeds which have never been surpassed: 21 knots in 1856, and if one has any doubts on this point, one has to bow before the distances covered each day. The *James Baines* had a run of 420 miles which gives an average of 17½ knots.

England, surprised as usual and slow to catch on, refused to be outstripped. She finally won the tea race and the records of that period have left behind them wonderful stories. The three-master was still predominant but reduced to the very essentials, to the finest of the fine, and construction and handling had been brought to such a pitch of perfection that the *Ariel* and the *Taeping*, after a race half way round the world, entered the Thames within a few minutes of each other after a voyage of four months. England has preserved as a relic the *Cutty Sark,* which was said to be the fastest of these sailing ships. A ship-owner bought and restored her to her primitive aspect and she is now to be seen at Greenwich as a monument to the glorious tradition of the Clippers.

* * *

One cannot conceal, however, the risks that these ships ran at these speeds which had to be maintained at all costs. The excellence of captains and crews, their abnormal qualities, prevented worse disasters. The men who commanded these ships looked down on other sailors and there was the greatest possible rivalry even among crews. There was nearly a riot

137. A Late Steel Clipper

when sail was reduced. They withstood squalls which would have sent any honest ship to the bottom. To begin with, whatever the weather, they sailed with all the hatches and all the companion-ways closed under tarpaulins. It became a routine. Thus they did not fear to ride the sea. They bore the battering of the waves and shipped seas where everyone clutched on like grim death waiting for the storm to abate. Certain Clippers are said to have remained on their beam ends for more than five hours, without a drop of water entering, and since the masts were designed to stand up to anything, they were merely made heavier by the water in the sails, which took only about a quarter of an hour to dry out. Among the skippers I must mention the famous Bully Waterman of the Howland Company who, whenever he went below, padlocked the topgallant halyards and sheets so that no one could take in any sail during the night.

*   *   *

Gradually a new form was born from these prototypes which, without competing with their essential qualities, profited by improvements brought about by both science and technique. The sailing ship, left to trade and long voyages, reserved for burdensome cargoes which had nothing to fear from deterioration, took on an aspect quite different from that of the old marine. It was no longer a question of facilities, but of overcoming difficulties. Profit, solidity and the reduction of crews was the goal; this resulted in that series of four-masted barques with a multiplicity of square sails (138) which many of us remember.

The *Great Republic* heralded them officially but was quickly surpassed. At first the hull was of steel, and of a primitive solidity which, by its very robustness more than by its shape,

138. Four-Masted Barque

still favoured speed. This hull was a brutal solution: with a craft like this one no longer had anything to fear from the waves. She cut her way through deep troughs which would have disturbed the ships of earlier days. Her length was an additional aid to carry her over several waves: she sailed across them. Her shape was of a great simplicity, a long rectangle tapered at both ends. The midship frame, which at one time was studied with jealous care and considered the most delicate part of the ship, is no secret here. There were two of them, one at the first-sixth and one at five-sixths of the length of the ship. The masts were hollow iron, without tops, with topgallant cross-trees. The yards were also of hollow steel and there was steel rigging with bottle screws giving complete support. The word 'barque' was added after the number of masts to denote the rigging of the mizzen when it carried no square sails but only a spanker with a gaff.

The silhouette was highly original. The three square masts were of the same height and very low in relation to the hull—entirely different from the proportions of the old ships, whose mainmasts were the same length as the ship. The difference is apparent in the *Quévilly*, 324 feet long and with a mainmast

156 feet in height. In certain others, which were even longer, the mainmast was only a third of the length. One can judge what a massive, stocky silhouette had replaced the finesse of olden times. Moreover, on account of the solidity of the rigging and the unbreakable masts, the sails had a tendency not to diminish in width as they rose to the tops. They formed almost complete rectangles.

But they were a beautiful sight all the same. One no longer thought of lightness, but took pleasure in a certain visible strength, an obvious power in their utility and reliability. The bowsprit had now grown shorter and was no more than an iron spar of 15 to 18 feet for a hull of 300 feet, crowding still further the general design and giving even more strength to the ensemble of the hull and the sails.

These sails were sub-divided aloft. Instead of four, the new sailing ship carried six with topsails and topgallants, a charming invention. The topsail was divided in two, the lower one being fixed, and the other mobile, handled from the deck. It could be lowered in a few seconds. Half the surface of the topsail could be reduced and three reefs could be taken in it in a few seconds without climbing the mast. In addition, the new ship was loaded with staysails which reinforced the silhouette. A last and rather touching memory; all the light hulls of these superb ships retained, painted in black, the gun ports of the old batteries. No one has ever known why, but it was magnificent.

The largest of all these constructions was the five masted *France*, built at Bordeaux, which was wrecked in 1922 on the New Caledonian coast after ten years' loyal service. She was 390 feet long and 51 feet in the beam, therefore almost eight times longer than she was broad. Of the same build as the galley, an immense spindle, and with in addition the symmetry of four masts and a fifth to relieve the whole, she gave a powerful impression of efficiency.

These ships are a thing of the past. They have disappeared in shipwreck or have been broken up, but I am told that a certain Finnish shipbuilder, Mr. Ericksen, for personal reasons, has collected all that remains of these old types and that one can still see outside his yards the last flock of these huge birds with their short, robust wings, waiting to make a flight which will never be undertaken.

139. New Zealand War Canoe

CHAPTER XVII

The Exotic

LET us now leave Europe and its dreams of individual hegemony—leading to dreams of destruction—and pay a visit to calmer nations which, at least on the surface, appear to be less aggressive. It will be interesting to find their solutions in the matter of sail and oar. Perhaps the journey across the hot or cold seas will be pleasant, as we encounter races more ardent and intuitive, more patient and less adroit, and perhaps also it will bring us the diversion that we need or, in the last analysis, the bitter taste of renunciation. We can cross the Isthmus of Suez on the back of a camel or on the arm of water which de Lesseps created through the sand. We are *en route* for the east, a word which conjures up a certain melancholy, a black word which, however, we can flood with light if we use its synonym the Orient. Admiral Paris, while he was still a lieutenant, did some magnificent work on these exotic ships and I propose to use his findings in so far as they concern the particular craft I have been able to study. From the same source also, thanks to our friendship, I have been able to collect certain more personal points of view, some anecdotes and comments.

*　　*　　*

The waters of the Indian Ocean in the vicinity of Africa and the Arabian coast are plied by the *sambuk* and the *baggala*, built for the most part at the ancient port of Muscat on the Oman promontory which has given its name to this sea. The wood for these beautiful ships is imported from a long way off, sometimes even from Java. There are no forests left in Arabia. Their preservation has always been the mark of a superior civilisation. It is quite possible that the decline of Greece can be largely attributed to deforestation.

In the stifling heat of the Red Sea and the animation of the

140. *Zarook*
above: Catamaran
below: *Pambau-Manche*

Persian Gulf, these two small craft manage to find a little wind. We know that in the Gulf the highest mean temperatures of the sea have been registered: 37° C. or almost 99° F. Today the *sambuk* and the *baggala* (141) are fishing boats; they collect fish, shells and pearls but they have not forgotten their old warrior habits and frequently become the most brazen pirates. Their peculiarity lies in the way they have retained shapes long since forgotten and which today they alone evoke. They actually resemble each other closely and differ merely in size and tonnage. They are characterised by a very long stem extending more than a third of the length of the boat, and by the shape of the immense cutwater which is joined to the keel at an angle of 45° and forms an absolutely straight line. Henri de Monfreid pointed out to me a certain curve in the bows of the *sambuk* and showed me that it is only at its upper extremity that the stern rises and forms a sort of truck. A deep draught and an almost lateen sail mark the *sambuk* while the *baggala*, also a two-master, carries lugsails. The stern of these boats is very original: the *sambuk* is loaded and decorated with all sorts of complications giving it a real carrack stern or perhaps more accurately that of a pink, while the *baggala* gives one the complete illusion of being a high-built ship. The *baggala* has windows aft (141a), galleries and quarter-galleries, like the ships of the eighteenth century, and to give it a closer resemblance to these ancient types it is decorated with one or two rows of oar ports, the second of which is always supernumerary but which gives it a military appearance. The first row, the deck ports, was armed formerly with carronades but today, when more scien-

141. *Baggala*

tific inventions for killing are universal, it only carries oars. For the first time we find here real seams and the word loses its symbolical meaning. The carpenters of the north solved in this way the problem of the continuity of the planking and its different strakes, and in the Arab ships we see the hull planking joined by cross-whipping.

A small ship worthy of mention is the *zarook* (140), because it is very new in form and already heralds entirely native solutions. Its midship frame has been set up right aft, thus forecasting already the Chinese junks. Its very strange keel is composed of three straight lines; the first, forming the stem, rises forward; then the actual keel, absolutely horizontal; and finally the heel rising aft. The position of the rudder on a large raked stern post is as original as the lever and tackle device used to control it. This and the large stern shows a Chinese influence.

India favoured the *pattimar*, reminiscent of the *baggala*, but lacking its proud warship stern and slightly smaller—between 200 and 300 tons. The great interest of these coasting vessels lies in their very ancient construction. The midship frame, the stem and the stern post alone are built in the shipyard—nothing else. To these three strongpoints are attached the ship's sides which are allowed to bend with their natural elasticity. There are no eccentric bulges because of the consistency and size of the teak, and once these strakes are in place they are made fast inboard with strong, pliant laths. This gives them unequalled suppleness and lightness.

*   *   *

313

But at Goa we meet a ship which, far from recalling western shapes, employs, on the contrary, new premises that have been adopted only in the east. It is the canoe with outrigger. I only mention this sensational discovery here, because I shall discuss it at length later when I deal with the admirable *warka-moweas* (142). In these waters one also sees *pambau-manches*, serpent

142. *Warka-Mowea* with Outrigger

ships, immensely long bark canoes which sometimes exceed 60 feet in length with a draught of less than four foot. Their pliancy allows them to undulate, and this is not an optical illusion but

143. Catamaran. *Pambau-Manche*

is in effect torsion at various points along the hull. It is an undeniable fact, of which we will not discuss the theory, but with 30 to 40 tough natives pulling on their paddles, this craft achieves between 12 to 14 knots, a quite phenomenal speed for a boat. In any case, as we move further eastwards, we come up against certain practical results which put some of our European ideas in the shade.

A little higher on the Coromandel coast, every sailor talks of the *chelingo*, but I propose to ignore it, for it is a hideous craft, a sort of floating chest which only advances thanks to the oars.

Higher still up the coast appears the catamaran (143), well known in Europe for its buoyancy. This is an intelligent raft capable of going anywhere because it is manned by Lascars, who are such good sailors that their name has become a house-

144. *Balon*

hold word. Everyone knows what the term 'a tough Lascar' implies.

* * *

One really ought to make a journey to Siam to study the famous *balons* (144), sumptuous canoes covered with gold and glassware, studded with carbuncles and jacinth, edifices of rich and dubious taste which sparkle along the river. But these processional ships are classic and travellers soon tire of them. A strange Norman compatriot, Abbé de Choisy, extolled their lavish opulence during his term at the Embassy in 1685. He wrote in his journal of the 18th October: 'The Ambassador took the letter and put it on a gilded *balon* to which the King's son had no access. This despatch *balon* followed the others laden with gifts and was accompanied by a convoy of eight. The Ambassador followed on his own in another....'

We see therefore that Louis XIV's letter to the King of Siam had a ship to itself.

'All these *balons* were gilded and carried delicate, bright gold bells; 60 men on each side with small gold oars, who kept perfect rhythm. They were a magnificent sight in the sun.'

The Chevalier de Chaumont called them 'the most beautiful ships in the world'. He describes them as made out of a single tree, and yet 'so light that the helmsman, by pressing his foot on the poop, could rock the whole *balon* and make it look like a prancing horse'.

315

These *balons* had already been praised by Forbin, who was Admiral of the Siamese fleet under the melodious name of Opra-Sac-Disom-Cram, and Paul Morand describes them in his *Bouddha vivant*.

*   *   *

Our next stop is Cochin China, where many curious types of boat are to be found; numbers of canoes which remind one of

145. *Gay-Yus*

Assyria and its pitch-smeared *couffas*, canoes of rattan as light as leaves, caulked with waterproof mastic and so perfectly woven as to be solid as iron; beautiful, bizarre *gay-yus* (145), junks which combine the Chinese form with the Malay outrigger. They are flat-bottomed but very tall, with almost straight sides, and they sway like crescent moons. The thwarts of their benches protrude and give them support. Horns at the extremities and, on an outrigger, a huge mobile stone that can be adjusted to the strength of the wind, maintain the balance of this delicate sailing ship.

And then there is China.

*   *   *

There are some words which possess a magic of their own. To me, China is one of these words. This is not only due to the idea of still-unexplored immensities in an age when we know everything; nor is it the incredibly vast population of which so little is known; the trembling deserts whose dust the wind brings even to the beaches; nor the Imperial cities with their gilded tiles; the pagodas of a thousand delights and a hundred thousand sorrows; the beautiful art treasures, the lacquers and priceless porcelain: it is all these, dominated by a supernatural, almost inhuman calm, a serenity which in the old days was really Celestial. All this appears and disappears, to be rediscovered in the odour and the perfume of those Chinese bales whose pungent scent I breathed as a child with such an infinite nostalgia. My first toy was a Chinese doll and I kept it for fifty years for the pleasure I always found in her smooth face, her admirably stylised hands and the soft red and green material of her dress. I cannot really express everything China means to me for even hyperbole is inadequate. One has to descend into the abyss to bring up jewels and nuggets. My joy always increases when I see a Chinese boat, and the shore of the Yellow Sea is still one of my ivory towers.

Among so much excellence, China is still remarkable for her science and her taste for shipping. She alone possesses more boats than the rest of the world put together. Obviously I am not speaking of those lethal machines, those battle fleets with their infernal installations. I am merely referring to the ship which brings life rather than death and the brutal destruction modern man seems always to be plotting and which he appears to cherish as the most magnificent attribute of his superiority.

China is the mother of boats. She alone today gives the ship its true place as the home on the water. Entire towns form aquatic groups instead of clusters of land dwellings. Even the great cities have more amphibian citizens than pedestrians. Boats encumber the waterways, the reaches of the river and the creeks, and they are so closely huddled together that one sometimes has to cross 20 hulls to reach the slipper-boat one wants to visit. A chain of gangways leads from one to the other in a watery maze. Everything has been written about China except the story of these lacustrian dwellers, these millions of humans who are born, live and die in their narrow little ships with their movable partitions and roofs, with their altar and their kitchen side by side. In Hong Kong alone nine hundred thousand live piled up on their sampans. Active and indolent, busy as bees or dozing lazily, they hurry about or sleep, incomprehensible, before their joss or their ovens. Chinese faces are eternal masks for Europeans, who imagine that they can diagnose by his features the virtues or the vices of a living being.

For my part I find an irresistible attraction in these rivers that give sanctuary to so many; in these inland lakes which delight the eye and the spirit; these seas covered with huge multi-coloured birds, winged ships. The length of the China seaboard and the abundance of her rivers has necessitated this busy marine life. The coast stretches between latitudes equivalent to the distance from Ireland to Mauretania or Britanny to Senegal. It is obvious, therefore, that an enormous quantity of shipping was necessary and that it would include all manner of different craft. The rivers are some of the longest in the world, traffic is intense and in addition to this, the custom of using the junks as dwellings must be taken into account. Moreover, we are dealing with a people which, although it has dispensed with mechanical civilisation, has remained one of the most patient, observant and industrious on our planet. I am therefore justified, I think, in not nursing that self-satisfied and precocious contempt which their boats inspire in some Europeans. Two little stories gave me a glimpse into the possible qualities of Chinese craft. An old naval officer once told me that off Formosa in his beautiful frigate, the very latest in western design, he had met such a violent sea that he had been forced to heave-to. While he was bearing the shock of the waves on the beam, in a most undignified position, he was passed by a junk from Foochow which held its course and whose crew seemed highly amused. This smile from blackened teeth had particularly humiliated him and if he had ever despised Chinese shipping, from that evening he respected and made a study of it. He passed on his admiration to me.

Another rather significant story. Admiral Courbet, fanning himself with his famous little straw hat with the tally bearing the name *Bayard* in letters of gold, was pacing the deck of the *Volta* in his patent leather boots and white gaiters. When, on the 23rd August, 1884, he gave the signal to attack the Chinese squadron in the river Min, he had not the slightest idea that the 11 despised wooden junks would give him so much trouble. After all the others had been sent to the bottom, the junks went on firing.

He had to admit that in his astonishing ship John Chinaman was a magnificent sailor.

*　　*　　*

The rivers and the seas offer an infinite variety of boats and no one can boast of knowing them all or of being able to

146. Foochow Pole Junk

recognise them. Each village has its own colours and its individual characteristics. As a general rule, the river boat is narrower and less colourful and carries a higher mast than its ocean-going brother: narrower because of possible collisions and for up-stream work; less colourful because fresh water is less corrosive than salt; and with towering masts because only part of the sail is used on the river—the upper part which clears the banks and looks for the wind aloft.

The ocean-going ships can be divided into two main groups, the northern and the southern. The former are heavier and more stocky with almost rectangular sections; the latter, with their slimmer lines, can compete with our finest hulls. The northern vessels are squarer and better defended because of the sea they have to sail in; flatter because of frequent beachings on sand banks which they flout by 'sitting on top of them' as the mariners say. In any case, even for the ships of the south, running aground is a trifle. The junks are built to find on a sand bank all the facilities of a harbour. It is their only form of dry dock.

The bow of the junk is one of its main characteristics. The junks of the north, the oldest and most specifically Chinese, have bows in the form of a box (147), square like the river junks. The

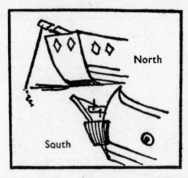

147. Bows of Northern and Southern Junks

sides are more or less curved. The southern junk (147) is provided with 'wings', it has an open bow with sweeping curves on each side. Between these two wings are secured the windlass and the big wooden anchor ballasted with a stone. Obviously there are exceptions to this, as in Swatow and Amoy, where we find speedy ships.

An important difference allows us to classify more easily the northern and southern junks: the shape of their sails. The Chinese sail is a third before the mast and two-thirds abaft; it is the sail of a lugger or a *chasse-marée*. In the north it is absolutely rectangular. In the south the upper part and the part abaft the mast is more or less strongly rounded; thus, in the ships of Chaochow and Shantung, a cross between north and south, although the foremast carries a regular oblong sail, the mainmast sports one with a rounded top.

I think the midship beam of the junk is almost invariably placed far aft. It determines these broad, very high poops (149) which justly call forth European condemnation since they should apply to an entirely flat boat; but for the Chinese, who knows his business, they are a primary necessity. They allow him to live in comfort on these ships in which he has been born, lives and will die. They prevent him from being drenched by the waves when going before the wind, for the junks in principle are designed for this point of sailing on their long journeys, descending with the northern monsoon and returning with the southern. From such a height one has a good view both of the course and the rigging, and if a mishap occurs, since it

148. Foochow Pole Junk

is provided with a sort of stern sail, the junk never gets broad-side on to a gale.

The sterns are also very different and reveal the origin of the boat. Their conception is quite remarkable and essentially Chinese; there is absolutely nothing European about them. They are designed to avoid all the possible troubles arising from a stern wind. They all have a 'well' (146a), a water-tight compartment to which the sea has free access and through which the rudder passes. The effect of this is that when a huge wave strikes the stern, part of it is swallowed up in the well and instead of making the bows dip and causing pitching, the water of the well has a tendency to raise the bows; by the time the wave reaches the bows, the stem is out of the water. The water acts as ballast and when the wave has passed, the junk settles down and dipping under the pressure of its sails rejects the water which has been shipped through specially arranged scuppers.

321

Thus, in the difficult point of sailing before the wind, a sort of balance and suppleness is established, an ingenious creeping movement very far removed from ploughing the waves; rather a gliding over them.

In the boats of the south a similar effect is achieved in the bows by the opening of the wings (148, 149); thus, when the

149. Wenchow Fisher

junk is at anchor, the waves do not make the ship rock. They are split, and those which arrive on deck prevent the vessel from pitching. Furthermore, knowing the advantages and disadvantages of this disposition, many southern junks have a second deck, a kind of grating where the sailor stands and even if his feet are not dry he does not paddle about in the water streaming beneath him before reaching the scuppers. The bows in these junks are also protected by a particularly Chinese adjunct which we find, for example, on the ships of Fukien or Shitau (150); a kind of curved shield which parries a wave or a dangerous collision and protects the stem.

The hull is made of soft, easily curved wood which maintains a certain useful inertia. The junk is the vessel which has the smallest number of submerged surfaces in proportion to its sail; it flies and does not cut. It has modelled itself on the water fowl and its stern imitates the bird's raised posterior. It is swiftly and simply built while retaining, thanks to a system of bulkheads, a solidity which can stand up to any ordeal. The

beams are replaced by criss-cross watertight partitions. In fact
with this curious ship the Chinese were 500 years in advance of
Europe and as early as 1687 Père Lecomte, speaking of the
advantages of the Chinese ship, quoted this division into compartments which made it practically unsinkable.

As a result of this interior arrangement, it is not the weight

150. Shitau Bay Trader

which serves as a basis for the price of cargo, but the volume. A
compartment is hired, the centre ones being the most expensive because they are the safest. That is why the junks of the
river Min, riddled by Courbet's cannon balls, were the last to
disappear beneath the waves. In addition to this, the spongy
wood of which they are built does not catch fire easily and its
softness and plasticity allow a leak to be repaired very swiftly
with a billet which expands and closes the hole almost her-
metically.

Everything is the reverse of what one finds in Europe, of
course, but is it after all so clumsy? Thus the beams, instead of
being beneath the deck are above it, leaving more room for
cargo and quarters. The planks are superimposed upwards. One
begins to see why the study of the junk must arouse our respect.

I may add that the rigging is almost a work of genius.
Chinese rigging is the most simple and the most handy that has
ever been devised. Remember what a complicated business
it was for our vessels to stay their masts. There was a double
system of stays which secured them forward and shrouds which
secured them aft. All these rope tensions over-loaded the ship.
A first-class ship of the line had to reckon with more than 20

tons of standing and running rigging and the shrouds cluttered up nearly a fifth of the deck space. Stays and shrouds hamper the bracing of the yards to such an extent that in the old marine the two forward shrouds were mounted on tackle-blocks and not on dead-eyes so as to ease the strain when they were braced right round.

151. Chinese Parrel

Well, the junk has neither stays nor shrouds and yet its mast never breaks. This comes from the system of securing the sail to the mast. The Chinese sail, made of cotton or matting, is sub-divided into several stages by intermediate small yards and folds up in the manner of old Venetian blinds. Each of these stages is

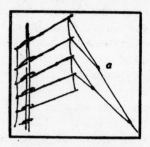

152. Another Parrel, and the Chinese Sheet

belayed to the mast by an individual parrel (151, 152). Thus the strain, instead of being concentrated at a single point as in our ships—a point which must therefore be stayed—is distributed over the whole length of the mast which can hold out without having to be braced because it is pliant.

The advantage is enormous. The Chinese sail can move around the mast according to the wind. One often sees a foresail, with sheets eased, turn round the mast, its sheet becoming its tack.

324

It then serves as a jib. When going before the wind these fore-and-aft sails, unhampered by shrouds, lie at right angles to the keel and work as square sails, while retaining their normal advantage for windward work.

153. Ningpo Trader

And as a matter of fact, when close-hauled the Chinese arrangement of sheets is perfect (152). It gives the sail complete

154. Hwang Ho *Ch'uan*

support and makes it utilise the wind to the maximum. The main sheet is branched by means of a bowline to each stage of the sail, to each small yard, thus preventing any pockets of canvas—those pockets which become dead-spots.

The luff of the Chinese sail is so taut that it works over its whole area. For centuries the Chinese have recognised the importance of the leading edge, with the result that certain of their sails are divided into strips which look like a series of separate sails. European constructors, after a study of the wind incidence on the sails of the Yangtze craft, have found that their curve corresponds to the optimum curve of the wings of modern

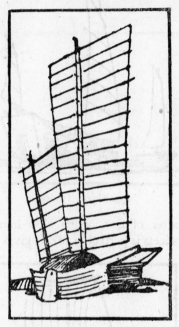

155. Tsungming Cotton Junk

aircraft. The same thing applies to the funnel effect, a very recent discovery in sail, where a mutually supporting effect is obtained between two parallel surfaces. The Chinese make use of this principle with their double or splayed masts.

But there is another advantage of the Far Eastern sail: it never has to be reefed. To reduce sail one has only to ease the halyard and one of the lower leaves folds back, to be secured to a cleat. Thus the surface can be reduced immediately without risk: one can imagine the terrible danger the European ran when he had to go aloft in a storm to take in sail. Of course the sailor in his usual heroic fashion thought nothing of it, but find me the Captain who has never turned pale in a squall before the manœuvre was finished? His men, with bleeding nails, battered, shaken and broken on their yard arm, clutching on for grim death. . . . With the junk a little movement of the hand-winch and it is all over. I use the word 'hand-winch' purposely, because from time immemorial the Chinese have used it to hoist their heavy sails, whereas even 30 years ago our topmen rushed along

156. *Kan Ch'uan*, Kiangsi

the deck to haul on the interminable halyards which joined the yard after passing through *six* sheaves.

* * *

From the artistic and picturesque point of view, as everyone has long since recognised, it would be difficult to find the equal of a junk. But a still closer study of these vessels brings no dis-

157. *Wai P'i Ku Ch'uan* or 'crooked stern boat'

illusion. The colour and the shape are complementary and I feel that an ebullient artist has always watched over their decoration. Some are over-loaded with colour, whereas others are content to rely on simplicity for their strength. Some of them have such unexpected shapes that the eye and the mind delight in an originality which may result from absolute necessity or perhaps from some ritual memory. A distinguishing and very striking mark of the southern junks is a big, black, white-encircled eye on the bow. 'How can you expect the boat to go straight if it can't see?' says the Chinese, while others assure you

158. Pechihli Trader

that this eye is put there to make the fishes think that the junk is only an animal. Scholars tell you that this decoration originates from the Phoenicians through the Arabs, who brought it from the Red Sea. Actually the junks of the north, which have never known the *sambuks* and the *baggalas*, do not carry these eyes, but the men of the north maintain that in these troubled, muddy waters, the junk has no need to see.

The coloured splendour of the junks is incomparable when they give full rein to their appetite for strident tones. The albums of rice paper, where butterflies and flowers swarm in blue frames, would not pale if for roses and insects the patient Chinese had substituted their southern ships.

How brilliant are the junks of Wenchow (149) with their red and white liveries, those of Fukien, and of Foochow (146), their sterns covered with phoenixes, the junks of Ningpo (153) with square blue poops like blocks of lapis lazuli, and the fishing junks of Hangchow (164), which have a human face painted on their square bows—an enormous human face, a gigantic mask with slanting eyes, bright wrinkles and flashing teeth.

*　　*　　*

The Chinese himself is invariably picturesque. For a *laodah* of quality, a captain of merit, a voyage is not merely a human undertaking; it remains a religious practice. Everything lies in the often malicious hands of the spirits of the sea. The date of departure is always fixed by a mystical conjuration and when he sets sail, he has to show many signs of friendliness to the

159. Chinchow Trader

personal god of the junk who is waiting for his homage. Then there will have to be respectful bows to the compass rose which points out not only the North Pole but also houses the secrets, the powers and the direction of the wind. The compass has been prayed to ever since it originated in China ten centuries ago. Before it are burnt silver papers in the shape of clogs, sticks of incense, and huge, square pieces of scarlet paper, several of which are saved to be stuck ostentatiously on the outside of the hull so that the spirits of the waves shall immediately recognise and respect them.

* * *

Among the river junks there are some most extraordinary examples which prove how the same needs have created the same forms, irrespective of epochs or latitudes. Earlier in this book I described the boats of the Euphrates, mentioned by Herodotus, which made only one journey. We find the same practice in China on the brutal Yellow River. They are floating crates of hastily-assembled planks and plates of tin, some of which still have advertisements printed upon them: well caulked, of course, with jute plugged in with a pair of scissors. The draught is only a few inches. These tubs sail up-stream from their place of birth to the spot where the river begins to be navigable. They go up slowly and calmly, then they are loaded, and where they have taken a month for the journey up-stream,

160. Amoy Fishing Junk

they only take five days to return with the current. Their life is over. They are demolished on arrival and the rather sorry, still usable parts will re-appear on new boats, new ephemerides. Donnelly describes them as ugly jigsaw puzzles. However, these Hwang Ho vessels (154), tied up with string and with patched sail, none the less manage to carry their 20 tons of trash in their rickety holds! A square sail, and for rudder a branch about 40 feet long from which the bark has not even been removed. . . . As one can imagine, these ragged ships are not particularly easy to steer.

*   *   *

Another type, on the contrary, is very beautiful, absolutely complete and studied down to every detail: the cotton junk of Tsungming (155) which sails on the Whangpoo down to Shanghai.

It is a long pine spindle, 60 feet in length and 8 in beam, almost exactly rectangular, without tapering and with a small cabin abaft the mainmast which is placed right in the middle of the junk. There are two masts but of a particular type: the foremast is a pole and the other, its big brother, is enormous and almost as long as the junk. The sail is strictly rectangular, divided by an infinite number of small yardlets which permit this gigantic wing to be handled with the utmost delicacy. It is, however, lowered and raised with great violence and Donnelly

161. Hong Kong Junk

relates that navigation on the Whangpoo is accompanied by huge flappings of the sails on the horse as they bow to a squall: since a hundred ships make their way downstream in company, these slaps make a deafening noise. Two minutes later, with the passing of the squall, the tall Venetian blinds climb up to the masthead again and the ships dip in unison and set off on their way. The leeboard is used here, carried on the side in the Dutch manner, no doubt learnt from the Chinese; it is a long outboard plank, fixed amidships.

*   *   *

I must now mention the *Kan Ch'uan* (156), one of the most successful and picturesque of the river craft: with a 30 to 40 ton capacity it is built exactly in the shape of a Canadian canoe. The same need to ply on a river with rapids has created the same characteristics. However, one must imagine a canoe 40 feet long with sides rising almost in a semi-circle fore and aft, while the waist brushes the water. Thus, the rapid little craft does not get out of control when it has to cross the eddies and the waves and its narrowness makes it extremely manœuvrable. It has two masts, one of which is a mizzen, right in the stern, its sail cut into long strips joined with seams on the cross and with slats like the Venetian blinds I have already mentioned.

And then the strangest product of all China, which shows

162. Duck Boat

how much is owed to experience in this country: the *Wai P'i Ku Ch'uan* or 'crooked stern boat' (157). It is met with only at Foochow on the Kungtan river, a dangerous and fast flowing stream. The ship has no sail and is drawn by a tow rope; it is designed entirely to allow easy steering and for struggling against the strong currents. It is equipped with two steering oars, one like a duck's foot, for the calm patches, well aft and very small, and the other, measuring 50 feet, to negotiate choppy waves. To carry it, the stern is set to starboard, with a hook on the top for the use of the gigantic oar. It is worked by a man on a small bridge to give him height.

This is the tangent principle European industry has used with bicycle spokes to radiate the thrust. The effect of the oar is to impart a twist and the Chinese twist it well and truly. Actually they insist that it is intended to hoodwink the evil spirits who, seeing such an ugly craft, will pass by in disdain.

* * *

The sea-going vessels in their dazzling variety need a more extensive work than any I have yet been able to discover. Here are a few of the more famous types.

Firstly, the king of them all, the five-master from Pechihli (158), evocative of the old Chinese navy, a powerful vessel with square sections, whose midship frame forms a rather rounded U. At the stern there is a protruding tail as on the galleasses of Don John of Austria, which serves as a deck from which to manipulate the after sails. It has a perforated, flat stern and a huge wale reinforces the whole vessel.

163. Flower Boat

It measures 140 to 150 feet, with a beam of 20. The five masts are stepped most skilfully and artistically. The very small foremast is right in the bows and out of alignment to port. The two mainmasts, which are of considerable size, follow the axis of the keel. Of the two mizzens, the tallest, to starboard, is right on the stern post, while the other is to port in the only spot where it does not disturb the movement of the helm. The reason for this dispersion must be the difficulty in making these long chests put about: it was found advantageous to separate the sails on the principle of a lever. This is the only Chinese vessel to carry topsails, particularly on the mainmasts. However, as soon as the wind falls it seems that the Chinese use everything they have, and the whole vessel becomes a sail in the most ingenious, capricious and tasteful manner.

The Pechihli five-master is very sober in decoration: a few carved planks in dark wood, made even more severe by a blackish-green varnish. To enrich the colour in a particularly charming Chinese fashion, broad vermilion discs (158) are painted on the deep, gleaming wooden mirror, each containing superb Chinese characters with the name and the port from which the vessel hails.

* * *

Of rather similar form are the junks of Chinchow (159), known as *Hung T'ou Ch'uan* or the 'Redheads'. This is one of the few ships of the north to be over-coloured and of grandiose proportions. The different colours are in heraldic hatchings. One should note the curious, powerful stern with the rudder lodged in its central cleft.

164. Hangchow Bay Fisher

The junk of Shitau (150) is another variety of the five-master for it preserves the box shape, although its bows begin to expand with the wings which give a new shape to the southern junks. In front of the opening is a strange shield, more ample than on any other types, with a large vermilion disc in the centre bearing the character *Fu*. The wings are green but the bulwark which prolongs them is red. Finally, under a double white wale, the eye appears on a black or violet ground. The foremast, following a usage which is found more and more in the south, is raked very much forward and eliminates the jibs.

Even more brilliant is the pole junk of Foochow (148), which brings the bamboos from the southern banks and which takes on a unique aspect when carrying this cargo. The poles are loaded in enormous light bundles outboard and on each side of the ship, forming rectangular blocks of 15 to 18 feet wide and 30 feet long. The ship is fantastically enlarged and when it appears by night or in a fog it makes an indescribable impression: a prehistoric animal, a sea mammoth, that mocks the worst seas and the most terrible hurricanes, for its load makes it absolutely unsinkable. It bobs like a cork.

Incidentally, this ship is one of the most exquisite in shape and colour, extremely elegant in its complication. It has the most beautiful stern in the China sea, on which, in addition to patterns of flowers, fruits and emblems, the flying phoenix triumphs. The background is white and gold, occasionally mauve or a faded pink, and this, contrasting with the highlights, gives it a rich, sophisticated quality. The Foochow junks are considered to be the best in China. They accomplished the famous voyage to London in 1848, which astonished the whole of Europe, and another to San Francisco in 1912, at a period when people had begun to appreciate them. To enable these ships to put about with such outboard loads, they have a little platform in the bows to starboard, where a very long oar can be used to help bring them round. Their sails, rounded aloft, are already southern.

The only ships to compete with them are the junks of Hong Kong (161), the most common in the China seas. They are of dark wood without decoration and are very manœuvrable. They have a flat bow and a very high rectangular stern, beautiful sails like the wings of a moth or a bat contrasting in their dark transparency with the brilliant southern depths.

Finally, let me recall the Amoy fishing boats (160), which since my childhood I have heard spoken of as the most shipshape vessels that have ever been built. They are crescent shaped, with very fine lines and streamlining as decisive as in our modern yachts, measuring, with an overall length of 75 feet, only 45 feet at the water line. They are the only boats used in the south with a lug sail, very tall and slender, with which they plumb the wind like no other ship. They are the swallows of the sea.

Their plumage has also something alive and definite about it: a black head, scarlet bulwarks and a white belly.

The war junks have nothing special about them. The traders are transformed very quickly into fighting vessels by means of a few well-placed guns and a large crew. In any case, China, on the sea as on land, is not a nation that has ever greatly prized military glory or the actions it entails. An Emperor at the end of the eighteenth century, yielding to a transitory enthusiasm of his people for the navy, sanctioned a national subscription to create one, but on second thoughts, when the money rolled in, he merely built on the lake of the Summer Palace, on an artificial sea, an exquisite junk of white marble, a place in which to seek coolness and relaxation.

Of course everyone is familiar with the flower boats (163) sometimes entirely gilded, with their cargo of pretty human flesh, and also the duck boats (162) which export millions of eggs.

* * *

It is time to end. The moment has come to embark and leave these rivers full of danger and endeavour, these haunted shores to descend to the south, where nothing counts except the present, to make a landfall off the happy, lazy regions still slumbering in the sunshine. There one hopes that the spirit may rediscover its original indolence, far removed from sin and remorse, far from serious conversation. One descends the other slope of the world cradled on the soft, gentle breath of the northern monsoon, on the ochre seas of old China, on waves heavy with the sand and mud spewed out by vast Asia. Europe is only the small western peninsula of an Asia whose immensity becomes more menacing each day, unless in her prodigious vastness, she should bring repose in dissolution.

It is pleasant, after coasting so long round the shores of overtense nations, to glide towards burning and secret solitudes, to be propelled in silence by sails of slats and cotton towards the great unspoiled domes of blue, the indigo sea, bonitos, exquisite flying fish, indolence. A limitless archipelago is at hand, last refuge of the harassed and the anxious. Privileged retreats have been growing more remote and now they are relegated to the ends of the world, reduced to those island heads which stud the sea like fallen fruit. The last vestige of steam has disappeared and true schooners without topsails link the orchards of copra.

Here, no more cargo vessels or big transports, but boats for regattas or jousts, fishing boats which seem to chase fish as if in sport. No warriors: they no longer fight or practise piracy. Slender ships borne away by the breeze, which almost take wing. This is Polynesia, bright with a thousand isles, atolls known to every reader from countless descriptions of their coraline beauty. The ship we discover here does not disturb our dreams. In itself it is a trifle fantastic and the eye that catches a glimpse of it is surprised before the mind is awakened. It is the

165. Junk, Eighteenth Century

canoe with an outrigger, already met with in Indian waters, but which finds its perfection in Oceania.

*   *   *

Cook describes these craft in great detail, thus showing his obvious surprise. Those he met no longer exist; they had huge raised bows and astonishing sterns curving in the air like reptiles' tails, or the heads and necks of serpents, some of them ending in a 'V' looking like open jaws.

Off Tahiti he was stupefied to be received by a real navy of war *prahics:* 'A hundred and sixty double canoes of 40 to 50 feet long, well manned and well armed. In addition to these warships there were 170 double canoes, not so large but all with a small cabin and sails which were not to be found on the war canoes. I estimated that there must have been at least 7,600 men in this flotilla.'

The *prahic* (166) is quite unsinkable, thanks to the addition of a second canoe which we have already encountered among the very ancient nations with their bundles of reeds.

The canoes of the Sunset Isles are similar, but here they are even more ingenious for they are faster and their form gives them an incomparable supple strength: two uneven canoes with the small one serving as outrigger (167). Of special interest

166. *Prahic*, Tahiti, Eighteenth Century

is the fact that we find here a method of construction which was used by the Vikings. Each side is fashioned to leave inboard rivets, pierced cleats which allow the passage of the whipping attaching the planking to the frame. Outboard, there is a projection on the edge of each plank for a cord which binds them together.

But the real discovery is the outrigger of this craft, which is never met with in Europe. The canoe is fitted with a parallel float supported by longerons. To windward, this offsets the heel of the canoe by its weight, and its buoyancy counteracts heeling over to leeward.

Yes, this is a surprising invention our sailors never thought of; it can double the speed of the craft. Thus the English Admiral Anson, who was certainly neither an oaf nor a braggart, estimated the speed of the Malay *prahus* (168, 169, 170) to be 20 knots. Twenty knots for a 30-foot craft is a speed which any western builder would say was impossible. The effect is obtained by this strange form of rig and the stability it maintains. The

canoe is a virtual spindle, a bobbin hardly two feet wide, and it
is its outrigger alone which enables it to remain stable under an
immense sail.

And finally, a few words about the speed *prahu* (170) which is
really a crack racing yacht. This most remarkable type could

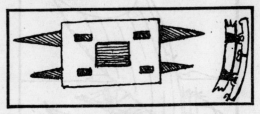

167. Tonga Isles

still be seen 30 years ago in the Carolines. It consists of a
spindle-shaped float of light and solid wood, to which are sewn
bark sides. Its outrigger, also of solid wood, always remains to

168. Mahian *Prahu*

windward and on the poles which join the apparatus to the boat
are planks allowing a cabin or a roof. A gigantic sail—the canvas surface is 300 times larger than the section of the midship
frame—is carried forward and propels the small ship at a
fantastic speed. The strange thing is that it never goes about.
The side of the hull to leeward is practically flat and counteracts
drift. When the tack is completed the bow becomes the stern
and it gets under way in its new direction, thus saving considerable time. Our boats could never catch it. By loading the deck
of the outrigger, they made the best use of the sail.

The *prahu* is the most sporting boat in existence, the most
simple and the most speedy. A strange thing that with these

Polynesians, whom one is inclined to despise, we are forced to admire a nautical invention which is unique. Nor must one

169. Santa Cruz

forget the New Zealand serpent ship (139), the undulating boat.

Why return to Europe, to its murky towns and airless streets? This is the place to live. When it is too hot you can take one of

170. Speed *Prahu*

these sinewy canoes and speed over the waves, beach on some shore where no one will come and bring you depressing and threatening news which may be false or only too true. Go into hiding when Alain Gerbault passes and wait peacefully until you set sail on the ultimate voyage of discovery.

GLOSSARY

ABAFT. Behind, toward the stern relative to another object on the ship.

ABEAM. Alongside, bearing at right angles to the side of the ship.

AFT. Toward the stern, or in the stern. *See also* FORE.

ALOFT. In the mast and rigging, above the deck.

AMIDSHIPS. In the middle of the ship, usually meaning halfway between bow and stern, but sometimes meaning on the centreline fore-and-aft.

ANTENNA. The yard of the lateen sail. *See* LATEEN.

ATHWARTSHIP. Across, from side to side.

BEAKHEAD. A structure projecting forward from the stem, under the bowsprit. Often decked and surrounded by rails, it gave the bows of sailing ships their characteristic appearance until early in the nineteenth century, when it began to be planked in solid with the hull. Later it was abandoned altogether as a member independent of the stem, though often a suggestion of its curve was retained.

BEAM. The width of the hull; hence, the midpoint of the sides, and a ship's being on her BEAM ENDS—lying over almost flat in the water, with one side entirely submerged.

BLOCK. Nautical word for a pulley. A BLOCK AND TACKLE is two sets of blocks with the rope running between them, which multiplies any force applied to the rope.

BONNET. A strip of canvas laced to the foot of a squaresail to increase its area. *See also* REEF.

BOOM. The spar to which the foot of a sail is secured.

BOWSPRIT. The spar projecting forward from the bow, on which HEADSAILS are set, and, earlier, the SPRITSAIL.

BRACE. A rope that controls the swing of the yards on a square-rigged vessel. A ship is BRACED UP SHARP when her yards are at a narrow angle fore-and-aft, to sail close to the wind.

BRAILS. Ropes for gathering up the sail before furling.

BRIG. A two-masted square-rigged vessel, formerly a class of naval vessel. The distinction is made in rig between BRIG, carrying a square mainsail as well as the fore-and-aft spanker, and BRIGANTINE, carrying no square mainsail, or, in English usage, no square sails at all on the mainmast. In American usage, this last type is a HERMAPHRODITE BRIG.

BRIGANTINE. A light Mediterranean small craft. Later, a particular rig. *See* BRIG.

BROADSIDE. The guns mounted along the side of a ship, often on several decks. Also, the salvo fired by such guns, all firing together.

BULKHEAD. Nautical word for a wall inside a ship.

BULWARK. A solid rail, the extension side of a ship above the level of the deck.

CARAVEL. A smaller version of the CARRACK, often lateen-rigged.

CARRACK. The 'great ship' of early European war and commerce, this was the first oceanic form of the sailing vessel. It was supplanted by the narrower and more seaworthy GALLEON in the sixteenth century.

CARVEL BUILT. Planked smooth, with planks laid edge to edge rather than overlapping one another. *See* CLINKER BUILT.

CENTREBOARD. A movable plate lowered through a slot in the keel to reduce leeway when sailing to windward.

CLINKER BUILT. Planked so that one plank laps over the next like clapboards on a house. This is a light, strong method of planking, usually reserved for smaller vessels. *See* CARVEL BUILT.

CLIPPER. A term originating in American Chesapeake Bay small craft, applied to the large, very fast class of square-rigged ship built first on the American East Coast in the late 1840s: hence, any large, fine-lined square-rigged ship.

CLOSE-HAULED. Sailing as close to the wind, as nearly into the wind, as possible. The term originates in the fact that sails must be hauled almost flat to work effectively on this point of sailing.

CORVETTE. The small sailing warship rating next below the FRIGATE. The name was also adopted for a minor escort vessel in World War II.

CUTTER. A term for small craft, particularly for a middle-sized rowing boat carried on naval vessels; also, in the early nineteenth century, for a class of fast, single-masted, armed vessel in England; and since then for a class of steam warship performing similar duties (the U.S. Coast Guard cutter), and a particular rig for sailing yachts, single-masted with two or more jibs. *See also* SLOOP.

CUTWATER. The part of the hull that cuts the sea, where the stem enters the water.

DECK. The covering of the hull on top, and floorings within the hull. Nomenclature has varied, but the MAIN DECK is customarily the highest complete deck running from one end of the ship to the other. The FORECASTLE is the raised deck forward; the QUARTER-DECK is the first raised deck aft; the GANGWAYS, and later a deck called the SPAR DECK, run between these two; the POOP is the highest deck in the stern. The deck below the main deck is the LOWER DECK, or the GUNDECK if it carries guns.

DROMOND. The largest class of Byzantine warship.

FALL OFF. To allow a ship's head to turn away from the wind without the use of the helm.

FORE. Towards the bow, forward on the ship. FORE-AND-AFT means lengthwise in the ship; it is particularly applied to the gaff rig as opposed to the square rig.

FORECASTLE. The raised structure in the bows of a ship, or the fore-part of the ship's deck where there is no raised structure. *See also* DECK.

FRAMES or TIMBERS. The ribs of the hull, crosswise members that run from the keel to the rail on each side and thus determine the shape of the hull. FLOORS, or FLOOR TIMBERS, run from side to side across the keel to reinforce the frames and stiffen the bottom of the ship. *See also* KEEL.

FRIGATE. From the Mediterranean term for a fast, light vessel propelled by sail and oar. The term still indicated a vessel of this type in Tudor times, but in the seventeenth century it became the term for cruising vessels of 24 to 32 guns. The type developed steadily in size and power until it became the classic fast warship of the Revolution and the War of 1812 in America, just below the ship-of-the-line in size but normally carrying its main battery on a single deck. *See also* SHIP-OF-THE-LINE.

GAFF. The spar at the head of a sail, pivoted on the mast aloft, and rising aft to the peak of the sail. From this the GAFF SAIL, a sail set from a gaff at the top, and the GAFF RIG, a rig built around gaff sails primarily. The gaff sail is the original sail of many types of small craft such as the CUTTER and SCHOONER.

GALLEASS. The heaviest type of rowing warship, larger and much bulkier than the galley, carrying sails and a heavy battery of cannon.

GALLEON. A fast, lean sailing ship developed in Europe in the sixteenth century. The usual beam-to-beam ratio of this type was 1:3, as opposed to 1:2 for the slower *nef* or carrack, the 'round ship' of medieval times and the 'great ship' of Tudor times.

GALLEY. A rowing warship, or more loosely any major craft designed for oars. Typically lighter, more slender, and lower in the water than the sailing ship. Also, now, the ship's kitchen.

GUNPORT. A square hole in the side of the ship, through which a gun is fired. The invention of gunports that could be secured against the sea made possible the warship carrying her battery on more than one level.

343

GUNWALE. The rail, the capping piece on the bulwark at the top of a ship's side, so called because guns were mounted with their muzzles protruding over it in early times.

HALYARD. The rope by which a sail or yard is hoisted up the mast.

HATCH. Any opening in the deck of a ship.

HEAVE TO. To bring a ship to the wind with some of her sails so trimmed that she lies almost stopped in the water; often practised under reduced canvas in heavy weather when it is no longer possible to continue sailing the course in safety.

HEEL. The leaning over of a ship from the weight of wind in her sails or from being hauled down.

HELM. The tiller or wheel by which the rudder is controlled; also the general action of the whole steering mechanism. A ship with WEATHER HELM has a tendency always to come up into the wind.

HOG. To droop at the bows and stern.

HULL. The body of a ship, independent of superstructure, masts or rigging.

JIB. A triangular sail set in the bows of a ship, often on a bowsprit. The jibs as a group are called HEADSAILS.

KEEL. The backbone of the hull, the longitudinal member running the length of the ship on the bottom, on which the structure of the FRAMES depends. Forward, the keel rises to join the STEM; aft, it terminates in the STERNPOST. See also FRAMES.

KETCH. A two-masted vessel with a tall mainmast followed by a short mizzen, usually fore-and-aft rigged. Originally, a square-rigged vessel, notably the BOMB KETCH, in which the normal foremast was suppressed to mount a mortar in the forepart of the ship, which thus had a clear field of fire forward.

LATEEN. A rig developed in the Mediterranean with a slanted yard and large triangular sail set on a short mast. This rig never enjoyed the popularity in the North that it did in the Mediterranean, and was replaced in the North by the GAFF RIG.

LEE. Aboard the ship on the side away from the direction of the wind. LEEWARD is the term used for objects not on the ship and lying downwind from her. LEEWAY is drift sideways through the water, caused by the pressure of the wind on the sails and the hull of the ship itself. See also WEATHER, WINDWARD.

LINE OF BATTLE. The formation known technically as line ahead, in which all the heavy ships are grouped in line, one following another, to be manœuvred together. The formation became dominant in Fleet tactics in the seventeenth century. See also SHIP OF THE LINE.

LUFF. To bring a ship's head nearer to the wind. Opposite to BEAR AWAY. Also, from this, the leading edge of the sail.

LUG. A tall rectangular sail set on a short yard which is peaked up aft; from which the term LUGGER, the small craft carrying such a sail.

MAINSAIL. The lowest and often the principal sail on the MAIN-MAST; also, in square rig, called the MAIN COURSE.

MAST. An upright spar, usually carrying sails. The MAINMAST is the principal mast on a ship, or the second from the bow where the height of the masts is equal. The FOREMAST is the mast in the bows. The MIZZEN MAST follows the mainmast, and is followed by the SPANKER MAST, or, on a ship with more than four masts, the JIGGER, SPANKER, PUSHER and DRIVER, in that order. (Only one seven-masted vessel has ever been built, an American schooner; this is the accepted order of the naming of *her* masts.) The masts on a large square-rigged vessel were customarily made up of three spars, the LOWER MAST, TOPMAST, and TOP-GALLANT MAST.

MOONSHEERED. *See* SHEER.

NEF. The big ship of Medieval Europe, characteristically of enormous weight and bulk in proportion to her length, propelled by sail.

ON THE WIND. *See* CLOSE-HAULED.

OVERHANG. The projection of the above-water part of bow or stern over the water; also, the angle of this projection.

PACKET SHIP. A ship running on regularly scheduled service between two or more ports— a term (and practice) that first came into service on the North Atlantic run between New York and Liverpool in the early nineteenth century.

PORT. The left-hand side facing toward the bow.

PORT. Any opening in the side of a ship, such as a GUNPORT.

QUARTERDECK. *See* DECK.

RATLINES. Lines running across the shrouds, forming ladders for the crew to go aloft.

REEF. A reduction in the exposed area of a sail, usually effected by furling part of it with REEFPOINTS, small ropes attached to the sail in rows, so that a new working edge is formed on one of these rows.

RIG. The characteristic arrangement of a vessel's mast and sails. In modern times ships have generally been named by their rig. *See* BARK, BRIG, CUTTER, KETCH, SCHOONER and SLOOP.

RIGGING. Ropes that support the mast or control the sails on a ship. STANDING RIGGING supports the mast, and is usually fixed. RUNNING RIGGING consists of halyards, sheets, braces and other gear to control the sails.

RUDDER. The flat hinged surface underwater that steers a ship, usually mounted on the STERNPOST.

SCHOONER. A fore-and-aft-rigged vessel with two (or more) masts, usually equal in height, or with the after mast taller. A schooner carrying square topsails above her fore-and-aft sails is called a TOPSAIL SCHOONER.

SHEER. The horizontal curve of a vessel's rail from end to end. MOONSHEER. A decisive rise, towards bow and stern.

SHEET. A line made fast to the lower corners of a squaresail and to the after corner of a fore-and-aft sail. Sheets are hauled taut or slackened according to the direction of the wind.

SHIP. The general term for any seagoing vessel navigating under her own power. Also, technically, a three, or more, masted vessel square-rigged on all masts. BOATS are small craft, technically those carried aboard ships. SMALL CRAFT is a general term for vessels smaller than what is loosely called a ship.

SHIP-OF-THE-LINE. Prototype of the modern battleship, the ship considered fit to fight in the line of battle, as opposed to cruisers and flotilla (small craft) which after the seventeenth century were not so considered. Typically the ship-of-the-line carried guns on two or more complete gundecks (aside from lighter guns on quarterdeck and forecastle), as opposed to the frigate, which carried guns on one gundeck (and, sometimes, on quarterdeck and forecastle), or the sloop of war, which was a miniature frigate without quarterdeck or raised forecastle.

SHROUD. A stay that supports the mast sideways, across the ship.

SKIFF. A small open boat for use in sheltered waters.

SLOOP. A minor naval vessel, the SLOOP OF WAR, rating next below the frigate; known in the eighteenth- and nineteenth-century French navy, and sometimes in the American, as a CORVETTE. To-day, the name of a rig; from an earlier, smaller vessel; a single-masted vessel carrying a fore-and-aft mainsail. Typically the small craft of this name was broader and shallower than the CUTTER; today the distinction is made between SLOOP, a single-masted vessel with only one jib, and CUTTER, a single-masted vessel with two or more jibs.

SPANKER. The gaff sail set in the stern of a square-rigged ship. *See also* MAST.

SPAR. A mast, boom, or yard; any piece of wood in the form of a pole used in the rigging of a ship.

SPRITSAIL. The squaresail set under the bowsprit, or on a short mast on the end of the bowsprit, in old ships; also a fore-and-aft sail set in a sprit instead of a gaff.

SQUARE RIG. A rig using squaresails primarily.

SQUARE SAIL. A sail, originally square in shape but later in other rectangular forms, which sets below a yard, equally balanced on each side of the mast. On a vessel carrying more than one such sail to a mast, the lowest sail is called the COURSE, and named by the name of the mast: FORE COURSE, MAIN COURSE, MIZZEN COURSE. Above these lower sails were set TOPSAILS, TOPGALLANTS, ROYALS and SKYSAILS.

STARBOARD. The right-hand side looking toward the bow.

STAY. The general term for any piece of standing rigging, in particular, standing rigging (such as a forestay or backstay) supporting the mast fore-and-aft. See RIGGING, SHROUD.

STAYSAIL. A sail, usually triangular in shape, set on a stay between the masts.

STEM. The centre piece in the construction of the bow; also loosely, the fore end of the ship. See also KEEL.

STERN. The after end of a ship.

STERNPOST. The upright member rising from the keel on which the stern is built. See also KEEL.

STRAKE. One breadth of plank, either within or without board, running from stem to stern of a ship.

STUDDING-SAIL. A narrow sail set temporarily at the outer edges of a square sail when the wind is light.

TOPGALLANT. The next sail above the topsail, in a square-rigged ship. Also, by an analogy very common in Elizabethan times, when this was the topmost sail, the uppermost member of any structure, as TOPGALLANT FORECASTLE, the upper storey of a two-decked forecastle.

TOPSAIL. The squaresail next above the lowest on the mast, for a long time the uppermost sail on a square-rigged vessel. In early times this was a small sail; later it became much the largest on the ship. It was split into UPPER and LOWER TOPSAILS in the later nineteenth century; the topgallant on the largest ships were also so split. A GAFF TOPSAIL is a triangular sail set above a gaff sail, from the end of the gaff to the masthead.

WAIST. The central part of the ship, particularly, the main deck between forecastle and quarterdeck.

WALE. A heavy reinforcing timber worked into the planking on the side of the hull. SKIDS are vertical pieces, like outside frames, that reinforce the side above water. Both were prominent in medieval shipbuilding.

WATERLINE. The line on which a vessel normally floats; large ships, and cargo vessels of all kinds, have a load waterline and a light waterline. WATERLINES refer to the shape of a vessel's hull entering and leaving the water.

WEATHER. Aboard the ship on the side toward the wind, as opposed to LEE, away from the wind. See also LEE, LEEWARD.

WINDWARD. Toward the wind relative to the ship, for objects not on the ship.

YARD. The spar to which a squaresail is secured at its head. Also, the spar to which a lateen or lug sail is secured. A YARD ARM is one end of a yard. *See* SQUARESAIL, LATEEN, LUG.